ANCIENT CULTURE AND SOCIETY

EARLY GREECE

The Bronze and Archaic Ages

ANCIENT CULTURE AND SOCIETY

General Editor

M. I. FINLEY

Reader in Ancient Social and Economic History in the University of Cambridge

---

C. MOSSÉ The Ancient World at Work

R. M. OGILVIE The Romans and Their Gods

B. H. WARMINGTON Nero: Reality and Legend

M. I. FINLEY Early Greece: The Bronze and Archaic Ages

Other titles in preparation

EARLY GREECE
The Bronze and Archaic Ages

M. I. FINLEY

Fellow of Jesus College and Reader in Ancient Social and Economic History in the University of Cambridge

W · W · NORTON & COMPANY · INC · NEW YORK

SBN 393 05410 1 CLOTH EDITION
SBN 393 00541 0 PAPER EDITION

 Library of Congress Catalog Card No. 78-95884. Printed in the United States of America.

1 2 3 4 5 6 7 8 9 0

To
Robert Cook
and
Geoffrey Kirk

CONTENTS

FIGURES

MAPS

PLATES

CHRONOLOGICAL TABLE

Note: All dates are B.C., and, except for a few at the end, they are all approximate.

		Greece	*Crete*	*Troy and Cyclades*	*Cyprus*
	40,000	Earliest known inhabitants			
	6200	Nea Nikomedeia			
	6000		Neolithic Age		First Neolithic phase
	4000			Neolithic (Cyclades)	
	3500				Second Neolithic phase
Bronze Age	3000	Bronze Age begins		Troy I	
Bronze Age	2800		Early Minoan I		
Bronze Age	2500	Early Helladic II	Early Minoan II	Keros-Syros culture—Troy II	
Bronze Age	2300				Bronze Age
Bronze Age	2200 or 2100	Early Helladic III ('Coming of the Greeks')			
Bronze Age	1900	Middle Helladic			
Bronze Age	1800		Middle Minoan	Troy VI	
Bronze Age	1600	Late Helladic I			
Bronze Age	1550		Late Minoan I		
Bronze Age	1500	Late Helladic II			Earliest dated tablets
Bronze Age	1400	Late Helladic IIIA	Late Minoan III		
Bronze Age	1300	Late Helladic IIIB		Troy VIIa	
Bronze Age	1200	Late Helladic IIIC		Troy VIIb	

Period	Date	Events	
Dark Age	1100		Salamis founded
	1050	Protogeometric pottery	
	900	Geometric pottery	
	800	Phoenician alphabet	
Archaic Age	776	Olympic Games instituted	
	750	Western 'colonization' begins	
	650	'Colonization' begins around Black Sea	
	630	Cylon's attempted *coup* in Athens	
	621	Draco's codification	
	594	Archonship of Solon	
	545–510	Tyranny of Peisistratids	
	520–490	Cleomenes I king of Sparta	
	508	Cleisthenes reforms Athenian constitution	
	490–479	Persian Wars	

Acknowledgements

The author and publishers are grateful to the following for permission to quote from copyright material: Clarendon Press, Oxford, for C. M. Bowra: *Pindar*; Cambridge University Press for G. S. Kirk and J. E. Raven: *The Presocratic Philosophers*; William Heinemann Ltd and Harvard University Press for *The Loeb University Library* edition of Hesiod: *Works and Days* translated by H. G. Evelyn-White.

Figure 1 is reproduced from Sir Arthur Evans: *The Palace of Minos* by permission of the Trustees of the Sir Arthur Evans Estate; Figure 3 from Marinatos: *Geras Keramopoulou* by permission of Myrtides, Athens; Figures 4a and 4b from Wace and Stubbings: *A Companion to Homer* by permission of Macmillan. Figure 2 is based on tables in J. Chadwick: *The Decipherment of Linear B*, Cambridge University Press, and in L. H. Jeffrey: *The Local Scripts of Archaic Greece*, Clarendon Press, Oxford. Figure 4d is reproduced by permission of the Agora Museum, Athens. Figure 4c is after Furtwangler-Losche and Figure 4e after Wide.

Plates Ia and Ic are reproduced by courtesy of the Ashmolean Museum, Oxford; Plate Ib the National Museum, Athens; Plates IIa and III Hirmer Verlag, Munich; Plate IIc Lord William Taylour; Plates IIb and IV the German Institute, Athens.

PREFACE

If there is a distinction between history and archaeology, this book is a *history* of early Greece. The largest part of the evidence is archaeological, and I have tried to assess, so far as I could within the space available, the present state of our knowledge. But the evidence is not the end in itself; my main concern has been with the historical analysis and conclusions, not with an archaeological survey. (I do not say 'narrative' because that is not possible to achieve in the ordinary sense of the word.)

I have been over the same ground in two chapters I wrote for the *Fischer Weltgeschichte*, volumes 3 (1966) and 4 (1967), published in German. They have been expanded and rewritten, in the Bronze Age section almost completely. The amount of rewriting reflects not only the volume of new archaeological discovery but also my own re-examination of many of the historical questions. Messrs. Weidenfeld & Nicolson and the Delacorte Press, holders of the English and American rights, respectively, in the *Fischer Weltgeschichte*, have kindly given me permission to make such use as I wished of my original text.

Warm thanks are due to friends—A. Andrewes, R. M. Cook, M. C. Greenstock and G. S. Kirk—who read and criticized the manuscript; to Jan Bouzek of the Charles University, Prague, who allowed me to read the manuscript of his forthcoming book, *Homerisches Griechenland*; and to my wife for her continuous assistance.

M.I.F.

Cambridge, 20 May 1969

A NOTE ON PROPER NAMES

No effort has been made to be rigidly consistent in Anglicizing Greek proper names, whether of persons or of places. Where modern place-names are noticeably different from the ancient, I have given the equivalents at the first occurrence and again in the index. Bronze Age place-names are often unknown. The use of later Greek names should not be taken as an indication that the same names were already in use in the earlier ages; it can sometimes be demonstrated that this was in fact not the case, and there are a few examples, indicated in the chapter on Crete, where the only available method of identification is the use of a modern name.

Part One
THE BRONZE AGE

1

Introduction

IN the study of man's early history, what is observed most clearly and readily is his technological progress. That is why it has been a long-standing convention to divide early history into broad periods according to the hard materials from which cutting tools and weapons were fashioned—stone, copper, bronze, iron, in that order. Then, as knowledge of the past increased, the long periods were sub-divided in different ways. When it was noticed, for example, that in due course the technique of giving a sharp edge to flint and other stones normally changed from flaking to grinding, the Stone Age was divided into Old (Palaeolithic) and New (Neolithic). Soon it became necessary to speak of Lower, Middle and Upper (or Advanced) Palaeolithic; of an 'in-between' Mesolithic period; of Early and Late Bronze, and so on; and also to separate each age according to region or civilization. A shorthand was thus created, and its use persists despite a growing awareness of its inadequacy, and even of its tendency to mislead. After all, wood, bone, potting clay, skins and textiles are no less important materials, but they are not all durable enough to survive till our day; their use crosses the stone-bronze-iron evolutionary line and they must be ignored in the conventional scheme. Furthermore, profound changes in the economy, the social structure and political power have occurred *inside* traditional ages: it is now agreed, for example, that the fundamental division between the Palaeolithic and the Neolithic was marked by the introduction of agriculture, not by a change in the way of manipulating flint. And, finally, there were very different time-scales in technological and social progress among different regions of Europe and western Asia, not to mention the other continents.

When all that is said (and more will be said later), the

fact remains that some such convention is necessary in the attempt to give an account of the thousands of years of prehistory. Before any particular civilization discovered the art of writing and then made use of it to record its activities, beliefs and history, the modern student has only archaeological evidence, material remains, to work with. He has no linguistic or national groupings, no royal dynasties or forms of government, no revolutions or wars to use as labels. Nor would it be meaningful to divide the period from 40,000 to 4000 B.C. by centuries. Not before about 3000 B.C. does prehistory end in Mesopotamia (modern Iraq) and Egypt, about 2000 B.C. in Asia Minor and Syria, about 1000 B.C. in Greece, still later everywhere else further west. More correctly, those are the dates, in very round numbers, when prehistory shades into history. The employment (and survival) of writing was for a long time so restricted that archaeological evidence remains essential, often predominant.

In Greece the Bronze Age began about or soon after 3000 B.C., initiated by the adoption of techniques developed further east and not by independent invention. Whether or not migrations into Greece were involved is uncertain and much debated. They are not required to explain the arrival of metals, but that they were possible is not subject to doubt: the Aegean Sea was a highway over which men and ideas travelled even in earliest Neolithic times (and perhaps long before). The cultivated grains and domesticated animals which mark the opening of the Neolithic Age were imported from the east, presumably from Asia Minor. How they travelled cannot be determined, but at the same time, by 6000 at the latest, the black volcanic glass called obsidian was used for tools in a region extending from southern Macedonia to Crete, and it all came from the island of Melos (as is proved by spectographic analysis of the finds).[1] Yet no traces have so far been found in Melos itself of a local population that early. It seems, therefore, that early Neolithic men from the mainland (and

[1] See C. Renfrew *et al.*, 'Obsidian in the Aegean', *Annual of the British School at Athens,* No. 60 (1965), pp. 225–47.

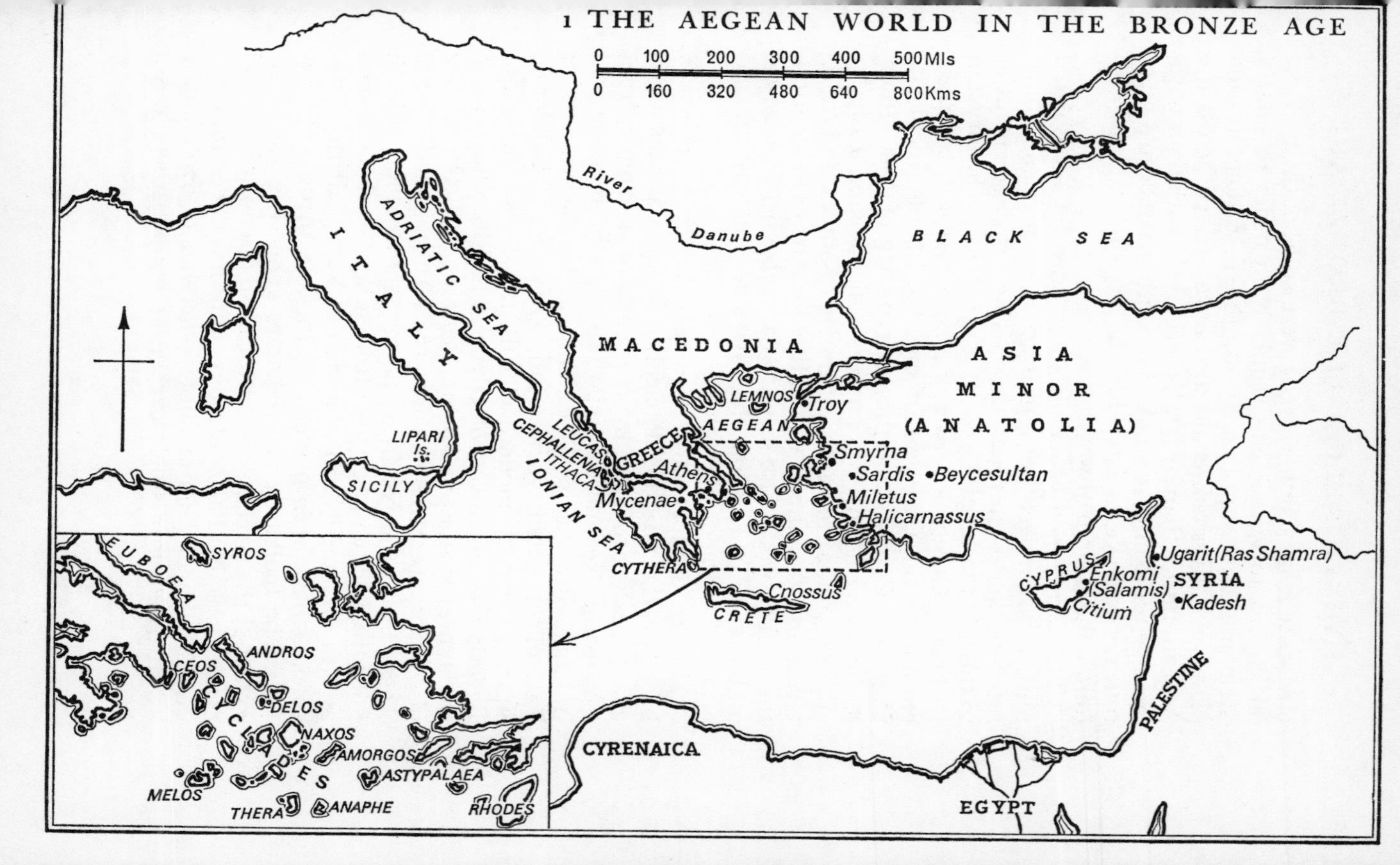
1 THE AEGEAN WORLD IN THE BRONZE AGE
0 100 200 300 400 500Mls
0 160 320 480 640 800Kms
River Danube
BLACK SEA
ADRIATIC SEA
ITALY
MACEDONIA
ASIA MINOR (ANATOLIA)
LEMNOS
Troy
AEGEAN
LIPARI Is.
LEUCAS
CEPHALLENIA
ITHACA
GREECE
Athens
Smyrna
Sardis
Beycesultan
Miletus
Halicarnassus
Mycenae
SICILY
IONIAN SEA
CYTHERA
Cnossus
CRETE
CYPRUS
Enkomi (Salamis)
Citium
Ugarit (Ras Shamra)
SYRIA
Kadesh
PALESTINE
CYRENAICA
EGYPT
EUBOEA
SYROS
ANDROS
CEOS
DELOS
CYCLADES
NAXOS
AMORGOS
ASTYPALAEA
MELOS
THERA
ANAPHE
RHODES

obviously from Crete as well) were sufficiently at home on the sea to visit Melos regularly in order to quarry their obsidian supplies. If so, the first domesticated plants and livestock could also have arrived across the Aegean, rather than by land, more likely with than without a genuine migration. And it would have been a mere routine 3000 years later for the art of metallurgy to follow the same pathway.

The Greek peninsula, in short, was not an isolated unit; it was indeed not a unit at all, in any sense, until recently (and even today there is no firm agreement as to the boundaries of 'Greece'). In both its prehistory and its history Greece was part of a larger Aegean complex, embracing the Greek mainland, the islands (including Crete and Cyprus), and the western coast of Asia Minor. In broad terms this was an area which shared a similar climate, similar terrain and similar resources, and therefore a similar material way of life. Because of its location, the Aegean world also served as a bridge between Egypt and the Near East on the one side and eastern and central Europe on the other.

Human occupation of Greece has now been traced back to the Middle Palaeolithic Age, 40,000 years ago (a date provided by one carbon-14 sample from Epirus). A Neanderthal-type skull has been discovered in Chalcidice, east of Macedonia, and concentrations of Palaeolithic sites have been found in western Macedonia, Epirus, Corcyra (modern Corfu), the Thessalian plain, Boeotia and northwest of Olympia in Elis. Only at one site, however, in Epirus below Ioannina, is there evidence of continuous settlement into the Neolithic and Bronze Ages. There the Neolithic pottery shows affinities with finds from Italy rather than from other Greek sites, such as Nea Nikomedeia in Macedonia. Nearly all these discoveries have been made since the late 1950s, so that it would be foolhardy at present to generalize about the extent of the Greek Palaeolithic or to discuss origins and connexions. No Palaeolithic remains have been found at Nea Nikomedeia for example, where about 6200 (a date again based on a single carbon-14 sample) there was a settlement which cultivated wheat, barley, lentils and peas, which kept sheep, pigs, goats and cattle, which manufactured baskets and four different styles of pottery. Nea Nikomedeia seems to have begun life with the whole gamut of new arts whereas other early Neolithic centres, such as Sesklo in Thessaly, at least went through a pre-pottery phase. Every new excavation supplies further variations and puzzles, demonstrating again and again that variation within the general Greek (not to mention the Aegean) complex is an essential part of its prehistory, though the explanations escape us, as they must when we are wholly dependent on material objects for our information.

So widespread are the known early Neolithic sites where pottery was being manufactured and agriculture practised, that it is difficult to escape the conclusion that these fundamental innovations were brought to Greece by a migration (or migrations). These first settlements were small, numbering their inhabitants in the hundreds, and their houses were single-roomed buildings scattered within the village area, unlike the dense, closely packed villages of the Near East. The next three thousand years then witnessed a considerable growth of population, demonstrated by the spread of habitation to new areas and by the greater thickness of settlement on older sites. There was growth and development in a number of ways, in the proliferation of varieties of food, in the refinement and further specialization of tools and weapons, of pottery and its decoration, of transport and architecture. If the inferences which have been drawn from other early and better known agricultural communities are valid, there was also some division of labour (not possible among hunting, food-gathering societies) and the beginnings of social stratification. And there were irreversible changes in the physical environment, not all of them necessarily favourable in the long run, caused by clearing of forests, by persistent cropping and grazing.

By about 3000 B.C., finally, they began to utilize the knowledge of metallurgy that was already well advanced in the Near East. In the immediately ensuing centuries, metal objects were still rarities in the Aegean; in some areas, such as Crete, they have scarcely been found at all. The majority, whether of bronze, lead or silver, were either weapons, decorative pieces, or objects perhaps connected with religion. Metal tools were hardly in evidence, and then only for the craftsman, not for the farmer. In short, metal began, and had a considerable life, as a luxury in the Aegean world, presumably available only to a wealthier social class that had arisen during the preceding Neolithic period. Stone, fired clay, bone and wood continued to be the hard materials (and it is worth reminding ourselves that they were never wholly displaced), until, finally, in the second half of the third millennium, there was a rather sharp increase throughout the Aegean, not only in the quantity of metal being used but also in the scale of its employment in production.

The coming of the true age of metals introduced radically new problems. A society which *depends* on metals, even partially, has to find a place in its social structure for specialists to a degree not required before, and it must concern itself, actively and continuously, with procurement of these scarce raw materials. The Aegean world is poor in metals. For the restricted needs of the first Aegean metallurgists, scattered small local deposits would perhaps have been sufficient; a few have been tracked down in modern surveys, but by no means in all districts where metal artifacts have been found. As demand grew, it became necessary to import tin and copper (and, to look ahead, iron), at first from the more advanced metal-using societies but then also from central and western Europe. The second stage was particularly complicated, for it meant that the Aegean peoples had themselves to prospect for the metals, then to organize the mining and smelting and to train local men in skills they did not possess on their own, and finally to move the copper or tin long distances. There is archaeological evidence of copper-mining in Transylvania (in the south-eastern Carpathians) and in Spain before 2000 B.C., for which Anatolian or Aegean prospectors must be responsible. The attractive suggestion has even been made that Troy, where metallurgy was practised in the first settlement, owes some of its early prosperity to its location as a bridgehead on the metal route between Asia Minor, the Aegean world and the lower Danube.

The rapid development of local metallurgical industries can be demonstrated for many Aegean sites, sometimes by deposits of slag and other direct traces of actual workshops, more often by variations in the style and technique of the finished products. The extensive intra-Aegean trade is equally well attested archaeologically, in marked contrast to the preceding centuries. The villages and hamlets of still earlier days now have a more solid 'urban' look about them, sometimes with fortification-walls of stone, sited by preference on low hills or knolls near the sea or near inland lakes. But that is the only available hint that the increased wealth, the greater specialization and the various requirements of foreign trade for metals together had a significant effect on the organization and class structure of society. Nor is there even a hint about the political relations between communities.

It is tempting to try to fill the gaps in our knowledge from the more or less contemporary developments in Egypt or Mesopotamia—but that is a temptation which must be firmly resisted. It requires no more than a glance at the archaeological record to see how rapidly and totally the civilizations of the Near East had outstripped those of the Aegean in scale and complexity, both of individual communities (and of the things they built) and soon of the extension of power from the single communities outward. Not even Troy is a proper exception; one must come down to the great Cretan palaces, after 2000 B.C., before one finds anything really grandiose in the Aegean world.[1] And above all there is the absence of

[1] To help fix the scale, Stuart Piggott, *Ancient Europe* (Edinburgh University Press; Chicago, Aldine Press, 1965), p. 122, has made the following interesting calculations: Troy II would fit inside the earthwork circle of the first phase of Stonehenge; the

any form of writing. Then, when writing finally made its appearance in Greece and Crete, its spread was slow and incomplete (never reaching Troy, for example) and its employment was so restricted that it is proper to speak of Greek prehistory, rather than history, even for the centuries in which the Linear A and B scripts (discussed in Chapters 4 and 5) were being used for palace records.

Non-literacy is a severe enough limitation on the society itself. For the modern historian it is crippling. The 'events' in the whole of Aegean prehistory can be counted on one's fingers; they are known only from very much later myths and traditions, and, as we shall see, they are highly problematical at best. Archaeology reveals cataclysms, but it cannot tell us the circumstances or even who the participants were, although in a few significant instances wide-ranging inferences can be drawn with considerable probability. Individual personalities are similarly lacking, not only because of the nature of the few written texts but also because of the remarkable absence of monumental portrayal. There are no beautifully inscribed obelisks, no individualized statues or wall-paintings, whether in palaces or tombs, in any way comparable with those of the ubiquitous rulers, nobles, warriors, scribes, priests and gods of the Near East. The rulers of Cnossus and Mycenae and Troy neglected to memorialize themselves. One is free to believe if one wishes that King Minos of Cnossus, Agamemnon of Mycenae and Priam of Troy were historical personages, not figures of myth; no one has found them on the spot in any shape whatsoever, not even as a name on a slab or a seal-stone.

A by-product of all these negatives is a severe frustration and uncertainty about the chronology. There is not a single dated object from the Aegean world which is not

---

Middle Minoan palace of Mallia in Crete is about the same size as the Roman villa at Woodchester in Oxfordshire; the palace at Pylos is about half as large in area as the Iron Age settlement at Glastonbury in Somerset.

an import (and there are precious few of those). All dates are archaeological. Relative chronology is established from the stylistic evolution of pottery and the strata or layers within the ruins on each individual site. The pivots, the 'absolute' dates, are then fixed by synchronizations, made possible by imported and exported objects, with a few known dates from Egypt or Syria. Schematically stated, the basic method is to spread a number of pottery styles—Mycenaean III A, B and C, for example—over a given period of years which is estimated from the quantity of objects recovered and the extent of stylistic change. Architectural developments provide a further check. And then, if datable Egyptian objects, for example, are present, the relative time-scale can be translated into actual dates.

The most serious weakness is the impossibility of fixing precisely enough the tempo of change either in styles and techniques of pottery and other objects or in the stratification. A margin of error must always be allowed, even in the new scientific tests, such as carbon-14, and though a margin of a hundred years may seem trifling when we are dealing with a millennium or more, it amounts to three full human generations. Hence an error of that magnitude can create false ideas about growth or change or migration, and the risks are multiplied whenever two or more cultures are brought into relation with each other. Therefore, when archaeologists produce dates as precise as 1440 or 1270 B.C., they are overstepping the limits of reasonableness and enveloping their calculations in a false glow of certainty.

Once the limits are understood, approximate dates are useful and indeed indispensable. The Bronze Age section of the chronological table opening this volume gives a synchronization for Greece, Crete, Cyprus and Troy. No greater claim is made for it than that it represents a scheme which many archaeologists would accept as reasonable in the present state of knowledge. By a harmless convention, the periods in Greece are called *Helladic*, in Crete *Minoan*, and in the central Aegean islands *Cycladic* (though the validity of this last as a category is being challenged). By another convention there is a further breakdown into double triads: Early, Middle and Late, each sub-divided into I, II and III. That may create an aesthetically pleasing pattern, despite the unevenness of tempo among Helladic, Minoan and Cycladic, and one can sometimes detect a fairly clear beginning, middle and end. On the other hand, the triadic system has insufficient warrant in many sites, and it has led to rather violent methods in the attempt to force the increasing and unwilling evidence into a frame which was created in the early days of Aegean archaeology. For individual sites, the preferable procedure is that adopted by the excavators at Troy and elsewhere of numbering each layer in turn, beginning with I and continuing as necessary. For larger areas, a more general scheme is desirable; the conventional triads have been retained for reference purposes in this volume, since no alternative is available at present.

2

The 'Coming of the Greeks'

THE weakness of the conventional, excessively symmetrical division of the Bronze Age into triads and sub-triads becomes apparent when it is recognized that the sharpest and most widespread break in the archaeological record occurs between Early Helladic II and III, rather than at the beginning of Early Helladic I or in the transition from Early to Middle Helladic (usually placed about 1900 B.C.). At a date which can be narrowed by pottery finds to about 2200 or 2100, more or less complete destruction is visible in a number of major sites in the Argolid—Lerna, Tiryns, Asine, Zygouries, probably Corinth—and Attica, and the Cyclades seem to have suffered too. Precisely how widespread the devastation may have been in Greece is still not determined. It was not universal, but one can hardly dismiss as coincidence the fact that burning and destruction in the last centuries of the third millennium are also in evidence across the Aegean, in Troy II, further south at Beycesultan near the headwaters of the Meander River, and in many other sites, even in Palestine.

The word 'break' should be understood in its strongest sense. Archaeological records are filled with changes of all kinds, but not often with anything so massive and abrupt, so widely dispersed, as occurred at this particular time. In Greece nothing comparable was to happen again until the end of the Bronze Age a thousand years later. Centres which were, for their time, rich and powerful, and which had had a long history of stability and continuity, literally came tumbling down, and what followed differed unmistakably in scale and quality. Archaeology cannot normally put names to the people or content to a disaster, but in this particular combination of disasters it is legitimate to ask whether they are not witness to the concurrent arrival on one side of the

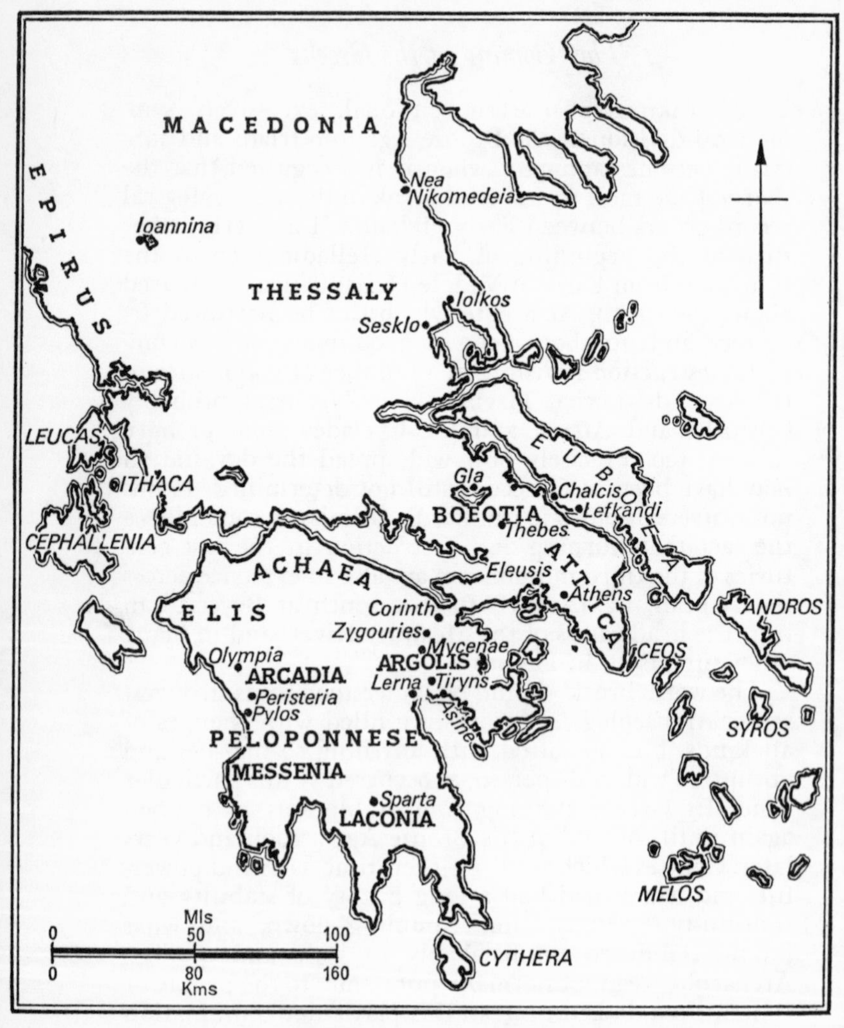

2 BRONZE AGE GREECE

Aegean Sea of migrants who spoke an early form of Greek and, on the eastern side, of people speaking other, inter-related Indo-European languages—Hittite, Luwian, Palaic.

There is an understandable reluctance to pose the question so directly. The tendency to equate language with race has bedevilled the study of prehistory and history ever since the discovery that the languages of Europe, Asia and North Africa can be classified into 'families', primarily according to structural similarities (often to be apprehended only by expert analysis). The numerous Indo-European family includes the ancient languages of India (Sanskrit) and Persia, Armenian, the Slavic tongues, several Baltic languages (Lithuanian, for instance), Greek and Albanian, the Italic languages, among which are Latin and its modern descendants, the Celtic group, of which Gaelic and Welsh have retained some vitality to our own day, the Germanic languages, and various dead languages once spoken in the Balkans (Illyrian) or in Asia Minor (such as Hittite and Phrygian). Serious students have now abandoned the romantic (or worse) conception of an 'Indo-European race', with a characteristic temperament, manners and institutions, sweeping over the land and replacing the cultures they found with one they brought with them from some hypothetical original home. Neither in Greece nor in Asia Minor is there evidence to justify anything like that. The institutions and culture of the great Hittite Empire, which in the second half of the second millennium controlled Asia Minor, and extended its influence beyond, about which we have many documents (written in the cuneiform script the Hittites adopted from Babylonia), were the products of developments within Anatolia (Asia Minor), not something fully pre-existing and brought into the area, in one piece, by a single conquering migration. Presumably the same was true of Greece in the period after 2200 B.C., for which we have no written documents before the Linear B tablets.

When that is said, however, a hard core of reality remains which must be accounted for. The time was to come, well before the end of the first millennium B.C., when much of Europe and large districts in western and central Asia spoke one or another Indo-European language. These languages were not native throughout this vast area from time immemorial, and there are sound reasons for believing that they had rivals within their own territories all through the Bronze Age (and demonstrably so into historical times in some regions). There is, in the end, no escaping the conclusion that some movement of peoples was involved, and archaeology has suggested—one might even say demonstrated—that the final linguistic map is the result not of one movement but of several, at different periods, from different centres and in different directions. Nothing else will explain, for example, the close affinity, within the Indo-European family, between Sanskrit and Lithuanian.

One of these movements seems to be reflected in the great destructions in Greece, Troy and elsewhere in Anatolia in the late third millennium B.C. There is no way at present to *prove* this hypothesis. Archaeological evidence often fails to throw any direct light on the history of languages and dialects, or even on migrations which are known from other sources or from unarguable inferences. There is, for example, no incontestable archaeological trace of the Dorians, either *en route* or after their arrival in Greece proper. Nor, as a much later example, have the Huns been clearly identified in central European archaeology. Yet someone had to introduce the Doric dialect into southern Greece, where it displaced 'Mycenaean' Greek,[1] and we know beyond doubt that the Huns made a devastating sweep into Europe. Our difficulties are further compounded by the unpredictable behaviour of language following a conquest. The Normans failed to impose Norman French in England, despite the thoroughness of their conquest and control, whereas Magyar (Hungarian), a member of the Ural-Altaic family, has survived to this day as a linguistic island surrounded by wholly unrelated Indo-European

[1] More will be said about the Dorians at the beginning of Chapter 7.

languages (German, Rumanian and several Slavic languages).

It is therefore necessary to define more closely what the suggestion of the appearance in the Aegean of Indo-European speakers before 2000 B.C. implies, and what it does not imply. To begin with, all racialist implications must be firmly rejected: it is absurd to imagine that they were already 'Greeks' having some mysterious affinity with the rulers of Mycenae 700 or 800 years later, not to mention Sappho or Pericles or Plato. Nor is it necessary to think that at the moment of entry they were speaking a language which could be easily recognized as Greek. More probably the Greek we know was finally fashioned in Greece itself, the idiom of the new arrivals being influenced by that of the older population of the peninsula. It emerged in the Mycenaean period at the latest (as is shown by the Linear B tablets), when two, or possibly three, closely related Greek dialects seem to have been diffused throughout the area, except in the isolated, mountainous regions of the northwest where the Doric dialect developed. The completely articulated classical dialect pattern—Ionic, Aeolic and Doric, with their variants and sub-categories, such as Attic—must then be attributed to the period after the breakdown of the Mycenaean world, that is, after 1200 B.C. (Map 4).

Much of the complex history of the Greek language can be explained as a purely linguistic evolution. It is therefore unnecessary to postulate successive waves of Greek-speaking immigrants into Greece, each with its own dialect, which used to be widely assumed. To say that does not preclude the possibility that there were further migrations after 2200 or 2100, from across the Aegean, for example, but it does not require them for the history of the language. Here we come up against the most notorious crux of all in interpreting the archaeological data. That important new culture-traits and impulses kept coming into Greece in the second millennium is evident on many sites. But how were they brought, by merchants and travelling craftsmen or by migration and conquest? The latter is the easy explanation—too easy. Two Middle Helladic innovations are worth closer consideration.

The first is the so-called Minyan ware, a characteristic style of pottery with a 'soapy' texture. It was remarkably widespread in Greece, the islands and parts of western Anatolia from about 1900, that is, from the beginning of Middle Helladic I, and many scholars have considered it an outstanding characteristic of a new culture brought by migrants, whom some have identified with 'the Greeks'. However, wheel-made pottery has now been found at Lerna and elsewhere in Early Helladic III which cannot be distinguished in any significant way from Minyan, except that it is an earlier, more primitive variety. There is thus no need to attach the great popularity of Minyan ware from about 1900 B.C. to a migration. All the archaeological evidence taken together now argues for the earlier date, 2200 or 2100 B.C.

Secondly, a new burial practice appears, widely dispersed, at the beginning of the Middle Helladic period. Shallow box-like graves (so-called cist-graves) were dug, sometimes lined with stone and strewn with pebbles, each containing a single body, and sealed with a slab. At first they tended to be so small that the bodies were placed in the contracted (or foetal) position; furthermore, no grave-goods were added. Eventually they became larger and richer. What is new is none of this—already widespread in the Cyclades centuries earlier—but the practice of placing the cist-graves of children, and occasionally of adults, within the house, under the floor or behind walls. A new outlook is indicated. But does that require a migration? If so, the new population would have had to be exceedingly numerous and all-conquering to impose a new funeral pattern so rapidly, and it is odd that cemeteries outside the village continued to be the rule for adults. The fact is that in the Aegean area throughout the Bronze Age, and in historical times as well, there was a bewildering variety of burial practices, varying regionally as well as in time, and often co-existing for long periods in the same community. Bodies were buried individually and in family groups, in different kinds of containers; they were sometimes dug up after decomposition and then the bones were re-buried; eventually cremation supplemented burial. The thinking behind the many shifts in practice usually escapes us, but one thing is certain, namely, that most of the changes arose without benefit of a migration. Hence there is no particular reason why the introduction of intramural burial should of itself imply a migration.

The Aegean was always a highway for ideas, techniques and institutions, at the beginning of the second millennium as at other times. It is a curious habit never to credit the people under consideration with any originality, always to make them borrowers and someone else the innovators. Anyway, originality never means creation out of nothing, and it is no less valuable and consequential when it starts from an idea borrowed from elsewhere. If, as appears, the Argolid was the centre of destruction by intruders about 2200 B.C., the further implication is that it was from this well-watered, fertile district that there eventually grew and spread the culture of the Early Helladic III and Middle Helladic periods out of which, in turn, there emerged the Late Helladic (or Mycenaean) civilization. That is a very different picture from the romantic one of the conquest which blanketed the whole, or even most, of Greece in one great swoop. The 'coming of the Greeks', in other words, meant the arrival of a new element who combined with their predecessors to create, slowly, a new civilization and to extend it as and where they could.

The destruction of earlier centres of power, such as the highly fortified Lerna, did not mean that its inhabitants were killed off or that comparable destruction took place in the hinterland. Some places were abandoned for longer or shorter periods, others not. Furthermore, the Bronze Age in Greece was not restricted to a few fortified towns such as Early Helladic II Lerna or Late Helladic Mycenae. Because the number of excavated sites is still a tiny fraction of the whole and because archaeologists naturally try to expend their limited time and resources on sites which promise to be most fruitful, an illusion of grandeur results. It is a sobering experience to read through a recently published catalogue of places now known to have been inhabited in the southwestern Peloponnese. On that small space, bounded by the Alpheus River, Mt. Taygetus, the Messenian Gulf and the Ionian Sea, the total of Late Helladic sites may be as high as 116, of Middle Helladic perhaps fifty-one on present evidence, which is certainly incomplete. Most of them were mere hamlets, and many were deserted for all time at the end of the Bronze Age.[1] These figures reflect both the 'inner colonization' of Greece from various centres and a steady increase in the absolute population figures. To attempt to separate the newcomers from their predecessors in such a development is impossible. And similarly with their respective contributions to the newly developing culture, or better, cultural complex. In sum, everyone contributed in one way or another, including people outside the Greek peninsula, in Crete, the Cyclades and Anatolia.

Unfortunately there is little that can be said about the new culture until the sudden outburst of power and luxuriant opulence revealed by the shaft-graves at Mycenae beginning before 1600 B.C. For five or six hundred years, from the beginning of Early Helladic III right through the Middle Helladic phase, the material remains are consistently so poverty-stricken that we are left unprepared for the great age that followed. The hamlets (for even Lerna can hardly be called more than that now) have a general uniformity of aspect: unfortified, usually sited on mounds or low knolls, irregular rather than laid out, huddled, lacking palaces or other really large buildings. Metal tools and weapons were pathetic, the latter rare altogether and too precious to be expended as grave-goods. Although pottery finds suggest some contact between the Argolid and the western islands of Ithaca and Leucas, perhaps even with the Lipari islands north of Sicily, the over-all impression is

[1] W. A. McDonald and R. Hope Simpson in *American Journal of Archaeology*, 68 (1964), pp. 229–45.

one of a grey uniformity and of isolation in the Middle Helladic period. Only the appearance, almost from the beginning, of Cretan objects and Cretan influences strikes a different note: an occasional imported Cretan cup or vase is found in a mainland grave, and potters in Athens and elsewhere began to introduce Minoan shapes among their wares.

Just what these Cretan connexions signify is hard to say. There is no reason to believe in any kind of Cretan authority over Greece in the eighteenth or seventeenth century. Nothing in the poor material remains reveals the developments in social organization and in ideas which, it is reasonable to assume, lay at the foundation of the subsequent Mycenaean civilization. Only the spread of settlement and the implied growth in population, already noticed, offer a hint that something significant was happening, however slowly.

3

The Islands

I. THE CYCLADES AND CYPRUS

THE eastern Mediterranean, unlike the western, is dotted with islands. Except for Rhodes and Cyprus, only occasionally did they play an independent role in historical times, if for no other reason because of their limited size and resources. Earlier, however, when population was small everywhere, when technology and social organization were less advanced, there were periods during which some of the islands (or groups of islands) were in the forefront of important developments in civilization. Crete was eventually outstanding, but relatively behindhand in the early metallurgical stage.

It is the Cyclades to which one must first turn. This cluster of small islands, extending in a southeasterly direction from Ceos and Andros, close to the southern tips of Attica and Euboea, respectively, to Thera (modern Santorini), Anaphe and Astypalaea, forms the central bridge across the Aegean Sea between Greece and Asia. Ranging in size from Naxos (170 square miles) to mere mounds of rock jutting from the sea, they have a forbidding appearance that is rather deceptive. Their coasts, inhospitable to modern ships with few exceptions, are dotted with bays suitable for Bronze Age vessels (both peaceful and piratical). And many islands possessed arable land: it was agriculture, fishing and the herding of sheep, goats and pigs that sustained the bulk of the inhabitants, rather than seafaring. On the other hand, it was seafaring, together with stone and metal working, that gave the Cyclades their importance in the present context. Appropriately enough, the most numerous of the early representations of Aegean ships have been found there—small models in lead from Naxos (*Plate Ia*), possibly to be dated before 2500 B.C., and engravings on flat circular terracotta objects (irresistibly named 'frying pans' by archaeologists) from Syros (*Plate Ib*), of a slightly later date. The ships have steep prows, no sails, and about a dozen oars on each side.

The Naxian models were unnoticed for nearly thirty years after their discovery,[1] and that is sufficient indication of the archaeological neglect of the Cyclades hitherto. Apart from one flurry at the turn of the present century, systematic excavation did not begin before the late 1950s. In consequence, all conclusions and general statements must be read as preliminary and tentative. Until recently, for example, no certain evidence had existed of a Neolithic phase. Now we have some from Ceos, and more ancient finds from tiny Saliagos, off Antiparos, going back perhaps to 4000 B.C. This late Neolithic culture seems unrelated to that of Crete or the eastern Aegean but similar to finds from nearby Attica, Euboea and Corinth. However one explains the affinities, it appears that migrants crossing the sea by-passed the Cyclades for 2000 years (as we have already noticed in connexion with the exploitation of Melian obsidian), that the first settlements were few and isolated, and that there was a sudden blossoming in the Early Bronze Age, after 3000 B.C. Not surprising, influences are visible from both Greece and Asia Minor, but the Early Bronze Cycladic culture formed traits of its own which cannot be mistaken. More correctly, one should speak of Cycladic cultures; in the material sphere, which is all we know, distinctions become more prominent as the volume of evidence accumulates, showing the development of local specialities in Syros, Amorgos, Naxos and perhaps elsewhere. The so-called Keros-Syros culture, contemporary with Early Helladic II and Early Minoan II, in the centuries beginning about 2500, marked the apogee. Metallurgical techniques influenced those of

[1] See now C. Renfrew, 'Cycladic Metallurgy and the Aegean Early Bronze Age', *American Journal of Archaeology*, 71 (1967), pp. 1–20.

Crete and Greece, as far as Epirus; metals may have been exported (at least silver and lead, relatively abundant in the Cyclades); manufactured articles in clay and marble were widely distributed. Yet there were scarcely any large settlements or heavy concentrations of people. Even Phylakopi on Melos, the most considerable Early Bronze Cycladic community known so far, remained unfortified.

The most notable of all Cycladic products were the marble 'idols', predominantly but not exclusively female, found in large numbers in graves, not only in the islands themselves but also on the mainland of Greece and in Asia Minor. Ranging in size from a few inches to, in one or two cases, five feet, these statuettes, often quite crude, are flat from front to back, with elongated oval heads. The sexual aspects are understressed, sometimes virtually absent, and the total impression is of an almost *avant garde* geometrical abstractness (*Plate Ic*). They were manufactured primarily to accompany the dead in their graves, and so they reflect some religious impulse or conception, which was shared outside the limits of the Cyclades. It is idle to pretend that we can grasp the thinking, just as we cannot yet understand a later Cycladic novelty, again in the field of religion. On Ceos in the Middle Bronze Age there was a building which appears to be a temple, at a time when such structures were unknown elsewhere in the Aegean world. In the ruins have been found hundreds of fragments of life-sized hollow clay female statues, the debris of at least nineteen individual figures, and possibly more than twenty-four. If they were goddesses, they had no known precedents in the Aegean, nor any successors for nearly another thousand years.

By the Middle Bronze Age the Cyclades had fallen off in importance. There are no signs of major disturbance; on the contrary, the remains reveal a continuous existence right through the prehistoric period, and the historical as well. But now their smallness reduced these islands to minor significance, to be noticed only on occasion, either because of some natural advantage or in relation to some larger and greater power. Thus the marble of Naxos and Paros retained its pre-eminence for many centuries. Thera, which suffered a major volcanic catastrophe early in the Late Helladic period, nevertheless became, in the Archaic period, a Dorian centre of sufficient prominence to be responsible for the first Greek settlement in Cyrene (Libya). Naxos and Melos were destined to occupy a special place in the historian Thucydides' account of the fifth-century Athenian Empire, and, still later, Melos gave us the best known of all Greek sculptures, the 'Venus of Milo' now in the Louvre. In all significant respects, then, the history of the Cyclades was an integral part of the history of Greece, outstanding for a fleeting moment at the beginning of the Bronze Age.

Unlike the Cyclades, Cyprus was integrated into the Greek sphere only for periods, and never fully. With its 3500 square miles, it was the largest island in the eastern Mediterranean (somewhat larger than Crete), and its location linked it to Anatolia and even more to Syria, rather than to Greece. The shortest run to Asia Minor is less than fifty miles, to Syria about seventy-five, whereas Rhodes, the easternmost Greek centre, is no nearer (250 miles) than Alexandria in Egypt. Good harbours, suitable for ancient shipping if not for modern ocean-going vessels (save for Famagusta), were most numerous on the east and south coasts, pointing to the Levant. The destiny of Cyprus was therefore shaped by two factors, neither of which the Cypriots could themselves control. One was the commercial and political situation in the eastern Mediterranean as a whole. Active trade between Greece and the Levant normally benefited Cyprus as a station on the way, but wars for possession of Syria or conflicts over naval supremacy (as those between Venice and Turks in the sixteenth century A.D.) could have destructive effects. The second factor was the extent of demand abroad for its copper ore, the key to Cypriot growth and prosperity in the Bronze Age. But one should not forget that, apart from the narrow mountain range on the north side and the extensive mountains of the west and southwest, Cyprus has not only much arable land but also good inland communications, a rarity in the Aegean. For thousands of years agriculture was the basis of Cypriot life; the substantial coastal towns did not emerge until the export of copper took on significant proportions.

The early history of population movements is obscure, not only for the usual reasons but also because of an unexplained volatility in the settlement pattern. Sites were frequently abandoned and not later re-occupied; the next inhabitants often preferred a fresh start somewhere nearby. The earliest pre-pottery Neolithic phase, which has produced one radio-carbon date soon after 6000 B.C., seems to have been thinly represented and short-lived. On present evidence, there is a complete gap between about 5000 and 3500, when a second Neolithic phase appeared, lasting a thousand years, with more than a hundred sites now identified. About 2500, catastrophe overwhelmed the island, apparently a natural and not a man-made one, wiping out (or driving away) much of the population, followed by another gap of some 200 years. Then, about 2300 B.C., the Bronze Age began rather abruptly, and such innovations as new pottery shapes and burial practices, considered together with the art of metal-working in a thinly peopled country, point to migration, conceivably coming from Asia Minor, through Morphou Bay in the northwest, as a backlash of the troubles in Anatolia mentioned at the beginning of Chapter 2.

The first four centuries of the Bronze Age witnessed slow but steady growth, revealed by the increase in the number and size of the settlements. Most were in the interior, in agricultural regions with good supplies of water, but native copper was being mined from the start, and at least one harbour-town, later known as Citium (modern Larnaka), was immediately established on the south coast for exports (an inference from a few Egyptian finds in the ruins). After 2000, westward trade began to pick up, not with Greece but with Crete; that island now looked further afield, beyond the Cyclades, pressed by its own growing need for copper. And trade with the Levant grew as well: cuneiform texts from Mari on the Euphrates River refer to copper and bronze imports from Alasiya (commonly held to be Cyprus) in the eighteenth century. Cyprus now entered her greatest period, which continued until 1200 B.C. The interior dwindled in importance, as genuine urban centres grew all along the southern and eastern seaboard, centres of manufacture as well as of trade. The graves give abundant evidence of wealth and luxury—and also of weapons, which Cypriots could now afford to expend in this way. The eastern orientation is unmistakable, until about 1400, when pottery from Mycenaean Greece began to invade the island. One calculation will indicate the scale of this new phenomenon, which lasted for two centuries. At the principal Cypriot Bronze Age site, near the village of Enkomi about three miles inland from Salamis Bay on the east coast, more large and expensive mixing-bowls and jugs of the Mycenaean III A type are said to have been found than in all the rest of the Aegean world together, including Greece itself.

These developments affected the power structure in a way that may have been comparable to those in Greece, but could not have been possible in the small islands of the Cyclades. The numerous weapons in the graves and the fortified settlements and hill-forts of the interior are pointers, the political interpretation of which rests heavily on the identification of the place-name Alasiya. The economic importance of Cyprus at this time is not in question. Its copper and bronze ingots are found or pictured everywhere, in Greece, in Egypt, even in Sardinia. The most dramatic evidence comes from the wreckage off Cape Gelidoniya, at the southwestern corner of Anatolia, of a 30-foot vessel which was sailing westwards with a cargo of at least one ton of bulk copper, bronze and tin, a quantity of tools and other objects, most of them carried as scrap metal, and unidentifiable perishable goods in jars. The closest date that can be assigned to the wreck is 1200 $\pm$50; there are reasons to think that the captain-merchant was a Syrian; and there can be no doubt that the metal (both the ingots and the scrap) was Cypriot in origin.[1]

But was there some centralized control over this wealthy island, and, if so, by whom, Cypriots or Asiatic mainlanders? This is the big question behind the identification of Alasiya. The name appears in Egyptian, Hittite, North Syrian and other Near Eastern documents throughout the second millennium, and most experts accept the identification with Cyprus, or at least with as much of the island as the rulers of Enkomi controlled. The 'king of Alasiya' was a considerable figure, who could stand up to the greater and better known monarchs of the Near East. He addressed the Egyptian Pharaoh as 'my brother'. The king of Ugarit (now Ras Shamra) in northern Syria called him 'my father'. He was a nuisance, and sometimes more, to the rulers of the Hittite Empire, who managed to bring him under control for a time, but not for long, and against whom he was able to hold his own in naval warfare. 'My brother' was mere diplomatic politeness, of course, and it can hardly be imagined that Alasiya was even faintly on a level of equality with the Hittite Empire or Egypt. But it *was* a power.

Unfortunately, a nagging doubt about the identification of Alasiya remains, and it will not be resolved until decisive written documentation is discovered. After 1100 the name Alasiya disappears. The Assyrians subsequently seem to have called the island Yadnana, and eventually Cyprus replaced all other names, though we cannot date it or identify its origin. Cyprus is also the word for copper (Kupfer, cuivre) in modern European languages, but not in Greek, which adds one last complication to the story. Nothing can really be said about the languages spoken on the island in the Neolithic and

[1] For a very full account of the discovery and its implications, see G. F. Bass *et al.*, *Cape Gelidoniya, a Bronze Age Shipwreck* (*Transactions of the American Philosophical Society*, vol. 57, part 8, 1967); more briefly in Joan du Plat Taylor, ed., *Marine Archeology* (London, Hutchinson; New York, Crowell, 1965), pp. 119–40.

Bronze Ages. There is nothing to indicate that Cyprus was penetrated by the migrations which brought Indo-European languages to Asia Minor and Greece before 2000 B.C. (If there is anything to the suggestion of a migration from Anatolia about 2300, it would have been of people fleeing from the ancestors of the Hittites.) Neither Alasiya nor Yadnana nor even, so far as we can judge, Cyprus is an Indo-European name. The only writing which has turned up consists of a few tablets found at Enkomi and in Syria (Ras Shamra), the earliest dated to about 1500 on archaeological grounds. Because the script (or possibly scripts) has affinities with Linear A, it has been labelled Cypro-Minoan, but it has not been deciphered and therefore does not help. The flood of Mycenaean ceramics between 1400 and 1200 was not accompanied by other Mycenaean culture traits and it is therefore unlikely that there was an influx of people from Greece along with the pottery.

The time was to come, however, when the Greek language was spoken and written by a large proportion of the Cypriots, and the form it took in the classical period gives the necessary clue to the date of introduction. The dialect is closely linked with that of Arcadia, the most land-locked district in the Peloponnese, and the writing was not only syllabic (when all the other Greeks had gone over to the phonetic alphabet[1]) but it retained seven signs from Linear B and others which were modifications of that extinct script. The Greek language and script were therefore established in Cyprus before the final disappearance of Mycenean civilization, and before the Peloponnese had gone over to a West Greek dialect. In Chapter 6 we shall see that the date was about 1200, shortly before Bronze Age Cyprus was devastated, the victim, like much of Syria and Asia Minor, of the so-called 'Sea Peoples'.

[1] In a syllabic script, most of the signs stand for syllables (a consonant and a vowel together), as in the classical Cypriot signs reproduced in Figure 2. A phonetic alphabet such as our own, in contrast, is made up for the most part of signs, each of which represents a vowel or consonantal sound.

4

The Islands

II. CRETE

THE other great island in the eastern Mediterranean, Crete (3200 square miles), had a very different development. Today it is a forbidding and largely barren land, the victim of gross mistreatment by man. If one approaches from the south, the view is rugged and spectacular, as the mountains come down to the sea. The White Mountains in the west are almost inaccessible. But in antiquity eastern and central Crete was justly famed for its meadows and pastoral uplands, its olives and vines, its oaks and cypresses, its protected beaches on the northern and eastern shores. Unlike Cyprus, however, Crete was poor in mineral resources and its was less favourably located for sea-borne traffic to and from Asia Minor, Syria and Egypt.

For more than 3000 years Crete gave no hint of what was to come in the Bronze Age. The earliest Neolithic habitations go back to about 6000 B.C., chiefly in the mountain caves with which the island is dotted, hundreds of which have remains of human activity. Although Melian obsidian has been found in Neolithic levels at Cnossus and Phaestus, the general impression is that Neolithic Crete lived in isolation. Metals made their appearance later than on the mainland, not before 2500 or even 2300 in any abundance. By that time the people had emerged from their caves, increased considerably in numbers and made great strides in technology. The more important settlements were at the eastern end of the island, but eventually there was a shift to the centre, and there were hamlets everywhere, even in the forbidding western region.

The development from the Stone Age to the Bronze is far from clearly understood. At Cnossus, Sir Arthur

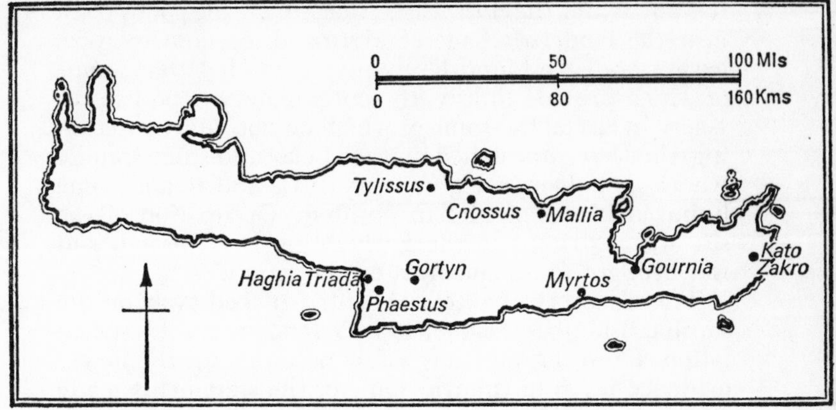

3 ANCIENT CRETE

Evans saw no sharp break and visualized the Early Minoan period (now dated from about 2800 to 2000 B.C.) as a long transitional one. More recently archaeologists have disputed his view, after taking account of the very different archaeological record at other sites. Evans, who first uncovered the palace at Cnossus in 1899, and then worked there with great skill and energy until his death in 1941, not surprisingly tended to impose a Cnossian stamp on the whole island. His division into periods conceals too much: Crete, like Greece, was at this time not uniform or monolithic in its culture. But Evans seems to have been right in conceiving of the Early Minoan phase as a direct evolutionary growth, not as a break from the late Neolithic culture. In many sites, the line between Early Minoan I and II, about 2500 B.C., is much more striking, as evidenced by the stone vases, rich jewelry and copper daggers of the later period. Regional variations are equally striking. For example, of the 500-odd Early Minoan II copper and bronze objects now catalogued, approximately two-thirds come from the south of the island, whereas the early silver and lead artifacts, far fewer in number, were nearly all found in the north and the northeast. At a site on the south coast near the modern village of Myrtos, discovered in 1962, excavators have found large quantities of pottery, some of which provide links with contemporary deposits elsewhere in Crete, but some of which do not. More interesting, they have unearthed masses of clay and stone spindle whorls and loom weights, very little metal and some hundred blades of Melian obsidian. Occupation of the site was restricted to the Early Minoan II period, and was brought to an end by a conflagration.[1]

The discovery of a 'textile centre' tucked away on the south coast opens the door to wide (and even wild) speculation. However, one may safely note that all the newer evidence helps to confirm some of the statements made earlier in this book about social development in general. The predominance of stone and clay tools long after the introduction of metallurgy is seen in the absence of metal tools for agriculture, and in the disproportion of daggers among the metal artifacts (perhaps half the total). This was linked with the development of a more ramified social structure and of specialization of labour. Fundamental was a division between town and country, which we may infer from the absence of farm implements in both the urban houses and the graves. There may also have been a trend towards specialization as between communities: a 'textile centre' is not intelligible in any other terms. The roots of these important developments lay in the Late Neolithic Age, within Crete itself, invisible though they now are to us. That is to say, although Crete had emerged from its long isolation to enter the Aegean Bronze Age complex, receiving influences from Greece and Macedonia, from the Cyclades, from Asia Minor notably, from Syria and even from Egypt (probably indirectly), the history of Crete, as we study it from its material remains, is neither one of mechanical imitation nor one of extensive immigration, but one of a society which absorbed new elements into a coherent internal development of its own.

[1] *Illustrated London News* for 17 February, 1968, pp. 25–7.

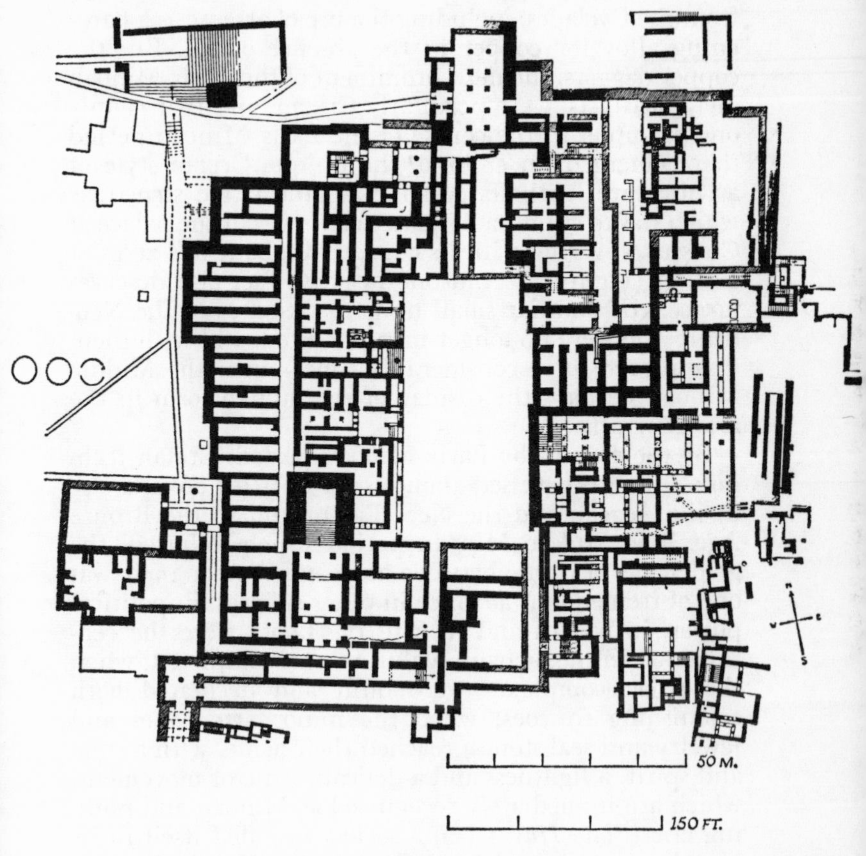

Figure 1 Palace at Cnossus

The signs of inventive originality are numerous and unambiguous. Vases and other small objects were regularly re-shaped and re-designed, not just copied, even when borrowing from abroad is most obvious. The basic techniques of metallurgy almost certainly were learned from the Cyclades, including the use of arsenic as a hardening alloy for copper in the absence of tin. But the copper daggers, the most prominent of the Early Minoan metal artifacts, were peculiarly Cretan, and that is only one example. In the course of the Early Minoan period there emerged, in embryo, the unique Cretan style of architecture, with its cell-like, agglutinative structure, which was to culminate in later centuries in the palace at Cnossus, covering with its courtyards about five acres of ground (Figure 1). And one negative fact also deserves notice: the familiar small human statuettes of the Neolithic Age were no longer manufactured, and with them disappeared for a considerable time—until the Middle Minoan period—the display of the human form in the arts generally.

By the end of the Early Minoan period, Cretan technology had progressed about as far as it (or anyone else in the Aegean and the Near East) could in the Bronze Age. The Middle Minoan period which followed, the golden age of Crete, between 2000 and 1600 or 1550, was one of tremendous advance in other spheres, in political power, in wealth and in artistry. Those were the centuries when the 'urban revolution' was completed; when the palace-complexes were built and decorated with astonishing frescoes; when the minor arts (vases and jewelry and seal-stones) reached their acme, with a style and spirit, a lightness and a delicate sense of movement, which are immediately recognized as Minoan and nothing else (*Plate IIa*); when a society revealed itself in its visual arts as one that, at least at the top, had a psychology and style of life quite unlike any other of its day (or of any other age in antiquity for that matter).

Perhaps the most remarkable manifestation of Cretan originality was in the field of writing. When one considers how few systems of writing have ever been

Ib Terracotta 'frying pan', 30 cm high, showing Cycladic ship, from Syros

Ic
Cycladic 'idol', 32 cm high, found in Amorgos

Ia Lead ship model, 42 cm long, Naxos, probably before 2500 B.C.

IIa Late Minoan seal-stones in semi-precious stone: *left* (impression) from Praesus, 2 cm in diameter; *right* from near Cnossus, 3 cm in diameter

IIb Thin gold disk, 5 cm in diameter, shaft-grave Circle A, Mycenae

IIc Clay snake, 20 cm in diameter, Mycenae, perhaps 1300 B.C.

invented anywhere and at any time in world history, the Cretan contribution, within a relatively short period, seems beyond comprehension. First came a kind of modified picture-writing which Evans labelled 'hieroglyphic' on the analogy of the Egyptian script. There then emerged, in the early Middle Minoan centuries, a more sophisticated script, called 'Linear A' by Evans, in which most of the signs represented syllables. Linear A was widely dispersed on the island, the largest number of texts having so far been found at Haghia Triada and Kato Zakro. Eventually it gave way at Cnossus to Linear B, an outgrowth in a complicated way from Linear A. Although Linear B, unlike Linear A, was also employed on the mainland of Greece,[1] so far no examples have been found in Crete elsewhere than at Cnossus. The question remains open whether we are faced with an accident of archaeology or with a phenomenon of Cretan history. If a recent claim stands up that spectrographic analysis of twenty-five 'stirrup-jars' with Linear B signs found in Thebes indicates that the majority were manufactured in eastern Crete,[2] the balance of probability would swing towards the accidental explanation. The question is important, for it is linked with such further issues as the extent and nature of Cnossian suzerainty in Crete, and the precise part which writing played in the society.[3]

[1] A few vases, clay lamps and other objects with from one to three Linear A signs have been found in Melos, Thera, Ceos and Naxos, but it is premature, to say the least, to draw any inferences about Cycladic 'literacy' from such weak testimony. It is not unfair to point out that archaeologists have not always been able to distinguish mere scratches from Linear A signs.

[2] H. W. Catling and A. Millett in *Archaeometry*, 8 (1965), pp. 3–85. But see the objections raised by J. Raison, *Les vases à inscriptions peintes de l'âge mycénien* (Rome, 1968), pp. 196–209, 233–40.

[3] Account must also be taken of yet another script, on a small disk from Phaestus, seemingly related to, but not identical with, the writing on a double axe found at Arkalochori in central Crete and to that on a limestone slab from Mallia, and of other bits and pieces. So far these isolated finds have produced a vast amount of commentary but no acceptable solutions.

CRETAN SCRIPTS			CLASSICAL CYPRIOT SYLLABARY		EARLY ALPHABETS		
Hiero-glyphs	Linear A	Linear B	(Sounds)		Greek names for letters	N. Semitic	Early Attic
			a		*Alpha*		
			ka		*Beta*		
			ta		*Gamma*		
			pa		*Delta*		
			la		*Epsilon*		
			ra		*Vau (digamma)*		
			ma		*Zeta*		
			na		*Heta*		
			ja		*Theta*		
			wa		*Iota*		
			sa		*Kappa*		
			za		*Lambda*		
			e		*Mu*		
			ke		*Nu*		

Figure 2 Scripts (none is complete)

Apart from signs engraved or scratched on pottery, seal-stones, libation-tables and various miscellaneous objects, Cretan writing is known to us in bulk only from small, leaf-shaped clay tablets totalling less than 4000, many of them mere fragments. Perishable materials, such as wax or papyrus, were certainly also used, but no trace of them remains. And even the clay tablets have survived by accident. They were not baked before use and they were discarded when they were no longer needed; only the conflagrations that accompanied the destruction of the palaces preserved whatever tablets happened to be on hand at the moment, all of them dating from that year. In consequence, we have something analogous to a cross-section of a cell under a microscope, lacking depth, any hint of development or change, of the element of time. And the texts themselves are both short and very restricted in range, consisting of lists of one kind or another, or of cryptic recordings of property relationships, ration allocations and the like. Even if all the known tablets could be read and translated with complete certainty, which they cannot, documents such as the following from Cnossus—'At Lasunthos (?): Two nurses, one girl, one boy' or 'Amnisos: One jar of honey to Eileithyia. One jar of honey to all the gods. One jar of honey . . .'—would soon exhaust themselves as sources of significant information.

The language of the tablets in Linear B, the latest of the scripts, is now known to be Greek (and more will be said about this below). But so far all efforts to decipher either Linear A or the still earlier hieroglyphic writing have failed. This is partly because the available texts are so few—the Linear B texts from Cnossus outnumber the Linear A tablets from all of Crete by about ten to one—but primarily because the language of the latter is certainly not Greek and probably not any known tongue. The suggestion that it is a Semitic tongue has little support. The more plausible suggestion of Luwian, inferred from such place-names as Cnossus and Tylissus, has failed to lead to an even partial decipherment. All we can say, therefore, is that the language of the Linear A script was that of the people who created the Minoan golden age; and that the script was originally invented for that language and later transferred to Greek, for which it was not very well suited. Our ignorance even extends to important place-names. If Cnossus and Gortyn and Phaestus maintained a continued, though unimportant, existence, and hence their names, throughout ancient Greek history, other centres were destroyed and totally abandoned in the Bronze Age. Haghia Triada and Kato Zakro, for example, have had to be given identifying labels from contemporary landmarks: their own names are still unknown.

The tablets, in sum, have provided important supplementary information, some of it novel (especially on the history of the Greek language), but our basic source is still the material remains. Perhaps the most important contribution of the tablets is to reinforce the power implications inherent in the archaeology. Indeed, it can be argued that the needs of a centralized administration were a far greater impetus to the development of writing, among the Sumerians (cuneiform) as in Crete, than intellectual or spiritual needs. Between the Late Neolithic era and the Middle Minoan period there was a rapid increase in human and natural resources and a concentration, both socially and geographically, of the power to employ them. Otherwise the great palace-complexes could neither have been built nor have functioned. There is not one tablet which indicates buying or selling of commodities; there is not even a word for either activity. On the other hand, there are many inventories, ration-lists and lists of personnel. The implication is that the whole society was run from the palace-centre, which organized the internal economy in every detail administratively, distributing people and goods, from the raw materials to the finished products, without the use of money or of a market-mechanism. Some confirmation comes from a demonstration that the numerous Cnossus tablets listing sheep and wool—all of them, it must be remembered, dating in the year of the destruction of the site—record an annual census of flocks and shearings and of the shepherds responsible. The total number of animals was about 100,000, and, insofar as place-names can be identified, they seem to have been pastured all over central and eastern Crete. It therefore appears that the palace at Cnossus had some sort of sheep-and-wool monopoly running to half the island.

The suggestion then comes to mind that wool may help answer an old puzzle: how did the Cretans pay for (or otherwise obtain) the copper, gold, ivory and other things they had to import? Wool is now offered as at least part of the answer. And it is true that the Cretans (called Keftiu) represented on Egyptian frescoes sometimes carry folded cloths. But they also carried gold, silver, ivory and other things which are not Cretan products, so that this bit of concrete evidence for wool as a major trading commodity is somewhat weakened. At this point the tablets are frustratingly, and surprisingly, silent. They say nothing about the outside world in any respect: that world might just as well not have existed so far as the tablets are concerned. And archaeology alone, it cannot be repeated often enough, rarely can reveal the *mechanism* of foreign relations even when it unearths great quantities of foreign or foreign-inspired goods.

Another approach suggested by modern scholars is to put the stress on empire and tribute, on the so-called Minoan thalassocracy (rule of the sea), references to which are found in classical Greek writers. There can be no dispute either about the wealth and power of Cnossus or about Minoan seamanship. There seem to have been 'Minoan' settlements on some nearby islands, notably on Cythera to the north, where the peak was reached in Late Minoan I, not very long before the site was abandoned (with no trace of destruction). However, the further step to a wide-ranging maritime *empire*, in the usual sense of that word, is neither simple nor self-evident, and it can be argued that the whole notion is very weakly based. The first Greek mention of thalassocracy is by Herodotus and Thucydides in the second half of the fifth century B.C., and that is far too late to be taken seriously by itself, without supporting evidence. The many Greek legends about prehistoric Crete have different emphases, mostly purely religious in character. The notable exception is the story of Theseus and the minotaur, which deserves special consideration.

The story runs like this. King Minos was married to Pasiphaë, daughter of the Sun, who developed an unnatural passion for a bull that had come out of the sea. She appealed to the divinely descended craftsman Daedalus, who constructed a contraption which enabled her to have intercourse with the beast. Pasiphaë then gave birth to a monster, half man, half bull, called the minotaur. On the king's orders, Daedalus built a labyrinth in which the monster was housed, and every year the Athenians, who were subjects of Minos, were required to supply seven youths and seven maidens to be fed to the minotaur. One year Theseus, the young son of the Athenian king, persuaded his father to include him in the annual consignment of victims. When Theseus arrived in Crete, he won the love of Minos' daughter Ariadne, and with her aid he slew the minotaur. The pair then fled to the island of Naxos; there Theseus deserted Ariadne, the god Dionysus found her and married her.

That tale, it has been claimed, reflects in mythical form Athenian subjection to, and then emancipation from, Cretan overlordship during the Bronze Age. But the objections to such an interpretation are grave. Although monsters of the half-man, half-animal type are common, particularly in Minoan seal-stones, only one or two harmless looking 'minotaurs' have been found. The bull, on the other hand, is amply documented as an important element in Minoan religion: as a sacrificial animal, or in the familiar 'bull-leaping' scenes, which are more likely to represent some form of ritual than a mere sport, or in small bronze statuettes found in some of the caves which were cult-centres. A possible explanation of the minotaur legend, therefore, is that it is a later tale devised to explain some ceremony, perhaps an initiation, linked with the worship of Dionysus, the original meaning of which had long been forgotten.[1] The alternative, that it is a concealed account of the overthrow of a foreign overlord, strains the imagination. History knows enough examples of traditional tales in which a people recounts how it once won independence, and they never disguise it so heavily as to conceal the fundamental point they are making. It may also be relevant that in the Middle Minoan period, Athens shows less trace of Cretan connexions, apart from artistic influences, than a number of other mainland centres.

Yet another puzzle is presented to us by the openness of the Cretan palaces, none of them citadels in the proper sense but unfortified 'civilian' complexes. The contrast with such mainland fortresses as Mycenae and Tiryns strikes every visitor. Minoan thalassocracy cannot be the explanation, often as it may be proposed. Threats from overseas have never been the only, or even the decisive, cause for fortification. They surely do not explain Mycenae or Tiryns any more than a medieval castle. Was there never any danger of conflict between palaces? Was there no need for compulsion and police protection at home? Yet everywhere one turns in Crete, peacefulness is the prevailing tone. The caves, which became havens of refuge in troubled times throughout Cretan history, ancient and modern, were uninhabited during the palace-era. Arms, armour and chariots are recorded in the Linear B tablets from Cnossus, but they are remarkably rare in the figured monuments of any nature or size. They are even rare in the graves; it is only after the occupation by Greek-speaking people from the mainland that one can properly talk of warrior-graves at all.

[1] This suggestion is buttressed by the persuasive arguments of Paul Faure, *Fonctions des cavernes crétoises* (*Travaux et mémoires* of the Ecole française d' Athènes XIV, 1964), pp. 166–73, that the labyrinth is to be identified not with the palace of Cnossus, but with a cave. He suggests the cave of Skotino, some miles east of Cnossus, where evidence of cult goes back to the beginning of the Middle Minoan period and persists into the Archaic Greek period. Religious continuity of such long duration is attested in not more than three or four Cretan caves.

Whatever the explanation of this phenomenon, it is one reason for stressing the uniqueness of Crete. The palace-centred society and its obsessively detailed records are reminiscent of Ugarit in North Syria or Mari on the Euphrates. But, as has already been said, the psychology and the values at the top were radically different in many respects, whatever may have been the case with the mass of the population, about whom we know nothing. Although not a line of writing exists, either from Crete or from the much more abundant documentation of her neighbours, near or far, which tells us anything explicit of the thinking of Bronze Age Crete, of their *ideas* on any subject, it is possible to draw some inferences from the material remains about their differences from the other centralized societies of their day.

Babylonian, Egyptian and Hittite rulers filled their lands with monumental evidence of their power, and of the power of their gods. Cretan rulers did nothing of the kind, neither in their palaces nor in their tombs. There is nothing majestic or central about the throne-room at Cnossus, whether in its size or in its wall-decoration (with its mythical animals and floral designs, but without a single portrait). Even the throne is not particularly regal. Not a single picture exists which portrays an historical event or which reveals administrative or judicial activity or any other manifestation of political power in action.

As for the gods and goddesses, they are difficult to discover at all. They seem to have been fairly numerous, but they were not housed in temples and so there was no need for the cult-statue characteristic of both contemporary Near Eastern and later Greek civilizations. Worship was carried on in small domestic shrines, in sacred places out of doors, and in about twenty-five of the caves in various parts of the island (by and large, not the more spectacular caves, and not all of them in use simultaneously). In the ceremonies, the stress was on an epiphany, on the temporary appearance of a divinity in response to prayer, to sacrifice, or—most characteristically and originally Cretan—to ritual dancing. In many of the scenes, it is the ecstasy of the worshippers which is central rather than the god in person; indeed, the act of anticipation alone is sometimes portrayed without the actual epiphany. The site of the epiphany was a sacred tree, a pillar, occasionally an architectural façade. Given this stress on the worshippers, on the human side of the relationship, it was appropriate that, except for a few frescoes and an occasional sarcophagus, these scenes should have been engraved on rings, seal-stones and small ceramic objects. Otherwise, the evidence for religion consists largely of such symbolic objects as the double axe and the 'horns of consecration',[1] the interpretation of which remains much disputed; of the equipment used in libations and sacrifices; especially in the caves, of the ashes and bones of sacrificial victims, bulls, sheep, pigs, dogs and other animals;[2] and of objects dedicated to the gods, including pottery, swords and shields, a variety of feminine articles, animal statuettes, and, eventually, human figurines, which were revived in Middle Minoan Crete after a long hiatus. Usually it is impossible to distinguish human from divine figures, except by the most subjective canons. If a few, such as the so-called snake goddess, are accurately attributed, they are anyway a late innovation, probably under eastern influence. And even then the traditional smallness of scale was strictly preserved.

This lack of monumentality is a fitting accompaniment to the absence of the external manifestations of war, to the specific qualities and the tone of Cretan works of art. Even the large frescoes are not effectively monumental (outside of Cnossus they are uncommon and almost entirely devoid of human figures). They have a lightness and mobility which are original and rare, if not unique, in the Bronze Age anywhere,

[1] There were no solar or astral symbols, it is worth noting.

[2] The complete skeleton of a bull has recently been found in a tomb, dated by the excavators soon after 1400 B.C., at Arkhanes, about six miles from Cnossus; see *Illustrated London News* for 26 March, 1966, pp. 32–3. This is the first example of a bull-sacrifice from a tomb.

qualities which are created with magnificent technical skill on the vases, gems and small bronzes (notably in the latter case those from Tylissus). But they tend, with their highly stylized subject-matter and treatment of such details as dress and posture, to a monotonous conventionality, a preciousness and prettiness inappropriate to their size. Life is all games and ritual, but one sees little human passion, personal joy or suffering. Life has a tinkly quality, they seem to say, without depth. Hence the minor arts are the greatest Cretan triumph after the bourgeois comforts of good drainage and sanitation, lighting and airiness in the palaces.

The impression, admittedly speculative, is that early in the Middle Minoan period Cretan society became institutionally and ideologically fixed, that it found an equilibrium which was not seriously challenged for centuries, which was safe in all directions, perhaps too passively safe. Thereafter a further refinement in skills, expansion of population, further additions to the palaces can still be seen, but it was mostly on a horizontal line, so to speak. That is why it is possible to picture this world without any reference at all to shifts from Middle to Late Minoan. Although that particular break is archaeologically valid, chiefly in the pottery, the style of life seems to have been little altered. Many parts of Crete were severely damaged by earthquake in the Middle Minoan III period, but the catastrophe was followed not only by immediate rebuilding, but by further growth, by the creation of new settlements, and by much closer contacts with the Greek mainland. But not by anything pointing to significant social or psychological innovations.

Then there came a time when, somehow, men from mainland Greece took control in Cnossus, and, through the power of Cnossus, of much of eastern and central Crete. The decisive proof is the fact that the language of the Linear B tablets from Cnossus is Greek (and indistinguishable from the Greek of the mainland tablets). Unfortunately, as has already been said, all the tablets date from the moment of destruction, so that they offer no clue as to the date of Greek penetration. All the indicators, however, suggest that this occurred at the beginning of the Cnossian stage, Late Minoan II (a century or so after the beginning of Late Helladic on the mainland), when there was a qualitative change in the tombs, among other things, following mainland models and including genuine warrior-graves for the first time in Crete. At about the same time, such centres as Phaestus and Mallia ceased to be 'royal residences', and the great palace at Kato Zakro on the eastern tip of the island, the fourth largest in Crete, was totally abandoned after a natural disaster (and it was not re-discovered until 1961).[1] The implication appears to be that the new rulers of Cnossus acquired some sort of suzerainty over a sizeable portion of the island, without themselves moving in large numbers to other centres (hence the persistence of the Linear A script elsewhere). That would explain why Late Minoan II is not discoverable as an 'independent' stage outside Cnossus.

Late Minoan II saw Cnossus at the height of its power. Ever since Evans, the end of that period has been dated to about 1400 B.C., so that it was a relatively brief era, ending in total catastrophe all over the island. Earthquake may have been a factor but it cannot be a sufficient explanation, because this time, unlike previous occasions; there was no recovery. Life went on in Crete, but the age of power and palaces was over forever.

[1] It is possible to link the destruction of Kato Zakro, on the coast, with the volcanic eruption at Santorini (depending on the date, variously estimated between 1500 and 1450 B.C.), which had a force several times greater than the eruption in 1883 of Krakatoa in the strait between Sumatra and Java, and which, like the latter, sent devastation through wind-blown ash and tidal waves in irregular movements over considerable distances. However, exaggerated claims of the effects of the Santorini disaster must be rejected. There are no signs of any long-term effects inland in Crete. Furthermore, scientists point out that, heavy as the loss of life may have been, there were no natural consequences which need have prevented men from returning and settling immediately. Volcanic deposits often enhance the fertility of the soil. The *permanent* abandonment of Kata Zakro must have had a social or political cause.

Henceforth the mainland was to occupy the centre of the stage. It had already taken over the preponderance of trade even in Late Minoan II, as is shown by the distribution of exported pottery in the northeastern and eastern Aegean, in the Levant and in the west. Perhaps a natural disaster, if that is really what happened, was followed by an expulsion of the Greek overlords through some sort of popular uprising, which also swept away the remnants of native power that the Greek intruders had seriously weakened a century or so earlier. But these are speculations for which no firm foundation exists. They would be undermined, it should be added, if recent suggestions could be substantiated that the fall of Cnossus is to be brought down to 1200 or even 1150 B.C., to coincide with the end of the mainland Bronze Age civilization. But the evidence, accepted by the preponderance of expert opinion, favours retention of the traditional dating.

5

Mycenaean Civilization

At a date which falls within the great Cretan palace-period, that is, towards the end of Middle Minoan III, about 1600 B.C., something happened on the Greek mainland which gave a radically new turn to developments there, and to the history of the Aegean generally. Precisely what happened remains mysterious, the subject of continuing speculation and controversy without agreement, but the visible consequences are clear enough. Mycenae suddenly became a centre of wealth and power, and of a warrior civilization, without an equal in this region. Soon other important centres arose in central and southern Greece, and influences then radiated to the Aegean islands and the coasts of Asia Minor and Syria in the east, and to Sicily and southern Italy in the west. The next four hundred years or so, both on the mainland and in many of the islands, reveal such uniformity in the archaeological record that, by an unfortunate convention, the label 'Mycenaean' has come to be applied to the whole civilization (though it was never used in antiquity). There is no harm done if the label is retained in an abstract sense, comparable to 'Islamic', but the danger must be avoided of sliding over to an implication of centralized political authority, of a territorially extensive society ruled from Mycenae, as the Assyrian Empire, for example, was ruled from Assur. There is, as we shall see, no justification for such a political implication.

The remarkable prelude to this civilization is fully attested only at Mycenae. It amounts to no more than two grave circles, an older one the pivotal date of which is 1600 B.C., excavated by Greek archaeologists late in 1951, now known as Circle B, and another perhaps a century later (Circle A), which Heinrich Schliemann found in 1876 (six years after his discovery of Troy) to

Figure 3 Grave stele from Circle B, Mycenae

make the fundamental breakthrough in modern study of the Greek Bronze Age. Both circles were part of a large cemetery, presumably outside the settlement proper. Three features are noteworthy: first, the circles were deliberately marked out and were intended to be significant; second, the grave goods were numerous, luxurious and in part warlike; and third, the idea of memorializing power and authority was wholly concentrated in these tombs, for no trace of the settlement has been found, which must mean that there were neither walls nor fortifications nor palaces built of stone. The actual burials were scattered irregularly within the circles, in ordinary graves or cists or deep burial shafts —some twenty-four in Circle B, only six in Circle A, all the latter of the deep shaft type.

The interments themselves were no radical departure from older practices, nor was the unceremonious pushing aside of earlier bones and grave-goods to make room for later corpses. But everything else was new. The graves were marked on the surface by upright stone slabs (Figure 3), many of them inscribed with figured decorations or animals or military and hunting scenes (but never with a name or a proper portrait or other immediate link with a particular personality, thus remaining strictly within the Bronze Age tradition of the anonymity of power). The circle must have had some sacral significance, which survived a long time. In the great building programme on the citadel after 1300 B.C., when the 1000-yard circuit wall was constructed, Circle A was brought within the precinct and retained as 'hallowed' ground, marked off by an elaborate double ring of limestone slabs. Whatever the builders of that period may have known or believed about the grave circle, the impulse behind their beliefs was a powerful one, since by that time the original surface was well underground and they would have given themselves far less trouble had they ignored it.

It would require pages to give an adequate account of the contents of the richest of the graves, numbers III, IV and V of Circle A. Karo's catalogue of grave III alone includes 183 numbered items, and that figure is an understatement, since many of the 'items' include more than one object, in one instance 'sixty-four small circular gold disks [engraved] with butterflies'[1] (*Plate II b*). All the traditional luxury materials were employed, gold above all, the latter in a quantity and workmanship for which the only ancient parallel is among the Scythian burial finds in southern Russia a thousand and more years later. Alongside much delicate, even feminine, gold-leaf and filigree work in ornaments of all kinds, there were masses of swords and other possessions of the warrior. What is missing is anything like the Cycladic 'idols', anything that is not obviously utilitarian in an earthly sense (weapons, utensils and ornaments). Both in the materials employed and in the artistic skills and styles, there are reminiscences of, and borrowings from, the civilizations outside. Yet fundamentally the whole is original in workmanship and style, a new creation of the rulers at Mycenae and their craftsmen.

Whoever the men and women were who were buried in these specially prepared graves, they were at the top of a power structure within the community different from any Greece had known before. It is tempting to link their emergence with the arrival of the battle chariot and the long sword, though the first graves in Circle B seem a bit early for that. In any event, chariots figure prominently on the slabs marking the later shaft-graves, as in the still later Linear B inventories from Cnossus and Pylos. The chariot was an import—the idea, that is, not the actual vehicles themselves—but that is no argument that the people who took advantage of this new military weapon were themselves migrants. Nor is the abundant gold, which might represent the fruits of mercenary service, for example in Egypt as some scholars believe, or of successful raiding, or of trade, or of all three in combination. For the present we must confess that the causes of the sudden

[1] G. Karo, *Die Schachtgräber von Mykenai* (2 vols., Munich, 1930–3), I, p. 43.

III Interior of the largest *tholos*-tomb, popularly known as the Treasury of Atreus, Mycenae

IV Bronze tripod and cauldron, 61 cm high, ninth century B.C., found in Olympia

upsurge in power and the possession of treasure are unknown.[1]

The shaft-graves and their contents reveal a steady increase in technical and artistic skills and in concentration of power. Similar growth occurred in many parts of central Greece and the Peloponnese during Late Helladic I and II (subdivisions which are hard to distinguish anyway), but outside Mycenae (and eventually in Mycenae too) the visible symbol was a very different kind of burial-chamber, the spectacular *tholos-* or beehive-tomb. These were circular chambers cut into a hillside, with a special runway (*dromos*) leading to them, roofed over by the careful building up of a dome-like frame of stones in ever-decreasing rings, ending with a capstone above the natural height of the hill. The whole structure was sealed and covered with earth, leaving an imposing mound in view. Some idea of the scale can be had from the dimensions of the greatest and one of the latest of them all, the popularly but inaccurately named 'Treasury of Atreus' at Mycenae (*Plate III*): 48 feet in diameter, 43 feet in height (both inside measurements), a *dromos* 118 feet in length, and a lintel over the entrance-door weighing perhaps 100 tons.

Nothing prepares us for such tombs. There is no architectural forerunner, either in Greece or anywhere else. But any doubt that they indicate not just power but more or less unique status in the hierarchy, kingship in effect, is removed by the co-existence with the *tholos*-tombs of many chamber-tombs containing rich grave-goods, the resting-places of families well up the hierarchical scale but not at the top. The spread and location of the new dynasties in central and southern Greece can be plotted on a map by following the erection of *tholos*-tombs, the largest number of which were constructed in the fifteenth century (Late Helladic II). The word 'dynastic' is justified by the evidence of successive burials

[1] A new complication has arisen with the discovery in 1965 of what may prove to be a grave circle contemporary with Mycenaean Circle A, also with buried gold, at Peristeria in the western Peloponnese (about which more will be said below).

over several generations (in the chamber-tombs as well), each requiring considerable effort to re-open and re-seal the chamber. It should be added that there is no way of telling whether the dynasties remained within single families or not: usurpers are not distinguishable in their graves.

The *tholos*-tomb period is also the age when mainland activity becomes clearly visible abroad, in the form of extensive pottery finds, at first primarily in the west (Sicily and southern Italy), but by the end of Late Helladic II also in quantity in the other direction, in Rhodes, in Cyprus, in Miletus in Asia Minor, and elsewhere, an activity which mounted to a crescendo in the final phase of the Bronze Age, in Late Helladic III A and B. It is at this point that the limitations of the Linear B tablets are particularly exasperating. They have been found in considerable numbers in Mycenae and Pylos (and a few in Thebes), and thus far nowhere else on the mainland. They are comparable in language and content to those from Cnossus, equally lacking in the dimension of time because they, too, date from a moment of destruction and conflagration. If the commonly accepted date of 1400 for the fall of Cnossus is right, then Greek speakers took control there at the height of the *tholos*-tomb period. But we do not know where in Greece they came from. It is a gratuitous assumption to suggest that they were from Mycenae itself. Nor do we know when and where on the mainland writing first made its appearance, in the Linear B script. To make matters worse, 'Mycenaean' pottery before the III C period tended to be so uniform in style and technique that it is always difficult and often impossible to distinguish among places of manufacture.[1] When, therefore, a modern writer refers to 'Mycenaean pottery' found, for example, in the Lipari Islands, he means pottery from somewhere in the Mycenaean world, which eventually included such places as Rhodes and Cyprus, and not necessarily from mainland Greece, let alone from Mycenae itself. (Or it may have been a local 'imitation'.)

[1] Perhaps scientific analysis of the clays will eventually make distinctions possible, but that study is still in its infancy.

This uniformity, it should be added, is most complete with the most important pottery of all, that of the Late Helladic III B period, the individual specimens of which are as difficult to distiguish in time (a span of about a century) as in place.

The question of the relations between the mainland centres and those sites in which pottery finds are particularly concentrated is therefore a most troublesome one. That there was extensive trade (and that even before 1400 the mainland was beginning to push Crete out) can be taken as certain. Some materials, such as amber and ivory, could not have been brought to Greece otherwise, nor, in all probability, could most of the gold, tin and copper. Scattered Mycenaean objects and motifs reached central Europe and as far as southern England (including Stonehenge), from about 1500 B.C., and their presence is to be explained by the Mycenaean search for metals. Amber is common in Greece from the shaft-graves to the end of the Mycenaean age, though rare in Minoan Crete and post-Mycenaean Greece, and much of it is Baltic in origin.[1]

But who were the traders and under what conditions did they operate? The Linear B tablets from the mainland are as silent on these questions as are those from Cnossus. Very likely the concentration of Mycenaean pottery at Scoglio del Tonno in the Taranto region of southern Italy reveals the presence of a 'Mycenaean' trading post, linked with the movement of goods from central and western Europe. It is not so easy, however, to find satisfactory criteria for assessing the view of some writers that Rhodes and Miletus were Mycenaean colonies. That the material remains in those two places (unlike Cyprus) look 'Mycenaean' is true, but that proves nothing about their *political* connexions with the mainland, one way or the other. If we had no more information than that about classical Rhodes and Miletus in the year 400 B.C., we

[1] This has been determined by infra-red absorption spectrophotometry; see the series of articles by C. W. Beck and others in *Greek, Roman and Byzantine Studies,* of which two have so far appeared, vol. 7 (1966), pp. 191–211; vol. 9 (1968), pp. 5–19.

might guess them to be colonies by the same reasoning, and we should of course be wrong. The decipherment of Linear B has thrown new light on the relations between the mainland and Cnossus; yet even now it is not certain whether the take-over of Cnossus by Greek speakers was followed by actual allegiance or subjection to a mainland power. Trade, migration, conquest and colonialism do not always interact in a neat package.

Nor are the political relations clear on the mainland itself. The notable fact has already been mentioned that the *tholos*-tombs are earlier than large-scale domestic architecture, that, in other words, the kings and nobles lavished their wealth and expressed their power, architecturally, in their burial-chambers before they turned their attention to their palaces and houses. The excavators at Pylos have found evidence of an extensive settlement of the lower town earlier than the construction of the great palace, but they cannot trace its history back very far, and that is the picture in Greece generally. We know that the population had grown considerably and that they were clustered in villages, usually on hillsides overlooking the farmland. (Some 400 Mycenaean settlements on the mainland have already been located.) And we know that society had become hierarchically stratified, ruled by a warrior class under chieftains or kings. Then, after 1400 (and in most places not until about 1300) there came the dramatic shift from concentration on impressive burial-chambers to the erection of a number of palace-fortresses. Such places as Tiryns and Mycenae in the western Peloponnese, the Acropolis in Athens, Thebes and Gla in Boeotia, Iolkos in Thessaly, now looked more like medieval fortress-towns than like the open, agglutinative Cretan complexes. There was still cell-like growth, but the nucleus was the so-called *megaron* type of house, consisting of a columned fore-porch or vestibule, a long main room and usually a store-room behind.

This stress on fortification and the warlike cannot have been merely a matter of taste. Something in the social situation required it, as presumably it was not needed, at least not on anything like such a scale, in

Crete. The mainland Linear B tablets record the same activities and the same kinds of inventories as at Cnossus, the same pattern of palace control and administration over the community and over the surrounding region (but not at any considerable distance beyond). However, the tablets give no clues about the warlike factor, for which we must try to draw implications from the distribution and fate of the fortresses themselves. In simplified form, the key question may be posed like this. Why were the Argolid and the region around Corinth relatively thick with fortresses, whereas in Messenia to the west, Pylos was only lightly fortified and twelve miles to the north there were large *tholos*-tombs and a heavily fortified hilltop site at Peristeria, the ancient name for which is unknown? There was a considerable settlement at Argos in the Middle Helladic period, and then again continuously from Late Helladic II on, but there was no palace, no fortification, not a single *tholos*-tomb, no arms in the graves. Apparently Argos was subject to Mycenae six miles to the north, or to the slightly less distant Tiryns in the south, and had no warrior aristocracy of its own. On the other hand, it is hard to imagine that Mycenae and Tiryns were on a par, dividing the Argive plain between them (or that Thebes and Gla were equal powers in Boeotia). In the generations following the early *tholos*-tombs, persistent raids and wars presumably raised a few successful dynasts to positions of superpower and suzerainty, with the lesser or defeated chieftains destroyed in some instances, and in others allowed to survive in some form of subordinate status. There are signs at several places, for example, Mycenae, Tiryns and Thebes, of heavy destruction and burning in this period, followed by changes in the building-complex and the fortifications. That suggests war damage. No doubt there were also inter-dynastic marriages to complicate the succession to the throne and the inter-state relations, as they always do.

The picture that emerges from such an analysis of the tablets and the archaeology combined is one of a division of Mycenaean Greece into a number of petty bureaucratic states, with a warrior aristocracy, a high level of craftsmanship, extensive foreign trade in necessities (metals) and luxuries, and a permanent condition of armed neutrality at best in their relations with each other, and perhaps at times with their subjects. Nothing points to an over-all authority on the part of Mycenae. That notion rests wholly on the Homeric poems, in which Agamemnon is commander-in-chief of a coalition army on an expedition against Troy (and in which his authority is easily flouted, it should be noted). But the contemporary evidence argues that, whatever the authority of the ruler of Mycenae over the Argolid may have been, Pylos owed him nothing, nor Thebes or Iolkos.[1]

Apart from some battle scenes, Mycenaean palace art fails to reflect in any direct way the warrior-society. That art is, indeed, astonishingly derivative (except in pottery), with the same love of abstract and floral decoration, the same monotonous processionals, the same conventionality and static quality as its Cretan prototypes. There is the same impersonality, too. Almost never, for example, is a 'foreigner' portrayed, distinguishable in features, dress, hair or beard. Nor was the monumentality of the architecture transferred to painting or sculpture, a fact which becomes all the more striking when one remembers that by the thirteenth century there had been close contact with both Anatolia and Egypt. There is not even anything comparable in scale to the Middle Helladic life-sized statues from Ceos (mentioned in Chapter 3).

Although the Linear B tablets abound with names of gods and goddesses, and with lists of what appear to be personnel in their service or of offerings to them, Mycenaean religion is archaeologically still less noticeable than Minoan. There are altars and there are representations of divinities and rituals on gems and seal-stones, most of them Cretan in origin without any

[1] The difficult problem of the worth of the Homeric poems as evidence for the Mycenaean civilization is discussed briefly in Chapter 6 and more fully in Chapter 7.

distinguishing features to mark them off as Mycenaean, but, until the summer of 1968, no clearly identifiable shrine or special room for ritual purposes had been found within the palace-complexes. That summer the excavators at Mycenae came upon a small sealed 'store-room' (about six feet square) in which were stacked, among other things, some sixteen hollow nude figures in clay, up to two feet in height, made on a potter's wheel, with short upraised or extended arms (but no legs), notional breasts (most were females), hair and facial features added afterwards, as was done with handles and spouts on vases. The room also contained six coiled clay snakes, realistically modelled. The latter are rather splendid objects (*Plate IIc*), but the statuettes are extremely 'primitive' and ugly, save for a single exceptional small one, which is clothed and painted and carries a design that points to a date not later than 1300 B.C. Nearby was another curious room, the excavation of which has only begun, in which there were platforms so arranged as to suggest the possibility of cult activity.[1]

In every significant respect this find is unique so far. Snakes are common in association with human figures, but these are the first known from anywhere in the Aegean in the Bronze Age to be portrayed independently. The statues are unlike any others in their over-all appearance (though similarities in technique of manufacture and in their posture have been suggested with one group of Cretan figures). And no other such 'store-room' has been found. All of which serves as a warning that most general statements about Mycenaean culture are tentative in the nature of the case. One is almost reluctant to record the fact that, at present, only at Eleusis, Ceos and Delos have reasonably certain traces been discovered of a 'temple' in the Mycenaean era; or to comment that it is perhaps not accidental that none of these places was a centre of secular power.

[1] See *Illustrated London News* for 4 January, 1969, and Lord William Taylour, 'Mycenae 1968', *Antiquity*, 43 (1969), pp. 91–7, a copy of which the author kindly allowed me to read in advance of publication.

6

The End of the Bronze Age

In the surviving Hittite archives there are about twenty texts, ranging in time from the late fourteenth century to nearly 1200 B.C., which refer to a kingdom of Achchiyawa. Ever since these documents were first deciphered more than a generation ago, there have been attempts to identify the people of Achchiyawa as Achaeans, the most common of the names in the Homeric poems for the Greeks in the Trojan War, and, therefore, presumably the name (or a name) by which they knew themselves in what we have come to call the Mycenaean age. The arguments are technical, complicated and not finally conclusive, but most scholars at present accept the identification. The texts show Achchiyawa to have been on the whole independent of the Hittites and troublesome to them, especially towards the end when the Hittite Empire was beginning to lose its grip. But where was the kingdom located? Again there is no decisive answer. Although some believe that the Hittites were contending with Achaeans from the Greek mainland—and one cannot deny that if this were true it would help resolve some of the difficulties—the probabilities are against such a view. Achchiyawa seems to have been based closer to the Hittite territory, perhaps on the island of Rhodes.

In any event, the Hittite evidence does not carry us beyond the one point that men of Achchiyawa, whether they were Mycenaean Greeks or not, shared in the buccaneering and warring that went on in the second half of the thirteenth century on the edges of the Hittite sphere of influence. The Hittite Empire was actually broken up by 1200 or 1190. Although we have no direct textual evidence from which to identify the people who accomplished that, there is a growing probability that there was some sort of link with the considerable incursions into the eastern Aegean by a loose coalition of peoples twice mentioned in Egyptian sources, from a careless reading of which they have acquired the misleading name of the 'Sea Peoples'. The first reference is to an attack on the Nile Delta by Libyans and their mercenaries—'northerners coming from all lands'—in the reign of the pharoah Merneptah, about 1220, who were thrown back, the Egyptians claimed, with losses in killed and captured running into five figures. Among the mercenaries were the Akawash (or Ekwesh[1]), whom it is tempting to identify with the Achaeans, from the name, despite the fact that the text makes a particular point of their being circumcised, a practice foreign to the Greeks of historical times and not attested for Bronze Age Greece either.

The second reference is far more serious. At the beginning of the twelfth century (perhaps as early as 1191), Ramses III stopped a full-scale invasion of the 'Sea Peoples' who were descending on Egypt by land and sea from Syria. 'No land could stand before their arms, from Hatti, Kode, Carchemish, Arzawa and Alasiya on.'[2] Pharaonic triumphal claims are wildly unreliable, but there is every reason to accept the hard core of this boastful account, that the Egyptians had thrown back a combined tribal migration and invasion reminiscent of the later Germanic movements into the Roman Empire, scything through extensive territory before being defeated or coming to rest. The Akawash are not mentioned this time, and, because of the complications already noted with foreign names written in hieroglyphics, there is no scholarly agreement about the identification of the various peoples save one, the Peleset, or Philistines, who after the defeat settled on the Palestinian coast, and gave that region the name it still bears.

Philistine sites are filled, almost from the moment of settlement, with Mycenaean III C pottery manufactured

[1] One difficulty in identifying names in Egyptian hieroglyphic texts is that only the consonants are given, not vowels.

[2] Translated by J. A. Wilson in *Ancient Near Eastern Texts relating to the Old Testament*, ed. J. B. Pritchard (2 ed., Princeton University Press, 1955), p. 262.

locally, whereas they have no III B. The importance of this is that the shift from III B to III C is everywhere—on the Greek mainland, in the islands, and also at Troy—the line which marks the end of the last great phase of the Bronze Age. That end was more abrupt than most breakdowns of past civilizations. From Thessaly in the north to Laconia and Messenia in the south, at least a dozen fortresses and palace-complexes were smashed, including Iolkos, Crisa (near Delphi), Gla, Pylos, Mycenae, and the one near Sparta lying beneath the ruins of the Menelaion of classical times. Other fortified settlements, and even cemeteries, were abandoned. Archaeologically all this destruction must be dated at about the same time, approximately 1200, and it is hard to imagine that it bore no connexion whatever with the activity of the 'Sea Peoples' and the destroyers of the Hittite Empire. The coincidence would be too remarkable, all the more so when the further fact is taken into account that there was turbulence as far east as Mesopotamia, and in the west, too, in Italy, the Lipari Islands and Sicily, perhaps even in France and north to the Baltic Sea. A large-scale movement of people is indicated, and there is a growing conviction among experts, based on archaeology and on inferences drawn from the further spread of Indo-European languages, that the original centre of disturbance was in the Carpatho-Danubian region of Europe. The 'movement' was neither organized nor concerted in the way a genuine coalition is. It appears rather to have been broken in rhythm, pushing in different directions at different times, as in the case of Egypt, attacked once from the west and a second time, a generation or so later, from the northeast. There was little stability in the inter-relationships among the migrants, uncertainty in the ultimate objectives. All that is analogous with the later Germanic movements, as is the fact that trading and cultural interchanges and influences, at least with Greece, had been going on for centuries before the raids began.

Insofar as the people of Greece were concerned, the attack came against them from the immediate north, wherever the ultimate beginnings may have been. It was perhaps in this context that a massive wall was built across the Isthmus of Corinth, traces of which are still preserved at the southeastern end. If so, it was of no avail. The intruders penetrated successfully and destroyed the fortresses of the Peloponnese, and with them the political organization and the settlement pattern they had been designed to protect.[1] Before the effects can be examined, however, it is necessary to consider a further complication, the story of Troy in the northwestern corner of Asia Minor.

The citadel of Troy, situated on a ridge a few miles from the Aegean Sea and the Dardanelles, overlooking and controlling a fertile plain, had no known Neolithic phase. It was first occupied at the beginning of the Bronze Age, about 3000 B.C., and was a fortress from the start. Throughout its long Early Bronze Age phase, down to perhaps 1800, Trojan archaeology reveals a remarkable continuity of culture. Not that the centuries were altogether peaceful: there were periodic catastrophes, hence the division into five clearly marked stages, but each break seems to have been followed by immediate reconstruction without any visible indications of a new element in the population. Troy II was the richest of the five, showing rather impressive goldwork (the first 'treasure' found by Schliemann) at least six centuries before the shaft-graves of Mycenae. What followed was poorer, not to say mean, but apparently without a break in the continuity. Archaeologically Troy's early culture is linked with contemporary finds in the northern Aegean islands and the Cyclades, in Thrace and Macedonia, and, curiously, far west in the Lipari Islands—but not at all with the Hittites or Syria (though further excavations in northwestern Asia Minor may yet produce parallels closer to home). No other clues are available since not one scrap of writing has been found

[1] The once standard view that the Dorians were the intruders who destroyed the Mycenaean world has less and less to support it, and is rapidly losing adherents. Something will be said about them in Chapter 7.

at Troy, nor is there a clear reference to the place in contemporary records elsewhere.

Then about 1800 B.C., came Troy VI, a new civilization that appeared without warning, as was the case with some of the important innovations elsewhere in the Aegean. It became much the most powerful of all the phases of Troy, culminating in a period of advanced technology, with complex fortification-walls, but lacking either treasure or aesthetically interesting work in any other field. The ruins are filled with horse bones, and it was apparently the horse that gave the new occupants a considerable, perhaps decisive, advantage over their predecessors. The quantities of Minyan ware and later of imported Mycenaean III A pottery indicate close connexions with Greece. After about 500 years, Troy VI was destroyed by a catastrophe so tremendous that earthquake is indicated rather than human causes. The immediate re-occupation, Troy VIIa, reveals no cultural changes, but, as after Troy II, a very reduced scale and standard in all respects. And it is this shrunken city which coincides with the last great phase in Greece, Mycenaean III B beginning about 1300. The date of *its* fall is then tied up with all the problems of the end of the Mycenaean world we are considering.

Troy VIIa was destroyed by man; that is clear from the archaeology. The date can be determined only by the pottery finds, and specifically by the fact that VIIa had only Mycenaean III B pottery, whereas III C turned up in the short-lived VIIb period (though unfortunately the finds are not sufficient to permit an answer to the question of how early in VIIb the new style made its first appearance[1]). Other things being equal, the conclusion would be drawn, at least tentatively, that the fall of Troy VIIa was part of the general cataclysm of about 1200 throughout the Aegean area. But other things are not equal because of the Greek tradition of the Trojan War, of a great coalition from the mainland that invaded and

[1] Nor, unfortunately, is it possible to fix precisely enough the appearance in Troy VIIb of 'knobbed ware', a kind of pottery which seems to have had a central European origin.

sacked Troy. If that tradition has any historical kernel in it, the Trojan War could have occurred, from the Greek side, only in the III B period, and therefore as a war against Troy VIIa. That the ruins are too paltry for Homer's great city of Priam is not a serious objection; so much exaggeration must be allowed any drawn out oral tradition. However, the date is a crux. Obviously no organized Mycenaean invasion of Troy was possible as late as 1200, for the Greek powers were themselves under attack or already smashed by then. To move the war back a generation would get round this difficulty, but to do that creates complications in correlating the dates of the finds at Troy with those from the major Greek sites. A small minority of scholars therefore propose abandoning the Greek tradition as essentially mythical, and removing Troy from its unique place in late Greek Bronze Age history, or indeed from any significant place in that history at all.

Whatever the truth about the fall of Troy, there is no dispute about the magnitude of the catastrophe in Greece. However, to speak bluntly of the end or destruction of a civilization is to involve oneself in ambiguities unless the notion is analysed and its aspects specified. Destruction meant in the first instance the pulling down of palaces and their fortress-complexes. With them, we have the right to assume, went the particular pyramidal social structure out of which they had been created in the first place. Thus, the *tholos*-tomb disappeared, with a few rather mysterious and out-of-the-way exceptions in Thessaly and perhaps in Messenia. The cist-grave now became the rule again, as it presumably had been for the lower classes during the Mycenaean period. The art of writing also disappeared. That may seem incredible, until the point is grasped that the sole function of writing in the Mycenaean world known to us on the available evidence was to meet the administrative needs of the palace. When the latter disappeared, the need and the art both went with it. And the palace disappeared so completely that it never again returned in the subsequent history of ancient Greece. Places like Mycenae,

Figure 4 Pottery styles

a Mycenaean IIIB (10 cm high, from Attica)

b Mycenaean IIIB (15 cm high, found in late Troy VI)

c Mycenaean IIIC (10 cm high, from Athens)

d Protogeometric (15 cm high, from Athens)

e

e Geometric (77 cm high, from Athens)

Tiryns and Iolkos were still inhabited in the III C period, after 1200, but the palaces were not reconstituted, and no Linear B tablets from this period have been found in Mycenae or anywhere else.

So basic a change, initiated by an invading population, necessarily altered the general settlement pattern. Not only was there an over-all decline in population at the end of III B, very sharp in some regions, but there were shifts and movements which went on for a long time. Some large centres were totally abandoned, for example Pylos and Gla. Others, such as Athens and Thebes, continued in occupation on a somewhat reduced scale. Still other areas—eastern Attica, the coast of Euboea nearest the mainland, Asine on the Argive coast, the district of Achaea on the gulf of Corinth (of which Patras is the modern centre), the island of Cephallenia in the Ionian Sea—now held larger populations than before. Some of this irregularity in the pattern no doubt resulted from further conflicts and expulsions that must have followed after the main initial shock, evidenced by still further damage at Mycenae and Tiryns about 1150. And there is reason to believe that smaller, subordinate communities—Argos, for example—received different treatment from the main centres of power.

In such difficult and confused times, one would expect some elements of the Mycenaean population to join in the marauding and the migrating themselves. If the Akawash among the 'Sea Peoples' in Merneptah's reign were in fact Achaeans, that would be proof enough. Somewhat firmer, if still controversial, evidence comes from Cyprus. It was said at the end of Chapter 3 that, whereas the imports of Mycenaean pottery in the centuries before 1200 were not accompanied by any real migration into the island from Greece, about 1200 there is a marked change in the archaeological picture which implies an influx of immigrants. The masonry walls of Enkomi are perhaps the most noticeable novelty, but there is also an upswing in craftsmanship, in both metals and ivory, and there is the mysterious script (already mentioned). Unfortunately, no Cypriot writing survives from this, or the immediately succeeding, centuries, but the most plausible explanation for the survival in classical Cyprus of an Arcadian dialect and a script based on Linear B is that they were brought there by Mycenaean Greeks about the year 1200. What then incites disagreement is the fact that in remarkably few years after the appearance of the new culture traits, the island was devastated, with immediate effects in the settlement pattern and the level of wealth and craftsmanship comparable to those we have already seen in Greece.[1] Again there is an 'if' in the picture. If Alasiya is correctly equated with Cyprus, there could be no doubt that this destruction was the work of the 'Sea Peoples' on their way to Egypt, as expressly stated in the Ramses account. It would then be tempting to imagine a first and considerable wave of Greek refugees, whose impact is seen in the new archaeological picture, followed within perhaps two decades by the destroying 'Sea Peoples'. But that would still leave the very difficult question of how refugees could have made such an impact in so short a time.

In Greece itself, one consequence of the new situation was that the separate communities turned in on themselves somehow. III C pottery was a direct outgrowth stylistically and technically from III B, but, unlike the latter, it quickly subdivided into local styles of marked diversity. Presumably this came about through the removal of the palaces as the controlling hand over the economy within their former power spheres, and through a considerable reduction in inter-regional communication and trade. Apart from pottery, the archaeological evidence for the next two or three centuries is very thin and unrevealing in any positive sense. Yet this very negative quality permits certain inferences. The population was smaller and very much poorer than before; that is to say not that the ordinary farmers and craftsmen were poorer, but that the upper classes were. There is

[1] Much of the controversy would probably disappear if the key archaeological finds could be dated very precisely round the pivotal year 1200.

no gainsaying the technical and artistic inferiority of the finds, the absence of treasure, and, above all, of large constructions, whether palatial, military or religious. Mycenaean society had been decapitated and those who remained proceeded, together with the new invading element,[1] to build a new kind of society. It is precisely this process which archaeology alone cannot illuminate very much. That it was a totally new society, however, is demonstrated later on, when writing returned to Greece and we begin to know something about the economy and the social and political organization.

The unavoidable concentration on material remains and technology should not be permitted to conceal the extent of the break that had occurred. Of course people went on farming and herding and making pottery and tools, using essentially the same techniques as before (but soon turning more and more to the new metal, iron, now available for the first time). They also continued to worship their gods and perform the necessary rituals, and presumably in this field of activity there was much continuity as well as change. But society was organized in a different way, it entered a very different path of development, and new values were created. The Bronze Age had come to an end.

[1] That some of the invaders remained in Greece is an assumption which it is impossible to prove. It is characteristic of this kind of combined invasion and migration that it leaves no archaeological record until it comes to rest somewhere permanently. (This point was briefly made in Chapter 2 with regard to the Dorians and the Huns, and will have to be made again about the Dorians in Chapter 7.) Some scholars have sought evidence in the fact that the Bronze Age Greek practice of burying the dead was replaced in most districts by cremation. There is no denying that it would be very satisfactory if a link could be established with the 'urnfields', cemeteries of cremated corpses deposited in urns, first noticeable in central Europe in the thirteenth century, and then widely dispersed in large sections of the continent, including Italy. However, the change in Greece came slowly after 1200, and was not completed before about 1050. Furthermore, it was indicated in Chapter 2 that dramatic changes in methods of disposing of the dead are known to have occurred without the impetus of a new element in the population.

Part Two

THE ARCHAIC AGE

7
The Dark Age

UNLESS life itself is destroyed in a region, there must always be continuity of some kind. In that sense, Greek history was a continuation of its Bronze Age prehistory. To make too much of that truism, however, is to put the stress in the wrong place and to overlook how fundamentally new the new society was to become. The Greeks of historical times had no tradition of a break and therefore no concept of a different civilization in the millennium before their own, although they did know in a vague and inaccurate way that other languages had once been spoken in Greece and the islands. Their 'heroic age', familiar to them from the Homeric poems and from much legendary material (such as the Oedipus story), was merely an early stage in Greek history. That is why Theseus could be credited with destroying the minotaur and with unifying Attica, both legendary actions, but one more appropriate to the Bronze Age, the other to the very different world of the Dark Age. Modern archaeology has discovered a prehistoric world never dreamed of by the Greeks of the historical era.

Archaeology brings to the forefront breakdown and decline about 1200 B.C., followed by poverty and a low quality of artistry and technology. What it reveals much less clearly, and in certain critical respects not at all, is that the centuries after 1200 point ahead, not only materially with the emergence of iron as the new and most advanced metal, but also socially, politically and culturally. The future of the Greeks lay not in palace-centred, bureaucratic states but in the new kind of society which was forged out of the impoverished communities that survived the great catastrophe. We cannot follow that process of growth in its formative stages, except in scattered hints strewn in the archaeological record and in later traditions, and we are not helped by the fact that in the contemporary written documents from Syria, Mesopotamia and Egypt there is no reference whatever to the Greeks. In the sense, therefore, that *we* grope in the dark, and in that sense only, is it legitimate to employ the convention of calling the long period in Greek history from 1200 to 800 a 'dark age'. And like the other 'ages' we are concerned with, subdivisions must be noted, one about 1050, a second in the course of the ninth century.

The confused archaeological record in Cyprus, already described, shows that the generations immediately after 1200 saw more than one movement of people, whether as a further influx from the north, or as internal transfers within the Aegean area itself, or both. The break-up of the Mycenaean states, the Hittite Empire and the small North Syrian states created a power vacuum, which made movement relatively easy, especially into depopulated districts. One new arrival of particular importance for Greek history was that of the Dorians in the Peloponnese and Crete. There are no archaeological identifying marks of Dorians, which is not surprising, since different dialects are sometimes spoken by groups who otherwise share the material culture that archaeologists discover. However, Doric is the one classical Greek dialect that requires us to assume an actual migration into Greece: some of the peculiar word-formations and phonetics cannot be explained, on strictly linguistic grounds, as an evolution from the Greek of the Mycenaean period. Presumably it was a dialect which emerged separately in the more isolated northwestern region of the Greek peninsula, outside the Mycenaean sphere, before it was brought into southern Greece and Crete. The eleventh century is as good a guess as any for the date of that movement. Elsewhere in the then Greek-speaking world, the catastrophe of 1200 did not introduce any new linguistic factor, but the process of local differentiation that followed had its effects, which we can see in the end-product, the historical Greek dialect pattern (Map 4).

Regional variations also make it difficult to present the

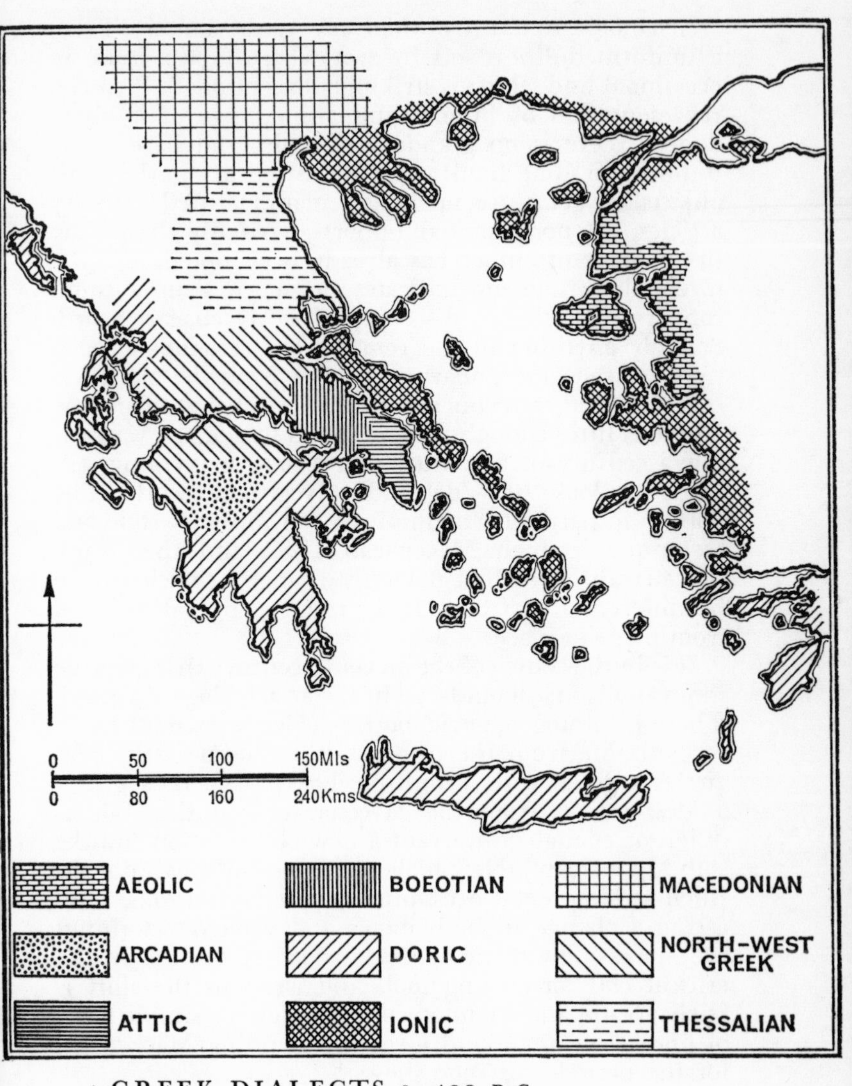

4 GREEK DIALECTS *c.* 400 B.C.

archaeological picture of the Dark Age succinctly. True, a uniform dullness sets in everywhere (apart from an occasional find which is strikingly exceptional). Pictorial representation of human and animal figures is abandoned; there is no grandeur of scale, and hardly any building in stone at all; nor is there delicacy in the small objects, as gems are no longer manufactured. Luxury articles, all non-essential imports, virtually disappear: the absence of amber has already been noted, and the rare gold ornament indicates no more than a tomb robbery or a chance discovery of a Mycenaean hoard. Scarcely anything in the remains has religious associations we can grasp, apart, of course, from the fact itself that the dead were buried with a few objects of utility. There is little enough which reflects war or the warrior. For a century or a century and a half, everything still tends to look like 'debased' Mycenaean work. The pottery in particular maintains a continuity of style and technique, though Mycenaean III C and then 'sub-Mycenaean' ware had not only changed sufficiently to be differentiated from III B products, but also varied from place to place.

It is in the course of the eleventh century that genuine innovations first loom large in the archaeological record. There is 'protogeometric' pottery (Figure 4), most easily recognizable from the compass-drawn circles and half-circles painted with a multiple brush. Experts see it as a 'descendant' from the Mycenaean, but the style is different enough to warrant a new classification (unlike 'sub-Mycenaean'). New tools, weapons and small objects (such as long metal dress-pins in place of buttons, indicating a change in both men's and women's clothing) are increasingly made of iron instead of bronze. In the critical class of cutting tools and weapons the shift is fairly abrupt and complete, as the following simple table of finds from mainland Greece (excluding Macedonia) for the period 1050–900 shows:[1]

[1] From A. M. Snodgrass, 'Barbarian Europe and Early Iron Age Greece', *Proceedings of the Prehistoric Society*, 31 (1965), pp. 229–240, at p. 231.

	Bronze	*Iron*
Swords	1	20+
Spearheads	8	30+
Daggers	2	8
Knives	0	15+
Axe-heads	0	4

There are, in most areas, changes not only in the grave structure but also in burial practices. Notable is the replacement of inhumation by cremation, completed in Athens, where the evidence is extensive and continuous, by about 1050.[1] All these changes were foreshadowed earlier in one way or another, and it would be wrong to suggest that about 1050 there was a sudden and uniform transformation throughout the Aegean world. Nevertheless, when the different kinds of evidence are taken together, a significant change becomes apparent at that point in time.[2]

Then, by the end of the same century, still another new feature emerges, the significance of which is far more obvious, namely the establishment by migrants from the Greek peninsula of small communities along the coast of Asia Minor and on the offshore islands. Eventually the whole western edge of Asia Minor became Greek, and the Aegean was converted for the first time into a Greek waterway, so to speak. The eastern settlements were grouped by dialect in three bands from north to south, Aeolic, Ionic and Doric, in that order (Map 4). But that required some three hundred years of complicated history which is largely lost to us—years of quarrelling and fighting with each other, and of ambiguous relations with the older inhabitants. We may suspect that few women were among the migrants, at least in the earlier days. In Miletus, writes Herodotus (I 146), the noblest of the colonists from Athens brought

[1] Infants and very young children continued to be interred regularly, and not cremated.

[2] It is important to note that these dates are all archaeological, as explained in Chapter 1. Protogeometric pottery is pivotal in establishing the chronology.

no women, 'but took Carian women, whose kinsmen they murdered. Because of the killing, the women laid down a law for themselves, which they swore an oath to observe and which they passed on to their daughters, never to dine with their husbands or to address them by name.' Just how Herodotus came to this story or what he was trying to explain is unclear, but in his own day intermarriage with Carians was a common practice in his native Halicarnassus. And we know (as Herodotus did not), thanks to recent and still preliminary archaeological investigation, that there were many separate migrations in small groups; that these were new settlements and not continuations or reinforcements of old Bronze Age or Mycenaean communities in Asia Minor (even where there was a return to previously occupied places, as at Miletus or Rhodes); that the first wave left Greece soon after the development of protogeometric pottery. Indeed, it is the discovery of quantities of protogeometric sherds in half a dozen or so sites which has enabled archaeologists to date the movements and to link some of the eastern sites with specific regions in Greece.[1] Aeolic and Ionic settlements were the earliest, the Doric somewhat later (not before 900, perhaps).

Exactly why any particular group chose to cross the Aegean *when* it did is anyone's guess, but there is no need to guess why they went where they did. The Asia Minor coast is a series of promontories with natural defences, backed by fertile river-valleys and plains, and in the eleventh, tenth and ninth centuries there were no strong powers or even large populations to block new settlers from establishing themselves. One site—Old Smyrna, so called to differentiate it from the later city of Smyrna, modern Izmir, nearby—provides a

[1] The unexpected recent discovery (see *Illustrated London News* for 6 April, 1968) of Mycenaean III C, sub-Mycenaean and protogeometric sherds in Sardis, the eventual inland capital of Lydia, raises new questions. There may be a link with the refugee movement of about 1200, as in Cyprus and Tarsus, followed by trading connexions, rather than another case of an actual Greek migration of the kind we are considering.

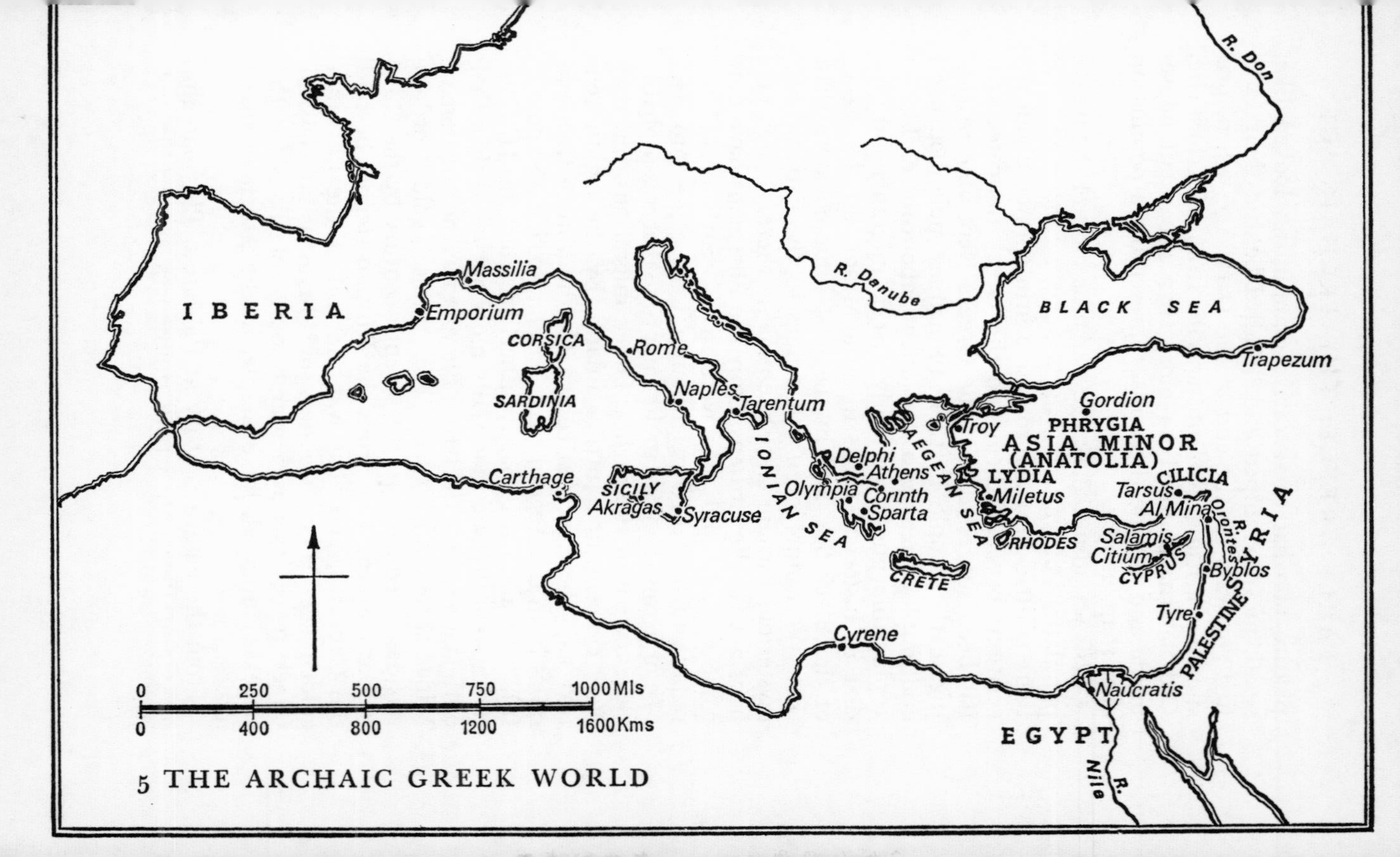

5 THE ARCHAIC GREEK WORLD

picture of what these early communities looked like: small, mean, cramped and huddled behind their fortified city-wall. At the end of the Dark Age, when, presumably, it had grown substantially from its earliest size, Old Smyrna counted no more than 500 small houses inside and outside the walls, representing a population of perhaps 2000.

This was also a 'dark age' as far as most of the native populations of western Asia Minor are concerned, and there is little on which to base a firm opinion about the relations between them and the Greek newcomers. It has been suggested that the Greeks were able to subjugate the people in their immediate neighbourhood and employ them as a dependent labour-force. This is a plausible guess—certainly Greek migrants did just that in historical times in Asia Minor, on the shores of the Black Sea, and in the west—but no more than that. We cannot even put names to the natives. The mysterious Carians were presumably there, though perhaps not yet the Lydians. Only the Phrygians have now come to light and they were in this early period too remote to be called neighbours. They came into Asia Minor across the Dardanelles at a time that was probably close to that of the earliest Greek migrations, but they were concentrated further inland. By the eighth century B.C., their greatest centre, Gordion, more than 200 miles from the Aegean coast, was large, rich and powerful, with a culture, partly inherited from the Hittites, technologically and materially more advanced than that of the Greeks. For the latter, Phrygia was the kingdom of Midas, whose touch turned everything to gold. Gordion was destroyed early in the seventh century by the Cimmerians sweeping in from the Russian steppes beyond the Caucasus, and that was the end of the Phrygian golden age. When we hear of Phrygians in classical Greek texts, it is as a major source of slaves for the Greeks, employed, for example, in the Athenian silver mines.

From the eighth century at the latest, Phrygian imports and Phrygian artistic influences are visible not only in Greek Asia Minor but also in Greece proper, and there were close relations with the civilizations further east. The archaeologists have discovered what appear to be traces of the Hittite 'royal road' across Anatolia, which the Phrygians then maintained. That, however, was not the main route of eastern influence to the Greek world of the Dark Age, but the sea route from Syria, with Cyprus as a major intermediary. Contact between Greece and the Near East was never completely broken; it could not have been, if for no other reason than the imperative Greek need to import metal—copper, tin, and then, increasingly, iron—which at that time came largely, if not wholly, from the east.

Although Cyprus had been devastated by the 'Sea Peoples', copper mining almost certainly never stopped, and by the eleventh century the island was also important for its iron metallurgy, the influences of which are visible on the Greek mainland in weaponry. Significantly, the main Cypriot centres were henceforth to grow on the eastern and southeastern coasts, closest to Syria. Enkomi was replaced by nearby Salamis, perhaps originally a Greek foundation of about 1100, and in the tenth century the Phoenicians made Citium their centre there. In the centuries to come, every Near Eastern empire conquered Cyprus in turn—first the Assyrians, then the Egyptians, and finally the Persians—though they could not always retain control. The result was a hybrid civilization which it is difficult to classify. Although Greek was the language of the majority of the population, an unidentified pre-Greek tongue remained in existence as well as Phoenician (the earliest Cypriot document in that language, a curse tablet, is dated to about 900). The art became more Levantine than Greek, as exemplified by the newly discovered 'royal tombs' of Salamis of the eighth and seventh centuries.[1] By then kingship had disappeared in the Greek world, but it survived in Cyprus as long as the island retained any semblance of autonomy.

[1] *Illustrated London News* for 18 November, 2 and 16 December, 1967.

It was presumably the close eastern connexion (and perhaps control) which enabled Cyprus to outstrip the Anatolian Greeks during the Dark Age. The discovery in excavations shortly before the last war of an ancient port at Al Mina, in the Orontes River delta in northern Syria (actually within the borders of Turkey today), brought to light one of the important link-posts on the Asiatic mainland. Cypriot and local pottery at Al Mina go back to the ninth century, and possibly earlier. By about 800, Greek pottery appears and then it becomes increasingly abundant, continuing after the Assyrian conquest of the area in the late eighth century. The source of the earliest Greek ware was not in Asia Minor but in Euboea and the Cyclades, later in Corinth and elsewhere. None of the evidence indicates what was traded in return, but there can be little doubt that metal was, as usual, a main Greek concern. The presence of so much Greek pottery suggests direct Greek participation—though it should be stressed that this was only a trading-post, not a permanent settlement of migrants as in Asia Minor—but it is not without relevance to recall that in the Homeric poems overseas trade was virtually a monopoly of 'Phoenicians', and that to Homer, as to Herodotus in the fifth century, 'Phoenicia' meant everything from the Cilician-Syrian border to Egypt.

No writing has been found at Al Mina and therefore its ancient name is unknown. It is just possible that it was the site of Posideion, according to Herodotus (III 91) the city which in his day was the northern boundary of one of the Persian provinces or satrapies. All that he could tell us about the past of Posideion was that it had been founded by one of the legendary Greek heroes, Amphilochus. And, in general, when the eastern Greeks finally came to write their history, which was not before the fifth century B.C., the earliest period was represented by little more than foundation stories built around individuals, and stories of isolated incidents, usually conflicts. They could offer no narrative going back beyond the sixth century, and they had no interest in a sustained account of social or institutional history. The picture they have left us is a schematic, sentimental reading back into the past of the values and claims of a later age, a 'mythical charter' for the present. Herodotus himself was uneasy. When he suggested (III 122) that Polycrates of Samos was the first Greek to seek a maritime empire, he explained that he was 'leaving aside Minos' and others like him, that Polycrates was the first 'in what is called the time of men'. We should phrase it as the first in historical, as distinct from mytheical, times.

Our only check, archaeology, cannot cope with stories about individual founders or specific incidents. However, archaeology has exposed as false a fundamental element in the traditions about the early Ionian colonization, imagined to have been a single action, organized by and starting out from Athens, where many refugees from the Dorians had congregated, including men from Pylos under King Neleus. That Athens had a role in some of the Ionian settlements is certain, but little else stands up. The Greek antiquarians who put the story into writing more than 500 years afterwards had no notion of the great breakdown of about 1200 B.C., no idea of a Bronze Age, and therefore no sense of the very considerable time-span of the Dark Age. They did not, and could not, know that there had been a gap of perhaps 150 years between the destruction of Pylos (which was not the work of the Dorians) and the earliest movements across the Aegean, far too long for a crowd of Pylian refugees to wait in Athens, an inherently improbable situation anyway. And the single colonizing expedition is pure fiction, whereas the paramount role of Athens in the development and diffusion of protogeometric pottery, which is fact, was completely forgotten (and it is doubtful that the later Greeks would even have recognized this pottery as their own).

It is fruitless to pursue in detail the later Greek traditions about the Dark Age in Asia Minor. Nor is the possibility substantially greater for Greece proper, where the traditions down to 800 or 750 B.C. are of the same kind and quality. We must turn instead to our earliest written documentation, the Homeric *Iliad* and

Odyssey, two epic poems, some 16,000 and 12,000 lines in length, respectively. What are we to make of them as sources of historical information? There is perhaps no question about the early Greeks which provokes greater controversy and less agreement, and here it is not possible to do more than state the position adopted in this book.[1]

The two poems were composed in Ionia, the *Iliad* perhaps in the middle of the eighth century, the *Odyssey* a bit later, by two different poets working in the same tradition. They were the culmination of a long experience in oral poetry, practised by professional bards who travelled widely in the Greek world. In the course of generations they knit together many incidents and local traditions, built round several main heroic themes, and they employed a highly stylized and formalized, artificial poetic language, in dialect basically Ionic but including Aeolic and other elements. No doubt there were bards in the Mycenaean world, too, but the tradition behind the Homeric poems was essentially a Dark Age one (and its existence provides an important corrective to judging the period solely from its *material* impoverishment). It was a tradition that deliberately looked back to a *lost* heroic age, and there are aspects of their own world which the poets successfully excluded. There is in the *Iliad* and *Odyssey* a considerable, though by no means perfect, knowledge of where the greatest Mycenaean centres had been located; there is not a hint that Asia Minor was now rather thickly settled by Greeks; there are no Dorians; there are indeed no distinctions, whether in dialect or in institutions, within the Greek world, other than differences in power. And there are the great palaces of the heroes, filled with 'treasure' (*keimelion*). When Agamemnon was finally persuaded to appease the wrath of Achilles, his offer included (besides seven cities and a daughter to wife with a great dowry) racehorses, captive women, 'seven tripods that have never been on the fire and ten talents of gold and twenty glittering

[1] In this chapter, our concern is with the society of the poems, not with the narrative of the Trojan War and its aftermath, already discussed in the previous chapter.

cauldrons' and a shipload of bronze and gold from the anticipated Trojan spoils (*Iliad* IX, 121–56). The Dark Age possessed no treasure like that. Then, even the warriors were allowed only one sword or one lance-head after death, not both together; as time went on, indeed, arms of any kind became increasingly rare in the graves.

Thus far, one might imagine that the bards had transmitted, from generation to generation down to the eighth century, a recognizable picture of the late Mycenaean world. However, on closer analysis it turns out that their palaces are in structure and details not Mycenaean palaces (or any other known ones), that their understanding of the use of chariots in warfare has become uncertain, that the social system of the poems differs qualitatively from that of the Linear B tablets (and in particular from the palace economy recorded in the tablets), that the very terminology of administration and social structure has been radically altered. Even their 'realistic' accounts of treasure betray at least one remarkable anachronism. The dowries, racehorses and captive women of Agamemnon's offer of amends are timeless, or at least undatable, but not so the bronze 'tripods' and 'glittering cauldrons'. Although such objects existed in the Mycenaean world, they were rarities, whereas in the Dark Age they became notable treasures, above all to be dedicated to the gods, especially towards the end of the period, when the *Iliad* and *Odyssey* were composed. A few complete specimens and many fragments have been found in Olympia (*Plate IV*) and Delphi, a smaller number in Delos, Crete and Ithaca, isolated examples elsewhere.

There is also significant change in religious practices. The Mycenaean world buried its dead; the Homeric poems cremated them, without exception. Again a difference within the Dark Age itself must be noted. By about 1050 cremation of adults had become universal in most of the Greek world (with the curious exception of the Argolid), but 200 or 250 years later, inhumation returned to the mainland while cremation continued in Crete, the Cyclades, Rhodes and Ionia. The *Iliad* and *Odyssey* remain firmly anchored in the earlier Dark Age on this point, although the paraphernalia and rites of mourning can be illustrated from later Dark Age graves and from scenes on 'geometric' pottery after about 800. That was the period when human and animal figures returned to Greek art for the first time since the Mycenaean age, a revival which did not go so far as an early return to portrayal of the divine. There are no epiphanies, no ritual dances, no initiation scenes; there are very few figures, either in sculpture or in the decorations on pottery, that one can imagine as gods even on a broad interpretation. This rarity in the plastic arts of the anthropomorphic spirit that dominates the Homeric poems is surprising (especially in contrast to the innumerable idealized Zeuses, Apollos and Aphrodites of later Greek art).

In sum, the Homeric poems retain a certain measure of Mycenaean 'things'—places, arms and weapons, chariots—but little of Mycenaean institutions or culture. The break had been too sharp. As the pre-1200 civilization receded into the past, the bards could not avoid 'modernizing' the behaviour and the social background of their heroes. All in all, there is an inner coherence in the way social institutions emerge from a study of the *Iliad* and *Odyssey*, despite the anachronisms at either end of the time-scale. That picture, it is suggested, is in general one of the Dark Age, and on the whole of the earlier half of that age, painted as a poet does and not a historian or chronicler, not precise or always accurate, surely exaggerated in scale, but not therefore a purely imaginary one.

The world of Agamemnon and Achilles and Odysseus was one of petty kings and nobles, who possessed the best land and considerable flocks, and lived a seignorial existence, in which raids and local wars were frequent. The noble household (*oikos*) was the centre of activity and power. How much power depended on wealth, personal prowess, connexions by marriage and alliance, and retainers. There is no role assigned to tribes or other large kinship groups. In the twenty years Odysseus was away from Ithaca, the nobles behaved scandalously towards his family and his possessions; yet his son Telemachus had no body of kinsmen to whom to turn for help, nor was the community fully integrated, properly organized and equipped to impose sanctions. Telemachus' claims as Odysseus' heir were acknowledged in principle, but he lacked the power to enforce them. The assassination of Agamemnon by his wife Clytaemnestra and her paramour Aegisthus placed an obligation of vengeance on his son Orestes, but otherwise life in Mycenae went on unchanged, except that Aegisthus ruled in Agamemnon's place. The king with power was judge, lawgiver and commander, and there were accepted ceremonies, rituals, conventions and a code of honour by which nobles lived, including table fellowship, gift-exchange, sacrifice to the gods and appropriate burial rites. But there was no bureaucratic apparatus, no formalized legal system or constitutional machinery. The power equilibrium was delicately balanced; tension between king and nobles was chronic, struggles for power frequent.

Telemachus, it is true, summoned a meeting of the assembly in Ithaca to hear his complaint against the noble 'suitors'. The assembly listened to both sides and took no action, which is what the assembly always did in the two poems. In general, the silence of the people is the most challenging difficulty presented to the historian by the poems. They are there all the time, even in the battles, but as a vague mass whose exact status is unclear. Some, chiefly captive women, are called slaves, but they do not appear to be worse off than the others. A few specialists—seers, bards, metalworkers, woodworkers, physicians—have a higher status. There is seafaring and a vital concern for trade, more exactly for the import of copper, iron, gold and silver, fine cloths and other luxuries. Even chieftains are permitted to go on expeditions for such purposes, but generally trade and merchandising seem to be the business of foreigners, chiefly Phoenicians. To be called a merchant was a grave insult to Odysseus; men of his class exchanged goods ceremonially or they took it by plunder. In part, all this vagueness about the ordinary people can be attributed to the poets' deliberate concentration on the heroic deeds of heroes. But perhaps it is also to be explained by the absence, in reality, of the sharp status categories of later societies, in particular of neat categories of 'freedom' and 'bondage'. The fundamental class-line between noble and non-noble is clear enough. Above and below that line the distinctions appear blurred, and perhaps they really were.

It would be idle to pretend that this provides the basis for a *history* of the Dark Age. All that can be suggested is that, following the elimination of the rulers of the Mycenaean world and with them of the whole power structure they headed, society had to reorganize itself with new arrangements and new values appropriate to the new material and social situation, in which migrants were presumably one factor to be reckoned with. If, as is probable but not provable, the destruction of the Mycenaean world also involved internal social upheavals, that would also have influenced the shape of the new arrangements. What happened in the centuries immediately following could not have been the same everywhere, despite the Homeric image of uniformity. In Asia Minor from the beginning (as in all subsequent Greek migrations to new areas), the settlements were small territorial units around an urban core. Judging from the archaeology, similar units existed from the beginning of the Dark Age on the Greek mainland and in some Aegean islands as well. The poets assume them to be the rule, but still in their day and for several centuries to come, whole areas of Greece—Thessaly and Aetolia, for example—in fact lacked urban centres and were loosely organized agrarian and pastoral societies. What was apparently uniform, however, was the class structure suggested by the poems, with an aristocratic upper class and a king or chieftain who was a bit more than 'first among equals'. How much more (or less) was a personal matter in each case, and, as we know from other indications, by the time the *Iliad* and *Odyssey* were composed the 'equals' had dispensed with the king almost everywhere and replaced monarchy by aristocracy. In some shadowy way, the common people also had an existence as a corporate body (whomever 'the people', the *demos*, may have included), but not as a political force in any constitutional sense.

Curiously, although the poets were conscious of a common bond uniting all the Greeks, a bond of language, religion and way of life (but not, either then or later, of a political bond or of a reluctance to war with each other), neither the *Iliad* nor the *Odyssey* refers to them by the name which has been theirs from at least the eighth century to our own day. They are Hellenes and their world is Hellas; 'their world', not in antiquity 'their country', because they were never politically united and therefore Hellas was an abstraction much like Christendom in the Middle Ages or Islam today. In the Homeric poems the Greeks have three different names, Achaeans, Argives and Danaans, the first two of which lived on as the names of specific localities in Greece (Map 6) while the third disappeared from use. It is virtually certain, however, that Hellas and Hellene were already current in the eighth century, and probably also the genealogies which were inevitably invented to explain the historical divisions according to dialect, 'race' or political organization: Hellen, son of Deucalion, had three sons named Dorus, Xuthus and Aeolus, and so on. In the eighth century, too, embryonic pan-Hellenic institutions were already in existence, notably certain oracles and the Olympic Games.

The eighth century, finally, saw the return of writing to the Greeks, in the form of the alphabet borrowed with modification from the Phoenicians. This fact the Greek tradition had right (though they had no idea of the date). We are in the position to pin the source down to the North Semitic script, and specifically the cursive writing used in business activity rather than the monumental characters of, for example, Byblos. Al Mina may have been the point of contact and diffusion, though that is

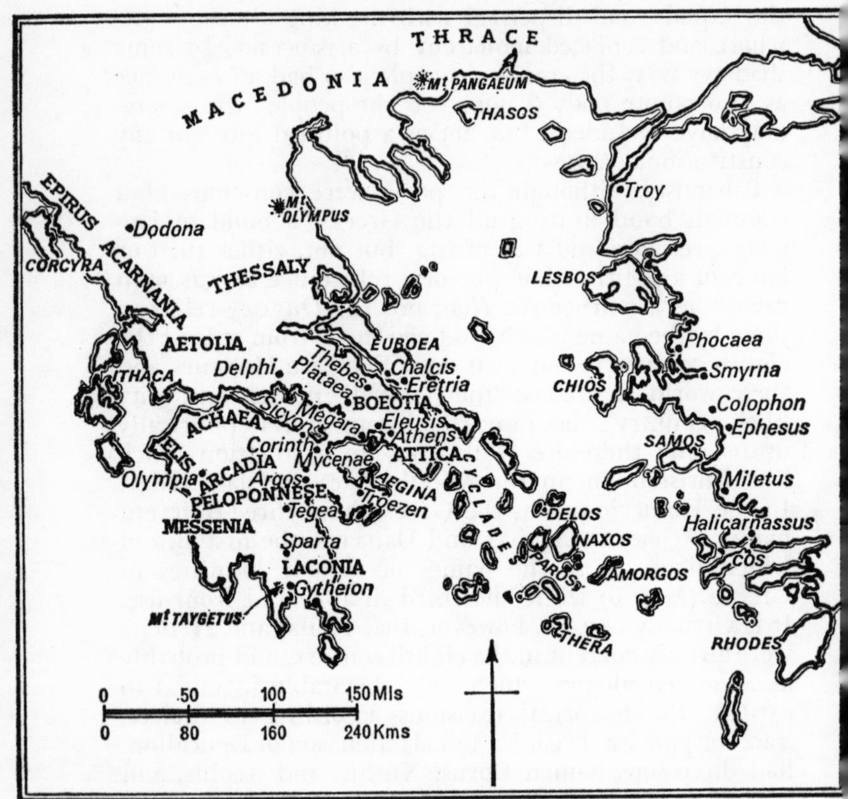

6 ARCHAIC GREECE AND THE ASIA MINOR COAST

only a guess, and the first borrowers were perhaps people from Euboea, Crete and Rhodes, more or less independently of each other, from whom the art then spread, by a complicated network of routes, to all the Greek communities. Neither the immediate reasons why the alphabet was acquired when it was (probably before 750) nor why it spread so rapidly are well understood. A long time was to go by before the Greeks made serious use of this new skill for chronicles or for religious texts, two of the chief uses of writing in the ancient Near East. Originally the Greeks seem to have concentrated on poetry and on what may be called labelling and mnemonic purposes, that is, inscribing names on pottery, gravestones and the like, on the one hand, and easing the burden of memory, on the other hand, by writing down lists that merited public notice and remembrance, such as Olympic victors.

The Homeric poems, in sum, looked back to the Dark Age and even a bit beyond, but they were composed at the beginning of a new era. By convention the next period (800–500 B.C. in round numbers) is known as 'archaic', a word taken from the history of art, and more narrowly of sculpture (as is the term 'classical' for the succeeding age). It is with Archaic Greece that the rest of this book will be concerned.

8

Archaic Society and Politics

Two phenomena which mark the Archaic Age are the emergence and slow development of the characteristically Greek community-structure, the *polis* (conventionally and not very aptly translated 'city-state'), and the vast diffusion of Hellas in the course of about two hundred years, from the southeastern end of the Black Sea almost to the Atlantic Ocean.

It has already been noted that in the Dark Age the community had only a shadowy existence as a political organism. How the shadow acquired substance is a process we cannot trace, but at the heart lay the creation of institutions which subjected even the most powerful men to *formal* organs and rules of authority. This was no simple task; tension between the organs of the community and the power drives of ambitious individuals remained a disturbing factor in Greek society not only in the archaic period but also in the classical. One step was the elimination of kingship,[1] a step which was curiously unnoticed in Greek legends and traditions. The contrast in this respect with early Roman history could scarcely be greater. In time, the Romans developed a very full and detailed story of the reigns of their kings, each in turn, climaxed by the expulsion of the last of them, Tarquinius Superbus in 509.[2] The abolition of kingship was a story of a revolt from Etruscan overlordship, and that explains something of its attraction and its tenacity in Roman legends. The Greeks lacked such

[1] One survival, in Sparta, will be considered in Chapter 9. It should also be noted that the word *basileus*, 'king', remained in use for such officials as the magistrates in charge of religious affairs in Athens, without any implication of royal status.

[2] See, for example, the first two books of Livy's history (available in the Penguin volume of Livy entitled *The Early History of Rome*).

a stimulus. And their silence about this aspect of their past suggests that anyway, despite the Agamemnons and Ajaxes of the Homeric poems, their real Dark Age rulers were petty chieftains within a framework of 'many kings', whose disappearance from the scene was undramatic and unmemorable. Without them, the nobles were compelled to formalize the previously informal advisory bodies we see in action in the Homeric poems. So there arose councils and offices (which we call 'magistracies', borrowing the word from the Latin), with more or less defined prerogatives and responsibilities, and with a machinery for selection and rotation, all confined within the closed group of the landowning aristocracy.

These communities were small and independent (unless subjected by force). Following the normal Mediterranean residential pattern, they had an urban centre, even if it were no more than a village, where many of the people resided (especially the wealthy). The town square, an open space, was reserved: it was flanked by the main civic and religious buildings,[1] but easy access was carefully maintained so that the people could all be assembled when required. That was the agora in its original sense, a 'gathering-place', long before shops and stalls began to encroach, so that the common 'market-place' translation of the word *agora* is rarely quite right and sometimes just wrong. Usually there was also an acropolis, a high point to serve as a citadel for defence. Essentially town and country were conceived as a unit, not, as was common in medieval cities, as two antagonistic elements. This was built into the language, which equated the community with people and not with a place. An ancient Greek could express the idea of Athens as a community or as a political unit only by saying 'the Athenians'. The word 'Athens' was very rarely used in any sense other than geographical; one travelled to Athens but one made war with the Athenians. Of course, the tempo of development among these farflung autonomous communities was very uneven, and there were considerable variations in the end-product. The community

[1] On the first temples see Chapter 11.

of the eighth and seventh centuries had a long way to go before it became the classical *polis*. Nevertheless, the embryo was there in the early Archaic period.

The fragmentation which characterized Hellas is partly explained by geography. Much of the terrain in Greece proper is a chequer-board of mountains and small plains or valleys, tending to isolate each pocket of habitation from the other. In Asia Minor the coastal region had roughly the same structure and therefore encouraged a comparable settlement-pattern. The Aegean islands were also mountainous and they were mostly very small. But the geography is not a sufficient explanation, and especially not of later Greek developments. It cannot explain, for example, why the whole of Attica was politically united whereas neighbouring Boeotia, which is not much larger, contained twelve independent city-states who on the whole successfully resisted the efforts of the largest, Thebes, to dominate them; nor why a tiny island like Amorgos had three separate *poleis* right through the classical era; nor, above all, why the Greeks transplanted the small community to Sicily and southern Italy, where both the geography and self-preservation should have argued for embracing much larger territories within single political structures. Clearly there was something far greater at stake, a conviction that the *polis* was the only proper structure for civilized life, a conviction which Aristotle (*Politics* 1253a7 *ff.*) summed up, in the last days of Greek independence, when he defined man as a *zoön politikon*, a being destined by nature to live in a *polis*.

Land communication from one pocket to another was slow and cumbersome, sometimes actually impossible in the face of resistance. Inland waterways were almost wholly lacking, and therefore the sea became the normal Greek highway, even for relatively short distances wherever possible. In antiquity the Greeks became the people of the sea *par excellence*, and yet their attitude to it was notably ambiguous: it was the home of those pleasant nymphs, the Nereids, but it was ruled over by Poseidon, whom men feared and appeased but never loved. Nevertheless, when they were forced into a continuous movement of expansion, from the middle of the eighth century, they took to the sea, going west and northeast. By the end of the Archaic Age, Hellas covered an enormous area, from the northern, western and southern shores of the Black Sea, through western Asia Minor and Greece proper (with the Aegean islands) to much of Sicily and southern Italy, then continuing west along both shores of the Mediterranean to Cyrene in Libya and to Marseilles and some Spanish coastal sites. Wherever they went, they settled on the edge of the sea, not in the hinterland.

The sea was not the only common environmental feature of these farflung regions. Ecologically they shared (with few exceptions) what we popularly call a 'Mediterranean' climate and vegetation, permitting and even inducing an outdoor existence still familiar in our day. Summers are hot and sunny, winters are tolerable and usually free from snow on the shores and in the plains, olives and grapes grow freely, flowers abound, the plains produce cereals and vegetables, the sea is rich in fish, and there is adequate pasture on the hillsides (rich in places), at least for the smaller animals. Nothing is as a rule luxuriant, and therefore agriculture and pasturage need constant attention, but on the other hand the requirements of housing, and especially of warmth, can be met by fairly primitive means. Only metals and wood suitable for such purposes as shipbuilding cause serious difficulties from short supply: they are available only in restricted, and sometimes rather distant, localities. Fresh water may also be a problem, hence the stress in legend and reality on springs and fountains.

Schematically the Greek 'colonization' movement may be conceived as two long waves (not counting the earlier settlement of Asia Minor). The western one began about 750 B.C. and continued in full swing until the middle of the next century, with a secondary wave going on for about another century, when the process was essentially completed. Migration to the northeast began before 700 with settlements in the Thracian region, in nearby islands such as Thasos and in the Troad in Asia Minor, followed from about 650 with further movement into the Hellespont area and then along both shores of the Black Sea, not stopping until the end of the sixth century, at the mouth of the Don on the north coast and at Trapezus (now Trebizond) at the southeastern end. Ancient accounts of these movements are not very helpful. One reasonably sober example, the accepted story of the foundation of Syracuse in Sicily as repeated by the geographer Strabo (VI 2, 4), reads like this:

> Archias, sailing from Corinth, founded Syracuse about the same time that Naxos and Megara [also in Sicily] were established. They say that when Myscellus and Archias went to Delphi to consult the oracle, the god asked whether they preferred wealth or health. Archias chose wealth and Myscellus health, and the oracle then assigned Syracuse to the former to found, and Croton [in Southern Italy] to the latter. . . . On his way to Sicily, Archias left a part of the expedition to settle the island now called Corcyra [modern Corfu]. . . . The latter expelled the Liburni who occupied it and established a settlement. Archias, continuing on his journey, met some Dorians . . . who had separated from the settlers of Megara; he took them with him and together they founded Syracuse.

Such mythical overtones and the stress on a few individuals and their quarrels, rather than on the broader social aspects, are characteristic of most of the traditions. On the other hand, these accounts are more 'historical' than the still vaguer and more confused ones about the drift to Asia Minor early in the Dark Age. Whereas the earlier migrations were probably more in the nature of chancy, haphazard flights, what was now happening was an organized shift of population, though still in small numbers; group emigration systematically arranged by the 'mother-cities'.

The common Greek word for such a new settlement abroad, *apoikia*, connotes 'emigration' and lacks the implication of dependence inherent in our 'colony'. As a rule, each *apoikia* was from the outset, and by intention, an independent community, retaining sentimental, and often religious, ties with its 'mother-city', but not a subject either economically or politically. Indeed, their independence helped preserve friendly relations with their old homes on the whole, free as they were from the irritations and conflicts commonly aroused under colonial conditions. The designation 'mother-city', it should be added, was often a slightly arbitrary choice; many of the new foundations were established by settlers joining together from more than one place in the old Greek world.

According to the commonly accepted chronological scheme, based on archaeology and Greek antiquarian efforts, the earliest colony was Cumae near Naples shortly before 750 B.C. (more precisely, the island now known as Ischia, from which Cumae was then founded), settled from Chalcis and Eretria, the two leading cities of Euboea (active at the same time at Al Mina in the Levant). Chalcis was also the mother-city of Sicilian Zancle (later Messina), of Rhegium on the Italian side of the straits, and of Naxos, Leontini and Catania (Katane in Greek) in eastern Sicily, all traditionally founded by 730. They were joined in Zancle by other Euboeans, in Rhegium by Messenian exiles, and in Leontini by Megarians. Syracuse was founded at the same time by Corinthians and unspecified 'other Dorians'; Sybaris in southern Italy in about 720 by men from Achaea with a sprinkling from Troezen in the Peloponnese; Gela in southern Sicily in 688 by Cretans and Rhodians. Thereafter foundations were further complicated by 'inner' migrations, as some colonies became mother-cities in turn, while emigrants continued to come from the east. Thus, Himera was established about 650 from Zancle with a contingent of Syracusan exiles; Selinus between 650 and 630 from Megara Hyblaea in eastern Sicily; Cyrene about 630 from the Aegean island of Thera; Massalia (Marseilles) about 600 by Phocaeans from Asia Minor; and Akragas (modern Agrigento) in 580 from Gela together with migrants coming directly from the latter's own motherland, Rhodes.

This list is not complete and none of the traditional dates is secure. Enough has been said to indicate the chronology of the movement, which has been archaeologically substantiated in its general outline, to underscore the way the settlements clung to the sea, and to reveal the number, diversity and geographical spread of the Greek communities involved. There is no need to repeat with a catalogue of the north Aegean and Black Sea foundations, for which both the literary and the archaeological evidence is much poorer. Settlement on the Thracian coast of the Aegean Sea began late in the eighth century, and again the cities of Euboea were in the vanguard, as shown by the name of the promontory Chalcidice (from Chalcis). Soon other Aegean islands came into the picture, Paros, Rhodes, and above all Chios. And then, as the movement went beyond the Aegean coast to the shores of the Black Sea, Miletus became the dominant mother-city (followed by Megara). If all the references to Milesian activity were taken too literally, that city itself would have been totally depopulated, and that is further proof of the restricted role of a 'mother-city'.

The lands to which the Greeks migrated, both east and west, were all inhabited, by a variety of peoples at different levels of development, that is to say, by people with different interests in the newcomers and different capacities of resistance. The Etruscans of central Italy were strong enough to stop Greek expansion at a line drawn from the Bay of Naples, and sufficiently advanced to borrow from the Greeks their alphabet, much of their art, and elements of their religion. The Sicels, however, like the Thracians or the Scythians in the north Aegean and Black Sea areas, were less advanced technically and socially. Some were apparently reduced to a semi-servile labour force, though the evidence is thin and confused. Others were pushed inland, where they maintained an uneasy and complicated relationship with the Greeks in the following centuries.

A study of the list of mother-cities (and of those which seem to have taken no part in colonization) shows that there was little correlation between type of community and colonizing city. In particular, there is nothing in the list to justify the once widely held view that the colonizing activity was *chiefly inspired* by commercial interests. Emphasis on the words 'chiefly inspired' is important. The intention is not to deny the commercial aspect of colonization altogether, in particular the oft repeated need for metals. The island of Ischia, the first western settlement, had some iron, and anyway it was a gateway to the relatively rich ore-bearing regions of central Italy. Foundations on both sides of the Straits of Messina soon followed, evidently to control that narrow roadway to the western Italian coast. The first settlers seemed to know where they were headed, and the information could have come only from traders who had already been in the area. When this is said, however, it explains very little of the centuries-long movement of dispersion. Sicily, for example, had no metal and little else to attract Greek merchants, except in occasional ventures, and the same was true of the Black Sea hinterland. Archaeological evidence of Greek activity earlier than the first colonists is almost impossible to find. In the end, the central question is that of the motivation of the men who actually migrated, who left their homes in Greece, the islands or Asia Minor, to settle permanently in unfamiliar, and sometimes hostile, regions, essentially independent of their mother-cities from the start. They were not the same people as the traders, who did not abandon their home-bases, and so their interests were far from identical. Nor did merchants constitute a significant element in the migrants who followed, to join the original settlers, or in the secondary colonies, such as Himera and Akragas, which in time split off from the earlier ones.

The distinction is emphasized by the small number of genuine trading-posts which were eventually established, such as the places called Emporium (which in Greek means literally 'trading-station' or 'market-centre') in Spain (now Ampurias) and at the mouth of the River Don; or the very interesting settlement at Naucratis in the Nile Delta, where the Pharaohs concentrated the representatives of a number of Greek states, chiefly in Asia Minor, who conducted trade with Egypt. The small number of these posts is revealing, as well as their relatively late foundation—Spanish Emporium was set up by Massalia, which was itself not founded before 600; Naucratis can be dated somewhat earlier than Massalia, whereas Russian Emporium was substantially later. But the most decisive point is that these were not proper Greek *poleis*, but, like Al Mina before them, meeting-points between the Greek world and the non-Greek, whereas all the other new settlements—to be counted in the dozens and eventually in the hundreds—were, from the beginning, Greek communities in all respects. That meant, above all, that they were basically agrarian settlements, established by men who had come in search of land. They settled near the sea and they welcomed good anchorage, but that was a subordinate consideration. Hence, numerous as were the Greek communities in southern Italy, there was none at the best harbour on the east coast, the site of Roman Brundisium (modern Brindisi). Hence, too, the aristocracy of Syracuse, which became the greatest of the new communities in the west, were called *gamoroi*, which means literally 'those who divided the land'.

In the final analysis, the one feature which all the mother-cities had in common was a condition of crisis severe enough to induce the mobilization of the resources required for so difficult a venture as an overseas transplantation—ships, armour and weapons, presumably tools, seed and supplies—and to create the necessary psychology as well. Behind the traditional stories of personal feuds, quarrels and murders which the later Greeks associated with some of the individual foundations, there lies a deeper and broader social conflict. One must not exaggerate the spirit of Viking adventurism in Archaic Greece.

A tantalizingly brief passage in Herodotus (IV 153) about the foundation of Cyrene from Thera gives us a clue, with the help of an early fourth-century inscription from Cyrene which purports to be the text of the pact of the first settlers.[1] What Herodotus says is this: 'The Therans decided to send out one brother from among brothers, selected by lot, from each of the seven districts of the island, and that Battos should be their leader and king. On these terms they dispatched two fifty-oared ships.' The inscription adds that the penalty for refusing to go was death and confiscation of property, and that volunteers were also accepted. Numbers were therefore small—two hundred at the most—and no women were included, which reminds us of the suggestion already made about the first movement into Asia Minor, that the earliest migrants took their wives from among the natives where they settled. And there was compulsion, although families with only sons seem to have been exempt. Why such pressure? We are not told. For Herodotus and for the people who later inscribed the 'pact' in Cyrene itself, the story is all tied up with orders from Apollo at Delphi and with a sanction for the Battiad dynasty which had seized power in Cyrene. That takes us back to the mythical explanations characteristic of most of the foundation stories. But the factual core remains, and though we do not know the precise situation, we cannot doubt the existence in Thera in the middle of the seventh century B.C. of an excess of population, and hence of the potential, if not yet the reality, of social conflict. Nor that the same was the case wherever active colonizing was being fostered, and probably often compelled.

Social crisis was rooted in the nature of aristocratic society and the ways it developed in the course of the Dark Age. Both increasing wealth and technical skills and a rise in population are demonstrable in the archaeology. With the elimination of kings in all but name, the aristocracy seems to have closed ranks, to have

[1] The text and a translation of the inscription (*Supplementum epigraphicum graecum* IX 3) will be found in A. J. Graham, *Colony and Mother City in Ancient Greece* (Manchester University Press; New York, Barnes and Noble, 1964), pp. 224–6. The colony concerned was not the city of Cyrene itself, but a slightly earlier settlement on an offshore island.

controlled much of the land (and in particular the best land), and to have created political instruments for monopolizing power. The stress on genealogies in the later traditions, with every noble 'family' claiming a divine or 'heroic' ancestor, is a certain sign of the tendency towards an exclusive aristocracy of 'blood'. Their wealth gave them a military monopoly for a long time. Metal was scarce and expensive, particularly the iron for swords and spear-heads. About the middle of the eighth century, there came innovations in helmets, body armour and weapons, partly inspired from both central Europe and the east. Within another hundred years or so, the full panoply was being regularly worn, from helmet to greaves, and that was far beyond the reach of anyone without means. Wealth was also essential for horse-breeding, now important with the rise of the cavalry, a peculiarly aristocratic military arm throughout history. The place of cavalry in Archaic Greece is obscure, and some historians tend to dismiss it as necessarily insignificant on Greek terrain. It cannot be denied, however, that horses and horsemen are very prominent in the painted pottery of the period; that such later Greek writers as Aristotle laid great stress on cavalry; that it was the Greek migrants who brought the cavalry to Italy; or that the ruling aristocracy of Euboea were called the Hippobotai, the 'horse-feeders', as late as the time of Herodotus (V 77). At the least, we must accept the value of cavalry in raiding and as a way of giving heavily armed fighters mobility in reaching a battlefield.

The aristocracy also used their wealth to forge bonds of patronage and obligation with commoners. It must be admitted that the status of the mass of these peasants and craftsmen is unknown to us except in nebulous terms. Apart from such classes as the Spartan helots (discussed in Chapter 9), the question remains open whether, and to what extent, the bulk of the labour force in the fields and pastures and in the noble households were free or half-free; or whether, indeed, such concepts are yet applicable in any meaningful way. Genuine slaves were to be found, captive women and fewer men, but the widespread reliance on chattels, on human beings who were property in the strict sense, was a phenomenon of the classical and post-classical periods, and therefore will not hold our attention in this book. But that does not imply that the lower classes were 'free' in our sense, or in a sense a fifth-century Athenian would have understood. Although they no doubt had personal and property rights that were protected by custom, and though they may still have been summoned to an assembly from time to time (as in the Homeric poems), it is more than probable that they were also tied in other respects, such as in an obligation to pay over a portion of their produce or to give an amount of unpaid labour, possibly even in a restriction on the right to move freely from their plot of land or their crafts. Perhaps this is the same kind of status that the Roman tradition about their own earliest era implied when the term 'clients' was used (not to be confused with the watered down meaning of the word in later periods).

We must allow further for a middle class of relatively prosperous, but non-aristocratic, farmers with a sprinkling of merchants, shippers and craftsmen. Their origin and history may be obscure, but they make their appearance in the fragments of lyric poetry that begin about 650 B.C., and they were the major factor in the most important military innovation in all Greek history, at about the same time. Once the panoply had been sufficiently refined, it was only a matter of decades before some commander—possibly the half-legendary Pheidon of Argos—saw the possibility of organizing heavily armed infantrymen, called hoplites, into a close formation in close ranks. Its advantages over the much looser organization of the aristocratic warriors were so great that by the end of the seventh century, the phalanx had become the normal formation in the Greek world. Furthermore, the advantages were enhanced by the simple device of increasing the levy, with profound social consequences. Hoplite arms and armour, which each soldier was normally required to provide from his own resources, were expensive. The innovation was therefore not a democratization of the army (that never occurred among the Greeks, except in a way in those states, such as Athens, which in the classical period used their navies, largely manned by the poorer classes, as a main military arm). However, the phalanx for the first time gave the commoners of more substantial means an important military function. It is tempting to link the disappearance of arms from the graves with this development, since arms no longer signified exclusive social status. On a less symbolic level, a place in the phalanx eventually led to demands for a share in political authority.

All classes thus found themselves involved in social conflict, or *stasis* (the generic Greek word), in varying combinations and alliances. Within the aristocracy itself, squabbling for honour and power was normal; the creation of formal institutions of political administration merely changed the conditions under which it went on. One need mention only the insistent Athenian tradition that the Alcmaeonid house were always breaking ranks and going their own way politically, or the monopoly of power achieved by the Bacchiads in Corinth. Then there were the wealthier among the outsiders, demanding a share in the prerogatives, a demand which obviously became more insistent and effective once they attained military weight in the hoplite phalanx. And finally there were the poor, the mass of the working farmers, whose position seems to have worsened with the general increase in wealth and prosperity. A growing population was itself a danger, if not an outright evil: much of Greece and the Aegean islands simply could not support a large population on the soil. The seventh-century poet Hesiod not only advises late marriage (at the age of thirty) but adds the following (*Works and Days* 376–8, 695–7): 'There should be an only son, to feed his father's house, for so wealth will increase in the home; but if you leave a second son you should die old.'[1] Furthermore, a

[1] Translated by H. G. Evelyn-White in the Loeb Classical Library (Cambridge, Mass., Harvard University Press; London, Heinemann).

rising standard of living among the wealthier classes will have led to greater pressure on the lower classes, through a need for a larger and more diversified labour force or through an expansion of their holdings even into poorer and more marginal land. In the end, as Aristotle wrote in his *Constitution of Athens* (II 1–2), 'there was civil strife between the nobles and the people for a long time' because 'the poor, with their wives and children, were enslaved to the rich' and 'had no political rights'.

That lapidary statement is oversimplified, with its loose use of the word 'enslaved', and too schematic. Nor are we in a position to say how universal the *stasis* had become. Nevertheless, the tradition of widespread demands for redistribution of land and cancellation of debts was no fiction.[1] Nor is it false to stress the aristocratic monopoly in the administration of justice (and of the priestly functions). Hesiod is pointed enough about the 'bribe-devouring judges' of his day (*Works and Days* 263–4). For the lower classes, unlike their betters, economic demands and a plea for justice took precedence over claims to political rights. The search for justice explains another facet of the tradition as we have it, namely, the role of the wise lawgiver. Law in the hands of a traditional and closed aristocracy, self-perpetuating and secretive, in a world which was just learning how to write things down, was a powerful weapon, and increasingly an intolerable one. There could be no justice, rose the cry, until the law became public knowledge and its administration open and equitable. Inevitably the men who were charged with this task when the demand became sufficiently insistent—such as Solon in Athens, Charondas of Catania and Zaleucus of Locri in the west—were reformers as well as codifiers. Lacking precedents, they invented freely, in a sort of compulsory originality which characterized every aspect of Archaic Greek life and culture. This can hardly be overstated. The political structure, made up of magistrates, councils and, eventually, popular

[1] See the account of Solon in Chapter 10.

assemblies, was a free invention. Some myths and cult practices may have been borrowed from the east; the combination was original, the literary formulations, as early as Hesiod's *Theogony*, wholly so, as well as the very notion itself that a poet, lacking a priestly vocation, had the right to systematize the myths about the gods. Even the phalanx was a new creation, whatever the foreign source of parts of the hoplite's panoply.

Two points about these archaic lawgivers need special mention. One is their self-reliance. They all agreed that justice came from the gods, but rarely did they claim a divine mission or divine guidance. Appeals to the oracle at Delphi may have helped seal their work with a sort of divine blessing, as similar requests had occasionally been made to approve a proposal for colonization. But the sequence was almost always the same: measures were formulated first, then Delphi was consulted. This ambivalence remained characteristic of the Greek community for centuries. Religious activity was frequent and ubiquitous; later ages even invented Delphic oracles to make up for the many failures in the past to bother to consult Apollo; divine authority over, and interference in, the lives of men and communities were accepted as a part of the nature of things. Yet at the same time, the community found the inspiration and justification for its actions in itself, in human terms.

The second point is the acceptance by the lawgivers of human inequality. Justice was not equated with egalitarianism or democracy at this stage. Solon wrote, 'I gave the common people such privilege as is sufficient.' As to those in power, he continued, 'I saw to it that they should suffer no injustice. I stood covering both parties with a strong shield, permitting neither to triumph unjustly' (quoted by Aristotle, *Constitution of Athens* XII 1). It is anachronistic to see even in Solon a democratic personality. The common people, the *demos*,[1] as a genuine political force may have lain just beneath the

[1] There is an ambiguity in the Greek *demos*: it may mean 'the people as a whole' or 'the common people', depending on the context.

surface by the beginning of the sixth century; popular sovereignty was not yet an issue.

What Solon's words serve to remind us is that the economic, juridical and political developments in Archaic Greece went on through a long period of struggle, confused, uneven, not continuous, but at the critical moments quite fierce. At first the opportunity to send out a sector of the population to new foundations served as a safety-valve. But the time finally came—and the middle of the seventh century seems to have been the turning-point in many areas—when external solutions no longer were available or no longer sufficed. The *stasis* flared up sharply, factious and ambitious individuals seized the opportunity to their own advantage, and there arose the specifically Greek institution of the tyrant. Originally a neutral word, 'tyrant' signified that a man seized and held power without 'legitimate' authority; it implied no judgment about his quality as a person or ruler. That judgment, unfailingly pejorative, came later, and then the Greeks, looking back to the age of tyranny, coloured its history to suit their new moral condemnation, though they never wholly concealed the fact that individual tyrants varied greatly, that some had even ruled benevolently and well.

It is impossible to understand Greek tyranny without first making an effort to free the mind from the connotation of despotism with which the word has been associated ever since the classical Greeks forged the close connexion. This will become very clear when we turn, in Chapter 10, to the Peisistratids in Athens. Not that the descendants of the first usurpers, in their efforts to maintain dynastic rule, did not customarily become brutal despots and get themselves thrown out—Archaic tyrannies were all short-lived in terms of generations—but the rise of the individual tyrannies and their role were rooted in the whole social situation, not simply in the moral quality of certain individuals.

Beginning probably after the middle of the seventh century, tyranny spread to many communities of mainland Greece and later to the Aegean islands, to Asia

Minor and to the western communities. Our chief source of information is Herodotus, who does not pretend to have an exact chronology, and the efforts in this direction by later Greek antiquarians and historians are unreliable, so that it is safer not to give precise dates in most instances. The earliest and in some ways most ambiguous of the tyrants was Pheidon of Argos, described by Aristotle (*Politics* 1310b26–8) as a king who rules as a tyrant, a pointed formulation suggesting that Pheidon was a genuine autocrat, unlike the hereditary kings before him; perhaps the introduction of the phalanx was his way of solidifying his power over the other nobles. Within a generation or so, more typical tyrannies appeared in Corinth, Sicyon and Megara, to cite the best known. That roster, as well as the sixth-century instances of Athens, Naxos, Samos or Miletus, all point to a high (though not perfect) correlation between tyranny on the one hand and more advanced economic and political development, in particular urbanism, on the other. Hence the most backward regions, such as Acarnania, Aetolia or Thessaly, rarely enter into consideration.

The common factor was the inability of the hereditary aristocracies to contain or resolve the growing conflicts, whether those within their own ranks or those involving the wealthier commoners, the growing urban population, and the debt-ridden and impoverished peasantry. Conflicts with other states were sometimes a further factor, as in Argos against Sparta or in Athens against Megara. It is no accident that in the 'colonial' areas the appearance of tyranny was later by a century and more, and then was often meshed in with the problems created by powerful neighbouring states, Lydia or Persia in the east, Carthage in the west. Polycrates of Samos benefited greatly by the need to organize resistance to Persia on an unprecedented scale and by his ability to achieve that. Others, in contrast, based their less spectacular tyrannies on Persian support.

Thus there was a military side to tyranny, but the bodyguards and troops, whether native or mercenary, must not be allowed to conceal its very considerable popularity. In every city there were elements who *wanted* a tyrant, expecting him to achieve by threats and force the social and political aims they felt incapable of achieving otherwise. In Athens there had been an unsuccessful coup by a man named Cylon about 630 B.C. A generation later there was a popular demand that Solon become a tyrant, on the model of the tyrannies of neighbouring Megara and Corinth. Solon refused—a rare and notable self-denial—and tried to bring about reform by other means, but the significant fact remains that there was a serious demand. And in many places tyranny did accomplish, at the expense of the traditional aristocracy, precisely what was asked of it. This is not to suggest that the tyrants saw themselves as the bearers of some mysterious historic destiny or as the forerunners of democracy or of anything else. They wanted power and success, and if they were intelligent and disciplined, they gained it for themselves by advancing their communities. They put an end, for a generation or two, to crippling *stasis*; they entered into alliances, by dynastic marriages and other devices, with other Greek states and were thus a force for peace where that was possible (as it sometimes was not); they nurtured peasant independence and perhaps fostered trade and manufacture (though this is far from clear in the available evidence); they strengthened the sense of community by public works and splendid festivals, focused largely around major cults. Above all, they broke the habit of old-fashioned aristocratic rule. The paradox is that, standing above the law and above the constitution, the tyrants in the end strengthened the *polis* and its institutions and helped raise the *demos*, the people as a whole, to a level of political self-consciousness which then led, in some states, to government by the *demos*, democracy.

The great weakness of tyranny was, of course, that its operations and tone depended so heavily on the personal qualities of the tyrant. Another was its seductiveness. The tyrant was not the only able and ambitious man in his state, but there was no place for the others commensurate with their claims, and there was no form which political rivalry could take other than conspiracy and assassination. Hence tyranny led structurally, usually in the second generation or at the latest in the third, to despotism, civil war and either abdication or overthrow. What followed differed from community to community. The centuries of uneven development in the Greek world had left a permanent legacy of considerable variation. Two states emerged as the most important, each in its way exceptional: Sparta, which avoided tyranny altogether, and Athens, which was to become the paragon of Greek democracy and also Greece's most important imperial power.

9
Sparta

NOT the least unusual feature of Sparta was the peculiar relationship between *polis* and territory: the *polis* of Sparta consisted, at least ideally, of a single class of 'Equals' (*homoioi*) residing in the centre and ruling over a relatively vast subject population. Sparta was located on the right bank of the Eurotas River, in a broken plain of nearly 700 square miles, the heart of the district of Laconia. After she conquered Messenia, her total territory amounted to some 3200 square miles, more than three times as large as Attica. Given the nature of Greek terrain, this figure is not very meaningful. What is crucial is that Messenia and, to a lesser extent, Laconia were more fertile than most Greek districts, so that the inhabitants were able to feed themselves without imports, except perhaps when there was heavy and prolonged fighting. Laconia also possessed iron mines, a great rarity in Greece, though it must be admitted that we do not know how early they were worked. The main weakness was poor access to the sea. Sparta herself was, strictly speaking, landlocked: the nearest available harbour was Gytheion some twenty-seven miles to the south, used both for merchant shipping and as a small naval base.

The Spartans themselves were not a very numerous group. The largest military contingent they ever mustered from their own ranks was at the battle against the Persians at Plataea in 479 B.C.—5000 hoplites. With them and serving in their army on that occasion were 5000 *perioeci*, men from the rest of Laconia (and perhaps a few from Messenia), who were free men living in their own small communities (such as Gytheion) but differing from the normal Greek pattern in that they lacked autonomy in the military sphere and in foreign affairs generally. In those respects they were subject to

Sparta, obligated to accept Spartan policy and to fight in the Spartan army at the latter's call and under Spartan authority. Although subjects and not to be confused with genuine allies, such as the Corinthians, the *perioeci* were at the same time citizens of their own communities, Doric in their dialect and entitled like the Spartans themselves to be called Lacedaemonians, after their eponymous ancestor, Lacedaemon, son of Zeus and Taygete (nymph of nearby Mt. Taygetus). They were thus sharply differentiated from the remaining and most numerous subject population, the helots.

The origin of the helot system has been the topic of endless unconvincing speculation ever since antiquity. There were parallels elsewhere in the Greek world, in Crete, in Thessaly and in the colonized regions both east and west, but even less is known about them, so that they do not help solve the helot mystery (which is connected with another puzzle, previously discussed, the entry of the Dorians into the Peloponnese). The usual practice, throughout most of antiquity, when a city or district was enslaved, was to sell off the inhabitants and disperse them. In Laconia, however, the Spartans adopted the dangerous alternative of keeping a whole population in subjugation at home, in what amounted to their native territory, and later (probably in the eighth century) they repeated the pattern when they conquered Messenia.

In that they lacked personal freedom, the helots were slaves, but they must be differentiated in several respects from the genuine slaves, who were chattels, the personal property of their masters. The helots were subjects of the Spartan state assigned to individuals, not free to move or to control their own lives, but possessing certain rights, which were normally honoured. Their basic obligation was to work the land and attend to the pastures of the Spartans to whom they were bound, and to pay over half the produce. They maintained their own family relationships and for the large part they lived in their own cohesive groups ('communities' would be too strong a word). Hence they were self-perpetuating: we never hear of Sparta importing new helots from abroad, and that fact alone sets them sharply apart from the chattel slaves elsewhere.

Whatever the origins of the system—how, for example, an original distinction was drawn in Laconia between the two very different subject statuses, *perioeci* and helots, or how the helots came to be monopolized by the Spartans and not also assigned to *perioeci*, who were in turn free to obtain and own genuine slaves if they wished—the consequences in historical times are intelligible enough. As we shall see, the helots, proportionally far more numerous than the slaves of any other Greek state, even Athens, were fundamental to the establishment of the unique Spartan system, and to the policies adopted by Sparta abroad.

Our ignorance of Dark Age Sparta extends still further, to the whole of its early institutional development. Archaeology has been even less helpful than usual here. The only prudent course, therefore, is to turn immediately to the Archaic period, from the early seventh century, putting aside all the efforts to reconstruct something coherent out of the blatant fictions permeating later traditions, including those which eventually became attached to the legendary lawgiver Lycurgus. Not that our evidence for seventh-century Sparta is abundant, but it at least has a firm anchor; some of it is contemporary and is subject to the normal controls of historical analysis. We can, for example, read the fragments of the lyric poet Alcman, which immediately suggest that Sparta in his time was still within the mainstream of Greek cultural development, as it later was not. Other signs point in the same direction, such as the archaeological finds or the plausible tradition about Sparta's leading role in the development of Greek music (whether or not one chooses to believe that it was a Lydian named Terpander, the inventor of the lyre, who migrated to Sparta and founded the musical tradition there). We can read the fragments of the poet Tyrtaeus, which reveal that seventh-century Sparta was also within the mainstream in its condition of chronic *stasis* (again as it later was not), involving struggles over land distribution, political demands by commoners (with the new hoplite army an important factor), and conflicts with other states in the Peloponnese, notably with Argos and with Tegea, the leading city in Arcadia.

There is even a curious story about a colony Sparta sent out to Taras (modern Taranto) in southern Italy about 700 B.C. Actually, there are two versions, each with variants, which were bitterly debated in antiquity. According to one (Strabo VI 3, 2), those Spartiates who had not participated in the conquest of Messenia, which took many years, were afterwards enslaved by the returning warriors, while 'children born during the war were called Partheniae [from the word *parthenos* meaning both "virgin" and "unmarried woman"] and deprived of civic rights. The Partheniae, being numerous, refused to accept their lot and conspired against the *demos.*' The plot was discovered, the Delphic oracle advised shipping them out to Taras, and there they joined with the barbarians and Cretans who were already settled on the site. In the alternative account, also recorded by Strabo (VI 3, 3), the Spartan women sent a delegation to the army after the war had dragged on for ten years, protesting the depopulation that was the inevitable consequence. The best young men were sent home to procreate, but when the full army finally returned, they failed to 'honour the Partheniae as the others but treated them as illegitimate. The latter thereupon conspired with some of the helots and revolted'; the plot was revealed by helots, and again the foundation of Taras was the final outcome.

Apart from Taras—and Spartan participation in its settlement is certain however one threads one's way through the conflicting tales—Sparta was never involved in the Archaic colonization movement. The reason lies in her extensive territory, especially after the conquest of Messenia, and this factor together with the system of *perioeci* and helots constituted a fundamental breach in the 'typical' Greek pattern of development. In the end Sparta had no choice but to take a road essentially different from that of any other state. The turning-point came in the so-called Second Messenian War, which, the tradition says, lasted seventeen years, and which is probably to be dated in the third quarter of the seventh century. Messenia revolted and the Spartans found themselves very hard pressed to put down the uprising, primarily, it would seem from Tyrtaeus, because of disaffection, disorder and near-rebellion in their own ranks.

During this struggle Tyrtaeus called for *eunomia*, 'obedience to the laws', which was to become, in the eyes of some Greeks, Sparta's greatest virtue in classical times. (It is worth noticing that in all his exhortations to patriotism and *eunomia*, Tyrtaeus never mentioned the lawgiver Lycurgus.) And once the Messenians were subjugated again, the Spartans proceeded to work out a common solution to their two most pressing problems, the elimination of *stasis* at home and the maintenance of a secure hold on the helots who greatly outnumbered the free men. We cannot trace the precise steps through which the solution—a compromise among various conflicting groups and demands—was finally achieved (and there were further changes in the following centuries within the framework of that compromise). There is no agreement among scholars, for example, as to the date or precise significance of a key document, the so-called Great Rhetra, preserved by Plutarch (*Life of Lycurgus* VI) in corrupt wording within a confused context. On any interpretation, that brief text, which distributes the power of decision-making among the kings, the council of elders, and the assembly of all the Equals, marks the first time in Greek history that the popular assembly was assigned formal, though restricted, powers, at a date which is probably earlier than the Second Messenian War. (The Rhetra makes no reference to the ephors, who were already in existence and who later, by the middle of the sixth century, became the most important executive authority in the Spartan government.) The measure of both our ignorance and the amount of development in Spartan institutions which must be allowed for, is thus sufficiently exemplified in this single text.

Eunomia was achieved, according to Herodotus (I 65), in the reign of Kings Leon and Agasicles, that is, early in the sixth century. 'Before then,' he writes, 'they were the worst ruled of nearly all the Greeks, both in their internal relations and in their relations with foreigners, from whom they were isolated.' If this has any foundation, it means that the two generations after the Second Messenian War saw the working out of the rather complex structure of historical Spartan society. The male Spartiates, the Equals, were now a full-time military establishment. Their lives were, in principle, wholly moulded by, and wholly dedicated to, the state. Even the decision whether or not a male infant should be allowed to survive was taken away from the parents and handed over to public officials. This was one of many devices which served, both symbolically and in practice, to minimize the bonds of kinship and thereby to reduce a major source of conflicting loyalties. At seven a boy was turned over to the state for his education, with its concentration on physical hardihood, military skills and the virtues of obedience. In childhood and adolescence he progressed through a series of intimate age-class groupings; as an adult his main association was with his military regiment and his mess-hall. Various rituals reinforced the system at fixed stages in a man's growth.

Concentration on the single purpose of the Spartiate's life was strengthened by his release from all economic concerns and activities. That was the responsibility of the helots and the *perioeci*, who, in their different ways, produced the food and armour and carried on the necessary trade. The helots worked under absolute compulsion, of course, but the *perioeci* were the beneficiaries of a monopolistic position, free from competition either from Spartans themselves or from outsiders. Spartiates were even prohibited from employing coined money, and outsiders were denied all access to the economy except through the mediation of the *perioeci* or the state.

This probably helps to explain why we hear little of unrest on the part of the *perioeci*, despite their lack of autonomy and their obligatory military contribution. It also explains the failure of Sparta to grow into an urban community. 'If Sparta were to be deserted,' wrote Thucydides (I 10, 2), 'and only the sanctuaries and building foundations remained, future generations would never believe that her power matched her reputation . . . for they live in villages according to the old Greek fashion.'

From childhood, too, the Spartiates were encouraged in competition among each other, not in intellectual achievement or for economic advantage but in physical prowess and stamina. The prizes were honorific rather than material in one sense, but among them were positions of authority and leadership. Already at the age of eighteen one might be rewarded by admission to the élite youth corps called *hippeis,* whose functions included serving as the royal bodyguard and carrying out secret governmental missions. Then came the chance for army commands and eventually government posts.

At the head of the governmental structure stood the two hereditary kings, an anomalous institution which is not easy to define (and the co-existence of two royal houses has defied explanation). They commanded the armies in the field. At home, however, they not only lacked authoritative royal powers but they were subject to supervision by the ephors. On the other hand, they retained certain traditional priestly functions; they received by right various perquisites; and on their death they were mourned on a scale and in a manner which Herodotus (VI 58) found so alien that he called the royal funeral rites 'similar to those of the barbarians of Asia'. They were *ex officio* members of the *gerousia,* a council of thirty elders, the others being men over the age of sixty elected for life. The kings seem not to have presided over the *gerousia* nor to have had any prerogatives in its deliberations beyond those of any other member. Nor did they preside over meetings of the assembly, which apparently could not initiate action or even amend proposals brought before it, but which nevertheless had the final vote in basic questions of policy submitted to it. And then there were the five ephors, elected annually from among the whole citizen-body and restricted to a single year in office, during which they had far-reaching powers in criminal jurisdiction and general administration.

The very existence of the two royal houses is one indication that the ideal of a community of Equals was incomplete in reality. The constitution may have hemmed the kings in, but the aura surrounding them encouraged and assisted the abler and more ambitious of them to extend their authority in a way that sometimes endangered the power equilibrium of the society. Herodotus is almost obsessed with stories about the susceptibility of Spartan kings to bribery. When Aristagoras, tyrant of Miletus, seeking Spartan support for the Ionian revolt against Persia, had raised his offer to Cleomenes I from ten to fifty talents, the king was saved from temptation only because his eight- or nine-year-old daughter Gorgo cried out, 'Father, the foreigner will ruin you if you do not withdraw' (V 51). Some ephors, too, found the extensive authority given to them very heady wine, which they sought to taste to the full in the one year of office allowed them. It often happened, according to Aristotle (*Politics* 1270b9 *ff.*), 'that very poor men attained this office, whose lack of means enabled them to be bought'; yet, such was their power, that even the kings 'were compelled to court them'.

All this may be grossly exaggerated (or, in Aristotle's case, it may refer to Sparta in its decline in the fourth century) but it nevertheless reveals that Spartan austerity was never as complete in reality as on paper. Besides there was inequality in wealth among the Equals. Some were even rich enough to enter teams in the Olympic chariot races, the paramount sign of outstanding wealth among aristocratic Greeks; surviving records list the names of nine Spartan winners (with twelve victories among them) between 550 and 400 B.C., one of them a king, Damaratus; another, Arcesilaus, twice a victor, was followed by his son twenty years later. Did men of such wealth never use it to advance their own interests in elections or those of their sons all along the line? That would be hard to imagine, just as it is difficult to appreciate the overtones of a meeting of the Spartan assembly, which was not heterogeneous like the Athenian but rather a meeting, in another capacity, of a highly disciplined army corps for whom obedience had been held up as the prime virtue all their lives. Could they have listened to debates with an open mind, disregarding the status of the speakers in the army hierarchy or their individual exploits on the battlefield?

Answers to such questions must be speculative because our ancient authorities are not concerned with them. Internal conflicts appear in the historical record we have, at least for the sixth century, only in accounts of the more spectacular careers of a few individuals, and then almost entirely in the context of foreign affairs. Herodotus will pause to tell (V 39–40) how first the ephors and then the elders brought pressure on the childless King Anaxandridas to take another wife in order to preserve his royal line, threatening him with some unspecified action by the Spartans as a whole should he persist in his obstinate refusal. But conflicts over broader issues or over control of affairs and something of the actual mechanics of policy-making do not really come to light until a man like Cleomenes I, king from about 520 to 490, employed his military successes and his diplomatic manœuvres to direct Spartan policy towards aggressive and dangerous adventures abroad.

It was accepted by ancient writers that the key to Spartan foreign policy was the presence of the helots. To hold them in check, Sparta had not only to keep peace in the Peloponnese, for an enemy state might stir up the helots, if not by design then by the mere fact of engaging too much of Spartan military energies and manpower, but she also had to be very careful before sending an army outside the Peloponnese. Spartan policy had not always been defensive and non-expansionist. But a defeat by Tegea and the inability to conquer Argos seem finally to have initiated the new policy by the middle of the sixth century. Wars and conquests were replaced by defensive alliances and non-aggression pacts, though naturally force was used to impose alliances when necessary and also to maintain them against defections. By the end of the century, virtually the whole of the Peloponnese had been brought into the network, except Argos which was too strong and Achaea which was too remote and insignificant. To strengthen the alliances, furthermore, Sparta supported friendly factions within the allied states, normally oligarchies, and in the process she gained the undeserved reputation of being the sworn enemy of tyrants on principle. In fact, Spartan behaviour towards tyrants was opportunistic, determined by judgments of self-interest rather than of morals and principles. She never moved against the tyrannies of Sicyon, Corinth or Megara, for example, whereas she interfered decisively to bring about the expulsion of Hippias from Athens in 510.[1]

The Athenian adventure is reported in our sources as part of the story of Cleomenes I, with the stress on the king himself. Perhaps he was the chief advocate or even the initiator of the policy, but there can be little doubt that he marched on Athens in his official capacity and with official sanction. Then came complications as two factions in Athens engaged in a civil war over the succession to the tyranny. Cleomenes returned to support one faction, led by Isagoras, against that of Cleisthenes. He suffered a defeat, left Athens and returned once again with an army enlarged by allied troops. When the latter learned why they had been mustered, they rebelled, under the leadership of Corinth, saying that intervention in Athenian domestic affairs was unjust and anyway no business of theirs. The other Spartan king, Damaratus, supported them, and the whole venture ended in a fiasco for Cleomenes, with important consequences.

Henceforth the allies were consulted, in more or less

[1] For the Athenian side of this episode, see the final pages of the next chapter.

formal meetings called for the purpose, whenever their military support was wanted, or at least when a large-scale joint operation was envisaged. A loose network of alliances between Sparta on the one hand and each of her allies individually on the other, was now converted into something approaching a genuine league. Modern historians actually call it the Peloponnesian League, though the Greeks always clung to 'the Spartans and their allies' and though its membership at various times included such states outside the Peloponnese as Megara, Aegina and Athens. In a sense the modern name goes too far: the 'league' never acquired any administrative machinery, not even a treasury, and its cohesion and effectiveness varied from decade to decade, and from issue to issue. Nevertheless, it was enough of a reality to give Sparta the added manpower she needed, and the peace at home, to become the greatest military force in Greece and the acknowledged leader of the Greeks against the Persian invaders.

10

Athens

GEOGRAPHICALLY the district of Attica, some 1000 square miles in all, is typically Greek, not so fertile as the best, such as Messenia, but with a number of good extensive plains nonetheless. Two features require special mention. Attica had a very considerable coast-line on the south and east suitable for beaching ships, and in the southeast, at Laurium, there was a rich supply of silver, which may have been tapped as early as the Bronze Age and was certainly mined more systematically from the late sixth century. But there was nothing in the terrain to promote the early and exceptional political unification of the district. Nor is the ethnic argument a sufficient explanation: neighbouring Boeotia remained politically fragmented, after all.

Not only was Athens the largest Greek city-state territorially, apart from Sparta, but, unlike the latter, she became a unified state without internal subjects, not even *perioeci*, let alone helots. All free men of Attica were equally Athenians, whether they lived in the main city or in Marathon or Eleusis or elsewhere in the countryside. The sharp class inequalities that existed were based neither on region nor on ethnic distinctions, but were repeated throughout the various demes or districts of the state; the slaves came from outside. To be sure, the size of the state meant that such larger 'villages' as Marathon had a semi-independent life of their own, with their own agoras, village officials, temples and cults. This regionalism, as some modern scholars refer to it, should not be exaggerated; in particular, it must be wholly differentiated from the more typical situation in Boeotia already noticed, with its twelve independent, and often quarrelling, city-states. The Athenians were themselves well aware that they were an exception in this respect, and in characteristic fashion they attributed the unification of Attica, or *synoikismos* as they called it, to a single heroic figure, King Theseus whom we have met before. That this is a mythical explanation (probably of the sixth century) is implicit in the vague and anachronistic account of the *synoikismos* given by Thucydides (II 15–16). Once Theseus, a sort of latter-day Heracles, is removed, there is no evidence that Attica was ever anything but a unit (though we must allow for possible disputes over such a border district as Eleusis), with a political development in the Bronze and Dark Ages—Mycenaean monarchy, breakdown, Dark Age chieftainship and finally aristocratic rule—that followed the lines already described for other Greek states, apart from the one aberration of size, for which no better explanation than the mythical one is available.[1]

Athens also took no part in the colonization movement. Though individual Athenians may have migrated, the city as such, unlike Sparta, had not even one Taras to her credit. Perhaps her large territory provided an outlet which other states had to find abroad. Besides, her continuous record of pottery production, from the earliest protogeometric, implies a better than average industrial development, which may have acted as a second safety valve against rural depression and overpopulation. In the end, however, Athens could not escape the universal *stasis* of archaic Greece, with the same issues, the same conflicting social groupings, the same call for a tyrant. The economic and political monopoly of the Eupatrid families (as the Athenian aristocracy were called, the word meaning 'well-sired') was menaced, both from within the closed circle and from the lower classes, in the second half of the seventh century, when the crisis appears to have arisen with some suddenness.

The first recorded episode was an unsuccessful attempt to establish tyranny in about 630 by a nobleman

[1] This reduction of the *synoikismos* of Theseus to a complete myth is not the view generally accepted by historians. It is based on the investigations of J. Sarkady, published in German in the *Acta classica* of the University of Debrecen, vol. 2 (1966), pp. 9–27; vol. 3 (1967), pp. 23–34.

named Cylon. Later Athenian accounts pretend that Cylon drew his support mainly from outside, in particular from his father-in-law Theagenes, tyrant of Megara; that the Athenians resisted *en masse*; and that the Eupatrid house of the Alcmaeonids brought a curse upon themselves by violating a safe-conduct and massacring Cylon's followers. The distortion seems fairly obvious. Tyrants everywhere had considerable internal support; even the Athenians had no choice but to admit that a generation later there was a popular demand for Solon to assume the role of tyrant. On the other hand, there is no inherent improbability in the family connexion between Cylon and Theagenes: such marriages were an essential part of inter-city relations and few aristocratic families had any reluctance in accepting a tyrant as son-in-law or father-in-law. As for the massacre following Cylon's surrender, there may have been a murderous vendetta for some years, which would explain the shadowy figure of Draco. He is supposed to have codified the law in 621—'a code written in blood, not in ink', a later hostile tradition said of it (Plutarch, *Solon* XVII 2), a tradition remarkably free from concrete data. What Draco probably did do was to lay down in detail the law regarding murder. Some of that law was still in force at the end of the fifth century B.C., and the little we know deals primarily with ways of putting an end to the traditional blood-feud. This is what the post-Cylonian blood-letting may have been responsible for. A total codification by Draco, however, is quite certainly fictitious. That was the work of Solon in the next generation.

With Solon we possess a body of genuine documentation for the first time, small though it is. He was himself a fairly prolific writer on ethical and political themes. Like all writers in this age of minimal literacy, he expressed himself not in prose but in poems, which survived for centuries. A few extensive quotations are still available. Besides, the original text of his law code, inscribed on wooden tablets, remained in existence for many years, though the confusion in the sources has led to disagreement among modern scholars about the details, even about how long they continued to be accessible.

Solon was a Eupatrid who in 594 was appointed archon, the highest office in the state, with plenipotentiary powers to put an end to the *stasis* by a thoroughgoing reform of the laws and the political system. Both the choice of Solon and the way it was made are significant. He did not seize power but was appointed to it, which proves that among the aristocracy itself a sufficient number were ready to accept major concessions to the clamouring opposition, many of them peasants in bondage and clientship (as explained in Chapter 8). The only hope for a successful compromise lay with an aristocrat who had taken his stand with the poor. Solon, we know from his earlier poems, had placed the onus for bringing the state to civil war on the rapacity and inhumanity of the rich. And he seems to have done so by public recitation, in the agora.

> Unrighteous are the hearts of the rulers of the people, who will one day suffer many pains for their great pride (*hybris*); for they do not know how to restrain their excesses. . . . They grow rich through unrighteous deeds, and steal for themselves right and left, respecting neither sacred nor public property. . . .
>
> (quoted by Demosthenes XIX 255)

The poor repaid him by an appeal that he become tyrant. This he refused, but he accepted the extraordinary archonship and proceeded to steer a complicated course between the extreme demands of the peasantry and the hard-bitten wing of the nobility.

His first action, the so-called *seisachtheia* or 'shaking off of burdens', was directed to the fundamental question of peasant bondage. Debts were cancelled, the many Athenians who were tied down as involuntary sharecroppers (*hektemoroi*) or who had been taken into bondage as a result of indebtedness were restored to freedom, others who had actually been sold abroad into slavery were bought back. A new law was then promulgated forbidding for all future time the practice of mortgaging the persons of free men or women as security for debts. Solon refused, however, to take the most revolutionary step of all, confiscation of large estates for distribution among the poorest peasants and the landless. Nevertheless, Aristotle (*Constitution of Athens* IX 1) was right to put the *seisachtheia* first among the Solonic measures in the interest of the common people. A free peasantry was to be the base of Athenian society all through her history as an independent *polis*. Serious weaknesses still remained in their position, but they were henceforth protected from the traditional forms of personal exploitation, a protection which Solon further strengthened by reforms in the administration of justice and by his codification of the law, an action which introduced clarity, certainty and public knowledge of the law into the community.

On the constitutional side the balance required was more complex, for in that sphere there were conflicts within the upper classes themselves. Solon's most decisive thrust was the creation of a formal status hierarchy based on wealth as the sole criterion. The citizen-body was divided into four classes according to wealth, measured, it is essential to stress, not in money but in agricultural yield. The highest offices, with a one-year tenure, were restricted to the first class, men whose land produced 500 dry or liquid measures.[1] One of these offices, the archonship, was the way of entry into the Council of the Areopagus, the traditional body of life peers with a general undefined supervisory authority over the state (reminiscent of the Roman Senate), which Solon retained. The next two classes were eligible for the minor offices and presumably for the new council of

[1] The dry measure was the *medimnos* (just under 1½ bushels), the liquid measure the *metretes* (about 8½ imperial gallons). The arbitrary attribution of equality in value to the two measures, like the failure to differentiate between one crop and another, or between wine and oil, reveals how far the economy was from a market-and-money system of evaluation.

400 which Solon created. The rest, the *thetes,* those who could not produce 200 measures a year, were restricted to the assembly.

Just how the assembly or the council of 400 functioned in the spheres of legislation and policy is the subject of much speculation. The sources have little to relate, apart from one very important new feature, namely, the grant to the assembly of apellate jurisdiction over the magistrates in some lawsuits. But the thinking behind the reforms and their general impact are clear. The wealthiest commoners became eligible for the highest offices and the Areopagus, thus breaking the Eupatrid monopoly though by no means removing the latter from power and influence, since they no doubt still constituted a majority of the largest landowners. The middle classes, including the hoplite soldiers who held sufficient land, were given a role in government for the first time. And even the poor, both urban and rural, were recognized as a working part of the *demos* as a whole, severely restricted though their position was. The great gaps in the structure of the rudimentary *polis,* which had prevented it from functioning as a viable community, were thus narrowed, though they were not yet sealed off.

Solon then left Athens for a long period, fearing that, if he remained, the dissatisfied extremists would put pressure on him to make further changes or to go on to become a tyrant. Factional disturbances continued. On two occasions it proved impossible to choose an archon. We hear no more of this kind of trouble after 580 B.C., presumably because the new constitutional machinery became formally accepted by most of the wealthier classes, Eupatrid and commoner alike. However, constitutional machinery alone could not give internal peace. *Stasis* could not be abolished by a stroke of the pen. The personal status of the peasantry had been secured by Solon, but not their economic position. Nor, apparently, could the city provide a livelihood for enough of the landless and the others who were unable to make ends meet in the countryside. Demands and counter-demands played into the hands of the more ambitious of the aristocrats able to draw upon retainers and followers in the continual jockeying for honour, power and wealth. Eventually one man rose above them all and achieved what Solon had tried to prevent. Peisistratus, an influential aristocrat who claimed a family tree going back to Homer's Nestor and who had gained public repute in a war with Megara, made his first attempt, according to the tradition, in 561. He was expelled after a time, tried again, was again expelled, and finally succeeded in 545. He then ruled until his death in 527 and was followed by his son Hippias, whose tyranny was not brought to an end until 510, and then only thanks to an invading Spartan army (Chapter 9).

There is no contemporary literary evidence about the Peisistratids. Our first account of them is that of Herodotus, writing in the middle of the next century, when every right-thinking Greek automatically condemned tyranny and all tyrants as an unmitigated evil. It is all the more revealing, therefore, that Herodotus and serious later writers were agreed that Peisistratus was an exception, a 'good tyrant' insofar as that phrase was not self-contradictory. 'He governed the city with moderation, as citizen rather than as tyrant' (Aristotle, *Constitution of Athens* XVI 2). They also agreed that one secret of his success, and of his son's, was that they left Solon's constitution in operation unchanged, except that they saw to it that the annually elected archon was always either a member of the family or a supporter. We should not understand this in a naïve way, though the statement is undoubtedly correct as bare fact. Peisistratus' first attempt or attempts to seize power (it is not certain that the tradition is right about two failures) seem to have been made with such support as he could muster within Attica. But the third time, equipped with funds he acquired from the silver mines of Mt. Pangaeum in Thrace, he came with a mercenary force, some of whom he retained as a bodyguard in his citadel on the Acropolis. His irreconcilable opponents were killed or exiled. Thus protected, Peisistratus could afford to allow the machinery of assembly, council, magistrates and courts, even the Council of the Areopagus, to go on functioning. On the other hand, no one could compel him to rule 'constitutionally'. That he did so from choice is a measure of his political intelligence, and in the end it is one key to his place in the evolution of the Athenian state.

The precise relationship between the Peisistratids and the other aristocratic families of Athens during their thirty-five-year period in power is not easy to define. Later traditions of the undying enmity of such families as the Alcmaeonids may be discounted as *post factum* attempts to purge the family records of their friendly associations with the departed tyranny. The Alcmaeonids did make an unsuccessful attempt to overthrow Hippias in 513, but, before that, one of them, Cleisthenes, had held the archonship under Hippias, and still earlier his sister had been married to Peisistratus. Relations were equally ambiguous and shifting between the Peisistratids and the Miltiades family. The latter were connected by marriage with the Cypselids, tyrants of Corinth, while Cleisthenes' mother was the daughter of the tyrant of Sicyon, in accord with the practice we have already noted in connexion with Cylon in the seventh century. Another of Peisistratus' wives was an Argive aristocrat who had previously been married to a tyrant in Ambracia, a member of the Cypselid clan. Other connexions of the Peisistratids are recorded in Euboea, in Thrace and Macedonia, in Thessaly and with Lygdamis, tyrant of Naxos. Aristotle's generalization, in his *Constitution of Athens* (XVI 9), that Peisistratus won the support of the majority of the nobility and the people alike, may thus be extended, so far as the nobility were concerned, to connexions abroad.

Much as the Greek aristocracy of the time may have preferred oligarchy to rule by one man from their ranks, they rarely carried their preference to a point of principle. Disputes between a tyrant and an aristocratic individual or family were generated primarily by considerations of personal honour or status. Even the assassination of Hippias' younger brother Hipparchus in 514, which led to the hardening of the tyranny into a more despotic rule, was motivated by jealousy in a pederastic love affair. The Athenians subsequently made national heroes of the two assassins, Harmodius and Aristogeiton, but that reflects public opinion in the age when the tyranny had been judged infamous in retrospect.

However, the Athenian aristocracy suffered a permanent defeat under the Peisistratids. Thirty-five years of the Solonic constitution at work, even with the tyrant as permanent overseer, could not be undone, especially when the period was also one of peace and growing prosperity for Athens. The leading families still held the main offices and still involved themselves in foreign relations, but they were also being tamed in the process, compelled and increasingly accustomed to function within a constitutional framework, in which the previous factional activities were curbed. When Hippias was driven into exile by the Spartans in 510, one wing of the aristocracy, led by Isagoras, sought to return to the good old days. They were defeated in a two-year civil war, after which Cleisthenes remodelled the constitution and laid the structural foundation of Athenian democracy. In this he was no doubt much aided by a 'national' spirit to which the tyrants had contributed actively and concretely. They built a great temple to Athena on the Acropolis (destroyed by the Persians in 480 and later replaced by the Parthenon) and began one to Olympian Zeus; they encouraged and embellished the major cults, introducing recitations from Homer into the Panathenaic festival which celebrated the birth of Athena, and the annual competition in tragic choruses at the Greater Dionysia; they patronized the arts generally and invited poets and musicians from abroad to their court in Athens.

The impact of these cultural factors cannot be overlooked even if it cannot be measured (and it is not lessened by acknowledging that the tyrants' interest was in their own glory as much as, or more than, in fostering a national self-consciousness). Part of the impact was on the economy. Athens was still a largely agrarian community and the prime test of economic stability was in the countryside. We know little about Peisistratean activity there, other than the support they gave to needy farmers by making loans available on easy terms, but all the evidence of the next century goes to show that the tyranny was the period when the class of owners of small and medium-sized farms became firmly and permanently entrenched. This would have been harder, if not impossible, to achieve, had there not been a considerable growth in the urban sector of the economy, providing an outlet for landless and marginal peasants, among other things.

The great attention to public buildings and festivals was one factor in the growth of the city economy. So was the remarkable upsurge in Athenian fine painted pottery, which about the middle of the sixth century rapidly acquired a virtual monopoly among Greek pottery exports to the other cities of Greece, to the western colonies, and to the Etruscans. Athenian coinage is still another sign: although it is not certain exactly when Athens began to mint silver, the decisive shift to the famous 'owls', the one genuinely international Greek currency, occurred either in Peisistratus' reign or in his son's. And, finally, more and more Greeks began to migrate to Athens from other cities, as new prospects were opened up for trade and manufacture, and as she blossomed into a pan-Hellenic cultural centre.

Later Athenians looked back to Solon as the man who set them on the road to democracy, whereas Peisistratus and Hippias were an uncomfortable and not very reputable interlude. Nevertheless, if we put aside moral judgments and considerations of intention or foresight, the historical role of the tyrants appears to have been equally important in moving the Athenians along that road.

11

The Culture of Archaic Greece

FOR all their geographical dispersion and their political fragmentation, the Greeks retained a deep-rooted consciousness of belonging to a single and unique culture—'being of the same stock and the same speech, with common shrines of the gods and rituals, with similar customs', as Herodotus (VIII 144) phrased it. They were right—and the phenomenon is remarkable, given the absence of a central political or ecclesiastical authority, the predominantly oral character of their culture even beyond the end of the Archaic period, and the inventiveness with which one community or another solved problem after problem in politics and culture. Perhaps nothing is so revealing as the rapidity with which a new idea was diffused. The Phoenician alphabet is an early example; others are the council-magistrate-assembly machinery of government, the 'Doric' temple and coined money. It seems not to have mattered whether an 'invention' was Greek to begin with or borrowed from outside. If it proved functional within Greek society in general and compatible with local conditions, then its value was quickly recognized in practice all over the Greek world.

One binding element was myth. The Greeks had a large stock of mythical tales. There was a myth behind every rite and every cult-centre, behind new city-foundations, and for more or less everything in nature, the movement of the sun, the stars, rivers and springs, earthquakes and plagues. Myth performed a number of functions: it was explanatory, didactic and prescriptive. It gave the archaic Greeks their sense of, and knowledge of, their past, their history in other words; it sanctioned cults, festivals, beliefs, the authority of individual noble families (with their divine genealogies), and so on through a range of practices and ideas. On the other hand, myth was not all-controlling. As we saw in discussing the lawgivers in Chapter 8, there was also much human self-reliance behind the evolution of institutions and ideas, a readiness to change and innovate without direct divine authority or revelation. Increasingly, the Greeks found themselves with separate, sometimes irreconcilable, mythical and non-mythical explanations and justifications, co-existing happily. The myths were believed to be true, though there was neither a sanctified priesthood nor any other pre-ordained authority with the prerogative to develop new myths or to certify old ones. From the sixth century B.C. on, an occasional voice was raised in doubt or scepticism; not many, however, for most people did not *study* the myths, they merely retold them or they performed the appropriate rites and that was sufficient.

The mythmaking process continued. Thus, as the Greeks dispersed east and west, Apollo, Demeter, Heracles and the other gods and demi-gods had to travel with them, and the myths were adjusted and enlarged accordingly. The Greeks in Sicily challenged the claim of Eleusis to be the place where Demeter, goddess of the fertility of the earth, first gave man the gift of corn. Heracles swam the Straits of Messina and then took a grand tour of Sicily which brought him as far as Eryx in the northwest, thereby sanctioning Greek claims to that part of the island. Aphrodite followed later, and it was from Eryx that her cult spread to Carthage and to Rome. In Old Greece, too, myths had to support shifting political relations and alliances, ideas of 'ethnic' cohesion (as with the Ionians), or the conflicting claims of certain shrines to higher status than others. The longest of the so-called 'Homeric Hymns' is about Apollo, and it has two distinct parts which are incoherent, if not downright inconsistent, one linking the god with Delphi, the other with Delos, his two most important centres. This example can be multiplied many times, as any modern handbook of Greek mythology reveals. The result was a considerable untidiness, to which another aspect of Greek religion contributed. Although all Greeks recognized and honoured the whole pantheon, no individual or community could conceivably perform all the rites to all of them. Each city had its patron deity and its special affinities with certain other gods and goddesses, who were accordingly celebrated even beyond Zeus himself, the unchallenged head of the pantheon, though no one denied Zeus's supremacy. Again there was the occasional sceptic, and again the people as a whole saw no difficulty.

Greek religion of the Archaic period was essentially a development from the basis already evident in the Homeric poems. By a variety of formalized actions, men sought to establish the most favourable possible relationships with the supernatural powers. That is to say, they tried to discover the will of the gods, and to placate and please them. The former required specialists, such as soothsayers, diviners and seers, but the rest of the activity was carried on by ordinary people, both privately, in their homes or through private associations, and publicly, by officials of the state. There were many officials called *hiereis*, a word which we translate as 'priests' despite the fact that they were normally laymen carrying on one particular public function exactly like all the other officials, civil and military. While kings still existed, they performed the state rites; now they were replaced by members of the aristocracy (and later by democratically chosen magistrates). And the rules were laid down without the intervention of a sanctified caste, backed only by tradition and myth. It was Homer and Hesiod, according to Herodotus (II 53), who 'first fixed for the Greeks the genealogy of the gods, gave the gods their titles, divided among them their honours and functions, and defined their images'. This may not be literally accurate but it points to the essential truth that insofar as the Greeks had an authority in these matters, it was largely the authority of poets, who may have claimed (and even believed) to be 'inspired by the Muses' but who cannot by any recognizable standard be equated with prophets or priests. Poetic inspiration is not prophetic revelation.

The activities through which the gods were honoured

and supplicated included table fellowship (sharing food and drink with them), singing, dancing and processions, allowing oneself to be possessed (maenadism and other forms of 'orgiastic' behaviour), and games featuring feats of prowess (for physical excellence was as much the gift of the gods as anything else). Religion, in sum, was not set aside in a separate compartment but was meshed into every aspect of personal and social behaviour. What was not included was a theology or spiritual exercise, not even in the 'mystery religions', such as the cult of Demeter at Eleusis. These involved hereditary priesthoods and a sort of personal communion, but the activity was nevertheless still restricted to formalized words, rites and spectacles.

Of all the rites, sacrifice, both vegetable and animal, was the most universal—it is hard to think of any significant action which was not preceded by a sacrifice—and therefore the altar was the basic piece of equipment, with the hearth in the house also serving as one. Altars were found everywhere, in conjunction with secular public buildings, assembly-places and temples, at the city-gates, in the countryside at sacred places. Often a 'shrine' consisted of nothing more than an altar surrounded by a bit of marked out 'sacred ground'. Then, as the material level advanced towards the end of the Dark Age, the temple made its appearance in the eighth century. Though the temple had been common in the Near East for two thousand years, it had been so rare and insignificant in Bronze Age Greece that we may properly speak of it as an innovation now. Its function was not to serve as a house of worship, at least not normally, but to be the home of the god, where his statue was kept together with the treasure he accumulated through dedications from grateful mortals. The earliest temples were of wood and rubble or sun-dried brick and are known to us only from a few terracotta models, narrow one-roomed buildings with a simple porch at one end framed by two columns supporting the gable. The first stone temples were built about 600 B.C., and with them came the great leap to the large structures that were ever after the hallmark of ancient Greek architecture, the oblong room (or rooms), covered by a pitched roof and ringed by rows of columns, with the spaces between the column capitals and the roof decorated by sculpted reliefs. The earliest surviving remains of Doric temples are as widely scattered as Argos, Olympia, Delphi, Corcyra (Corfu) and Sicily; none of these is later than 550 B.C.

In the course of the Archaic period certain religious centres acquired pan-Hellenic status because they had something extraordinary to offer. One group consisted of shrines where particularly effective oracles could be consulted. The ability to foretell the future was a very specialized and valuable skill. Diviners who 'read' the flight of birds, dream interpreters, seers who had visions, were usually private persons able to persuade clients that their powers were real and legitimate. However, nothing in this field could rival the direct voice of a god, especially Apollo, who had special shrines for this purpose in various places in Hellas, with Delphi unchallenged in pre-eminence. In all but one respect Delphi was just another small Greek community, whose religious life was administered in the normal ways. When the shrine of Apollo became oracular is unknown, nor is the procedure clear to us. On stated days, inquirers who had performed the required sacrifices and rites of purification (and paid a considerable fee) were permitted to address themselves to the god, either on their own behalf or as agents of their communities. Apollo replied through a female medium called the Pythia or Pythoness; her utterances were transcribed into often ambiguous verses by the chief priest, a lay official, and the inquirer then had to put the best interpretation on them he could. There was thus a mystical element at Delphi setting it apart from the usual rituals, though not from those at other oracle-shrines, each of which had its own particular method of operation. Most puzzling is the role of a woman as the god's mouthpiece, an uncommon practice among oracles, the singularity of which is further highlighted by the fact that all other women were denied admission to the temple.

The triumph of Delphi is evident not only from the many oracles mentioned or quoted by Greek writers and from the vast complex of 'treasure-houses', temples and statuary that grew up in the sacred precinct, but also from the way Delphic activity was retrospectively back-dated to a time when the shrine was certainly still only local in its importance. We have seen in Chapter 8 that not a few of the traditions about the consultation of Delphi in the foundation of early colonies were probably later inventions. It was in the seventh century, rather than the eighth, that Delphi was elevated to the greatest of the pan-Hellenic oracles. Although Greeks eventually travelled great distances to consult Apollo at Didyma near Miletus and at Claros in Asia Minor, or Zeus at Dodona in Epirus and at Siwa in Libya—to name a few main oracles—no other centre rivalled Delphi.

Delphi also organized games which acquired pan-Hellenic status, as did, for example, the temples at Nemea and Isthmia near Corinth. But in this field none could equal the quadrennial games in honour of Zeus at Olympia. The traditional date of their foundation is 776 B.C., which may well be exact and would give us the first fixed date in Greek history. Again the evidence suggests that at first the Olympic games attracted chiefly Peloponnesian Greeks, only later gathering momentum and drawing participants and spectators from all Hellas. In time the programme became very elaborate, including competitions in poetry, music and dance as well as public recitations and orations, but the main attraction was always in the athletics, chariot-racing, boxing and wrestling.

It was, then, in their cult activities, and in the poetry, architecture, sculpture and athletics associated with them, that the politically fragmented and often warring Greeks came closest to achieving some sort of unity in action. However, their religion was not a great force for *political* unity or even for peace within Hellas. Apollo was often consulted at Delphi before a war was undertaken, and it is not on record that he ever recommended peace as a good in itself, though he sometimes advised against a particular venture on its merits. The festivals themselves were times of truce, but their contribution over the long term to peace, or even to good will among the communities, does not seem to have been very tangible.

The origins of the practice of featuring athletic contests at important religious occasions are lost in the Dark Age. The elaborate account in the twenty-third book of the *Iliad* of the games organized by Achilles for the funeral of Patroclus is our earliest literary evidence, and it already reveals something of the complicated psychology involved. The Greek word we translate as 'contest' is *agon,* and ultimately its range of meanings included not only an athletic or poetical contest but also a lawsuit, a battle, a crisis or deep anxiety (hence our word 'agony'). In the present context, *agon* is best left untranslated; the *agon* was the outstanding, ritualized, non-military expression of a value system in which honour was the highest virtue, for which one strove even at the cost of one's life, and in which loss of honour, shame, was the most intolerable disaster that could befall a man. Honour-and-shame cultures have existed (and still exist) in other societies, as among the Bedouins or in Balkan and Mediterranean districts, and the values and attitudes can probably be found in some measure in every society. What stands out among the ancient Greeks is the intensity with which these values were pursued at the religious festivals. The greatest literary formulation, and also the latest to retain so much archaic traditionalism, will be found in the poems of Pindar, who died about 438 B.C. At a time when Athens was in the full bloom of its democratic culture, Pindar was still celebrating the victors at the games not only by singing their praises but also by gloating brutally over the defeated and their crushing dishonour:

And now four times you came down with bodies beneath
  you,
—You meant them harm—
To whom the Pythian feast has given

No glad home-coming like yours.
They, when they meet their mothers,
Have no sweet laughter around them, moving delight.
In back streets, out of their enemies' way,
They cower; for disaster has bitten them.

(*Pythian* VIII 81–7)[1]

Pindar's values were largely those of the archaic aristocracy, with whom the *agon* was intimately associated. Of all victories, the highest honour was achieved in the chariot race, the most expensive of sports, the one, therefore, that tyrants aimed for in particular. Pindar and other specialists in the epinician odes, as the poems in praise of the victors were called, put their art at the disposal of tyrants as freely as of other aristocrats. That is one way they revealed their rejection of the new social and political values which were appearing in the later Archaic age. Another was their total immersion in myth. If, however, we compare these odes with the *Iliad*'s account of the funeral games for Patroclus, an important new tone can be heard. Homer celebrates individual heroes, whereas in the odes the victors are linked not only with their ancestry and kin but also with their communities in the honour that has come to them. In short, in the archaic *agon* there emerges that dialogue, and ultimately that tension, between individual and community which has been an element in western society ever since.

Given the nature of our evidence, we know nothing about the attitudes of ordinary people to the values Pindar was still expressing, though there can be little doubt that the games attracted all sections of the population as spectators. Yet opposition to the aristocratic ethos was inevitable, on the one hand among moralists who began to move beyond the honour-shame syndrome, on the other hand among those who were engaged in the long struggle to break the aristocratic monopoly of wealth and power. Taming the Homeric kind of hero

[1] Translated by C. M. Bowra, *Pindar* (Oxford, Clarendon Press; New York, Oxford University Press, 1964), p. 183.

was not enough; it was also necessary to damp down the spirit of the *agon*, if not to destroy it altogether, as a negative and even disruptive factor within the community. We can see this clearly in the poems of Solon, respecter of the rights of the upper classes though he was. Even war, it should be added, had become a community affair and could no longer, with the coming of the hoplite phalanx, be conducted in the spirit of the *agon*.

The tension between the individual and public authority is already sharply expressed in the *Works and Days* of Hesiod. Although the language and metre of the poem are in the epic tradition and it retains strong mythical elements, the *Works and Days* is a 'private' poem, written in the first person. It is also one of the blackest lamentations ever composed, filled with horror at the 'iron age' of poverty and injustice in which men now live, bitter against the 'bribe-devouring judges', against the dangers of idleness and luxury and the ever present threat of poverty, an attitude which is all the more remarkable when one notes that the 'I' of the poem is both a bard, at least semi-professionally, and a farmer rich enough to own slaves and to look ahead to acquiring still more land by the fruits of his toil.

Two fundamentally new elements were thus introduced into Greek poetry, to remain dominant to the end of the Archaic period, though not necessarily always in combination as in the *Works and Days*. One was the personal element, the poet speaking in his own name. Although it may be a mistake to draw the inference automatically that he was therefore always being autobiographical, rather than merely employing an accepted convention that poetry is to be written in the first person, the poems nevertheless reveal 'what standpoints he wished to adopt, what emotions he preferred to express, and what topics he preferred to develop'.[1]

The topics often included social and political criticism, as with the Spartan Tyrtaeus, Solon, Alcaeus of Lesbos or Theognis of Megara, and that is the second new

[1] K. J. Dover in *Entretiens sur l'antiquité classique*, vol. 10, *Archiloque* (Vandœuvres–Genève, Fondation Hardt, 1963), p. 212.

element. This criticism was by no means all in one direction. One will find in the collection of elegiac verses attributed to Theognis, for example, a very different point of view and different overtones with respect to the aristocracy from those we have seen in Solon:

> In rams and asses and horses, Cyrnus, we seek thoroughbreds . . . but a noble man does not mind marrying the bad daughter of a bad sire if he gives much wealth, nor does a woman spurn to be bed-mate of a bad but rich man, for she would rather be rich than good. . . . The breed is mongrelized by riches.
>
> (lines 183–91)

> Never does slavery grow straight of head, but is always crooked and holds her neck askew. The child of a slave-woman never has the quality of the free-born, any more than a rose or a hyacinth grows on a squill.
>
> (lines 535–8)

The variety of ideas and standpoints reflects both the new 'individualism' and the growing complexity of, and conflicts within, the social situation. It also marks the emergence of rudimentary moral and political concepts. Poets and philosophers began, in this unsystematic fashion, to examine, and to argue about, the nature of justice, wealth, human inequality, rights and moral duties. In their own way they were looking abstractly at the problems that their fellow-Greeks were facing in the hard world of power struggles, of law reform and *stasis* and tyranny, and eventually of democracy.

The new poetry had to break not only from the heroic outlook but also from the heroic or epic style (which the poets knew very well and which they continued to echo freely). New metres were created and poems became much shorter.[1] Often the poems were also personal in the narrow sense that they abandoned the larger social canvas and concentrated on love, the delights of wine,

[1] The *Works and Days* was still more than 800 lines in length, at least in the text that has come down to us, the *Theogony* half as long again.

friendship and revelry. These developments are already visible in the earliest of the new-style poets whose work survives in any quantity (though even then mostly in fragments), Archilochus of Paros, whose mature work may be dated rather precisely to 650 or 640 B.C. The variety of his metrical forms indicates that behind him there lay a long experience in popular song, which co-existed with the epic tradition. This kind of poetry the world over is customarily linked with an occasion, whether a drinking-party, a village harvest dance or a great public festival, and more often than not it is also linked with song. (The very word 'lyric' implies that the poems were sung or chanted to an accompaniment on the lyre.) The occasion helped determine not only the style and subject-matter but also the conventions appropriate to particular kinds of poetry. None of this is very clear in the fragments of Archilochus, but it cannot be doubted for most of the lyricists who followed, ranging as they did in seriousness from the drinking-songs of Anacreon to the great choral odes of Pindar and his predecessors.

The writers of choral odes, in particular, travelled widely in the Greek world in search of patrons, but many of the other poets were fairly mobile as well. Archaic poetry was thus truly pan-Hellenic, and it is noteworthy that the poets themselves originated not only on the mainland of Greece and the Aegean islands, but also in Asia Minor and the newer centres of the west. When we turn to a quite different intellectual development, the rise of philosophy about 600 B.C., Old Greece appears to have played no role at all in the first phase. The beginning was in Ionia, and particularly in Miletus, and then, in the latter half of the sixth century, a second centre developed in Sicily and southern Italy, apparently inspired by political refugees. Xenophanes fled from Colophon to Sicily about the middle of the century, Pythagoras a bit later from Samos to Croton, where he seems to have founded a genuine school, which was at the same time a secret mystical sect.

One cannot avoid the word 'seems' in discussing these early 'physicists', as the Greeks called them from *physis* (nature), because the traditions that have come down to us about them are fragmentary, confused and in large part untrustworthy. However, whatever the truth may be about the details, there can be no disputing the revolution in thought they initiated, summed up in the familiar phrase, from myth to *logos* or reason. For a considerable time the revolution lay in the mode of thinking rather than in the answers given, which were speculative, and, in the light of later knowledge, often naïve in the extreme. Indeed, such questions as, What was in the beginning?, were not really new. But the answers had hitherto been mythical ones, specific and concrete, explaining both natural and human phenomena by reciting particular supernatural events or actions, in themselves unaccountable. 'Myth was a narrative, not the solution of a problem. . . . The problem found itself resolved without having been posed.'[1] The Ionian revolution, then, was simply that they posed problems and proposed general, rational, 'impersonal' answers.

How could the human species have survived in the beginning, given the long period during which the human infant is helpless? There is a genuine problem, posed by Anaximander of Miletus early in the sixth century. 'He says,' a late writer tells us, 'that in the beginning man was born from creatures of a different kind; because other creatures are soon self-supporting, but man alone needs prolonged nursing. For this reason he would not have survived if this had been his original form.' Details are added by another late writer: 'Anaximander of Miletus conceived that there arose from heated water and earth either fish or creatures very like fish; in these men grew, in the form of embryos retained within until puberty; then at last the fish-like creatures burst and men and women who were already able to nourish themselves stepped forth.'[2] Naïve as this specu-

[1] J.-P. Vernant, *Mythe et pensée chez les grecs* (Paris, Maspero, 1965), p. 291.

[2] Translated in G. S. Kirk and J. E. Raven, *The Presocratic Philosophers. A Critical History with a Selection of Texts* (Cambridge and New York, Cambridge University Press, 1962), p. 141.

lation may be, it is nevertheless separated by a wide gulf from Hesiod's mythical account (*Works and Days* 60–82) of the creation of woman:

> And he [Zeus] bade famous Hephaestus make haste and mix earth with water and to put in it the voice and strength of human kind, and fashion a sweet, lovely maiden-shape, like to the immortal goddesses in face; and Athena to teach her needlework and the weaving of the varied web; and golden Aphrodite to shed grace upon her head and cruel longing and cares that weary the limb. And he charged Hermes the guide, the slayer of Argus, to put in her a shameless mind and a deceitful nature. . . . And he called this woman Pandora, because all they who dwelt on Olympus gave each a gift, a plague to men who eat bread.[1]

That is a mythical explanation of the existence of evil, a problem Hesiod never actually posed as such. The revolution of the Ionian physicists, with their assumption of the existence of regularities in nature, and hence of the possibility of generalized explanations, subject to rational discovery and to rational argument and debate, in which they engaged freely, was therefore a necessary prerequisite for both philosophy and science (as distinct from merely empirical knowledge, for example, in metallurgy and navigation, of which the Greeks by now possessed a considerable stock). That is their importance, rather than the particular theories attributed to them. And behind them, as an immediate stimulant to their new approach, lay the practice of rational debate, free from supernatural interference and against the hitherto unarguable claims of aristocratic tradition, that was developing within the emergent *polis* in the social and political spheres.

The earlier Ionians seem to have concentrated their efforts largely on the cosmos and the nature of being

[1] Translated by H. G. Evelyn-White in the Loeb Classical Library (Cambridge, Mass., Harvard University Press; London, Heinemann).

generally. But Xenophanes, at least, was more of a moralist, and even a theologian; some of his famous aphorisms were radical and biting: 'Homer and Hesiod have attributed to the gods everything that is a shame and reproach among men, stealing and committing adultery and deceiving each other' (Kirk and Raven, p. 168). And the Pythagoreans turned their attention to the soul and elaborated a doctrine of transmigration and reincarnation. Their mystical doctrine somehow—though all this is now hopelessly obscure—drew them into the complicated politics of the Greek cities in southern Italy, where they became centres of faction and revolution. Thereafter Greek philosophy was to manifest an intense concern with, and involvement in, the actual life of the community, its politics and its social and ethical behaviour. One thinks especially of Socrates and Plato, of Aristotle or the later Stoics.

Finally, the history of the visual arts, too, is a counterpoint on the themes that have run through this chapter. Despite the many regional and local variations, the arts were pan-Hellenic, as evidenced not only by the ease with which sculptors and architects travelled—and their ideas as well—but also by the total impact. A seventh- or sixth-century Greek found himself in a relatively familiar environment, in this respect, wherever he went. Art, like poetry, was directly or indirectly functional; its canons were closely tied to its purposes. Art was meshed in with daily living, not set apart for occasional leisure time or for the enjoyment of rich collectors and aesthetes. It was found in the temples and other public buildings, not in museums. In the homes, there were beautiful vases, mirrors and jewelry rather than *objets d'art*. Even in the most private of the arts one rarely finds among the innumerable vases, pitchers and cups a non-functional, eccentric object.

By the sixth century potters, painters and sculptors began the practice of signing some of their works, a revolutionary step in the history of art, proclaiming the recognition of the artist as an individual (exactly like the lyric poet). Yet he did not become a rampant individualist, restlessly seeking novelty. In any given period and place he worked within the recognized canons (and his clients did not demand otherwise), placing his individual stamp on his output within that framework. Of course, in the continuous history of fine painted pottery, which goes back uninterruptedly to the beginning of the Dark Age, there were great changes not only in technique but also in fashion and taste. The most remarkable of all, perhaps, was the capture of the market in much of the Greek world, most notably in the west, by Athenian ware about the middle of the sixth century. The existence of canons and rules did not lead to mechanical repetition and sterility. Viewing the history of the potter's art whole, one therefore sees an effective interplay between the artist as individual and the artist as functionary or spokesman of his society.

The other visual arts have a much shorter history so far as our knowledge goes. Almost all painting from this period other than on pottery is lost, and architecture and sculpture are known in detail only from the time when stone, bronze and terracotta began to be employed in place of perishable wood and sun-dried brick, that is, from the seventh century B.C. What then strikes us forcibly is how heavily dominated these arts were by religious contexts and purposes. Greek architecture and sculpture were public arts in the strict sense. Archaic (and classical) Greece was a world without palaces or private mansions. Among public buildings, furthermore, the greatest effort and expenditure were lavished on temples. They were often decorated with sculptured metopes, pediments and friezes, and they housed statues of the gods to whom they were dedicated. Outside the temple, too, the connexion of sculpture with religion was more common than may at first sight seem the case. Statues of the victors in the great games come into this category: like the choral odes, these statues were a form of thanksgiving by the community (or tyrant) whom the athletes represented. Like the odes, too, the statues were not really concerned with the athletes as individuals; they were not portraits but ideal types, employed indiscriminately for men and gods. The familiar archaic statues of young nude males (*kouroi*) in stone or bronze, of which more than two hundred are now known beginning about 650 B.C., are sometimes labelled 'Apollo' by modern scholars and sometimes 'Youth'. But the distinction between god and man is legitimate only when there is external evidence, if the statue is funerary, for example, or if the base survives with an inscribed text. There is nothing in the statue itself from which to tell.

Such sculpture, like the temple, symbolized the triumph of the community, a demonstration of its growing strength and self-consciousness. Mycenaean rulers erected great palaces and tombs for themselves. Not until the age of tyranny were there again individuals in Greece who commanded enough power and resources to emulate them. Yet even tyrants did not customarily build palaces or splendid tombs in self-glorification. Peisistratus may have lived on the Acropolis for a time, but his 'memorial' there was not a palace but the temple of Athena Parthenos. This, like his Fountain-House, a complex structure, probably at the southwestern corner of the agora, which was a major feature of the city's water-supply system, reveals how far the Greek community had advanced as a living force, so that even a tyrant bowed to it. Homer's heroes lived on in the tales of their feats of prowess. The new 'heroes' immortalized themselves in public buildings.

In all this cultural history there were many Near Eastern sources and influences, on myth, in mathematics, temple-building and sculpture, pottery decoration. If nothing has been said about that here, that is not from any desire to deny the existence of these influences but with the intention of getting the balance right. Whatever the Greeks borrowed they promptly absorbed and converted into something original insofar as anything other than technique (in metallurgy, for example) was involved. They borrowed the Phoenician alphabet, but there were no Phoenician Homers. The idea of the free-standing human statue may have come to them from

Egypt (though that common view has been challenged),[1] but it was the Greeks, not the Egyptians, who then developed the idea, from the archaic *kouroi* and the female *korai* on to the great classical statuary. In the process they not only invented the nude as an art-form but, in a very important sense, they 'invented art' itself. 'It was the Greeks who taught us to ask "*How* does he stand?" or even "Why does he stand like that?".'[2] It is not far-fetched to associate such questions, which, of course, we do not know that any early Greek sculptor actually put to himself, with the kinds of questions the physicists were asking at the same time. The human self-reliance and self-confidence that permitted and fostered such questions, in politics as in art and philosophy, lay at the root of the *miracle grec*.

[1] R. M. Cook, 'Origins of Greek Sculpture', *Journal of Hellenic Studies*, 87 (1967), pp. 24–32.

[2] E. H. Gombrich, *Art and Illusion* (rev. ed., London, Phaidon; Princeton University Press, 1962), pp. 114, 120.

Select Bibliography

Introductory note: Books and articles mentioned in the footnotes are not repeated here. Full excavation reports have not been included; preference has been given to the more general summaries, when possible to the most recent, which usually contain good bibliographies of older publications.

As a general introduction to the study of early societies, V. Gordon Childe, *Man Makes Himself* (4 ed., London, Watts, 1965; New York, New American Library, 1952), has become a classic.

Volumes I and II of the *Cambridge Ancient History* are being completely rewritten. The new chapters are issued in separate fascicles as soon as they are ready, prior to the appearance of the volumes themselves. A few are cited here in an abbreviated reference: *CAH* followed by the fascicle number.

THE BRONZE AGE

The best survey (excluding Crete) is Emily Vermeule, *Greece in the Bronze Age* (Chicago and London, University of Chicago Press, 1964). The best illustrated work is F. Matz, *Crete and Early Greece* (London, Methuen, 1962), though special note must be taken of Max Hirmer's photographs in S. Marinatos and M. Hirmer, *Crete and Mycenae* (London, Thames & Hudson; New York, Abrams, 1960).

A. Snodgrass, *Early Greek Armour and Weapons* (Edinburgh University Press; Chicago, Aldine Publishing Co., 1964), carries his detailed inquiry into the Dark Age, as does W. K. C. Guthrie, 'The Religion and Mythology of the Greeks', *CAH* 2. For a subtle and complex study of the art which, despite the title, extends to Bronze Age Greece and Crete, see H. A. Groenewegen-Frankfort, *Arrest and Movement. An Essay on Space and Time in the Representational Art of the Ancient Near East* (London, Faber; New York, Humanities Press, 1951), summarized in simplified form in

BIBLIOGRAPHY

The Ancient World, written in collaboration with Bernard Ashmole, volume I of the paperback series, *The Library of Art History* (New York and London, Mentor Books, 1967).

On the archaeological and linguistic analyses by which the attempt is made to pinpoint and explain the 'coming of the Greeks', see J. L. Caskey, 'Greece, Crete and the Aegean Islands in the Early Bronze Age', *CAH* 24; R. A. Crossland, 'Immigrants from the North', *CAH* 60; John Chadwick, 'The Prehistory of the Greek Language', *CAH* 15, and *The Decipherment of Linear B* (2 ed., Cambridge University Press; New York, Cambridge University Press and Vintage, 1968). O. Gurney, *The Hittites* (2 ed., London and Baltimore, Penguin, 1954), is relevant on this and other topics in early Greek history.

On the Cycladic 'idols', see now C. Renfrew, 'The Development and Chronology of the Early Cycladic Figures', *American Journal of Archaeology*, 73 (1969), pp. 1–32. On Cyprus, see H. W. Catling, 'Cyprus in the Neolithic and Bronze Age Periods', *CAH* 43, or more fully, *Cypriot Bronze-work in the Mycenaean World* (Oxford, Clarendon Press; New York, Oxford University Press, 1964), which covers more ground than the title suggests.

R. W. Hutchinson, *Prehistoric Crete* (London and Baltimore, Penguin; Gloucester, Mass., Peter Smith, 1962), provides a good general survey. J. D. S. Pendlebury, *The Archaeology of Crete* (London, Methuen, 1939; New York, Biblo & Tannen and Norton (paperback) 1965), remains essential though antiquated. J. W. Graham, *The Palaces of Crete* (Princeton University Press, 1962), is the standard work. A brief account of the 'rediscovery of Crete' will be found in M. I. Finley, *Aspects of Antiquity* (London, Chatto & Windus; New York, Viking Press, 1968), ch. 1. On special topics: K. Branigan, *Copper and Bronze Working in Early Bronze Age Crete* (Lund, 1968), and 'Silver and Lead in Prepalatial Crete', *American Journal of Archaeology*, 72 (1968), pp. 219–29; J. T. Killen, 'The Wool Industry of Crete in the Late Bronze Age', *Annual of the British School at Athens*, No. 59 (1964), pp. 1–15.

Lord William Taylour, *The Mycenaeans* (London, Thames & Hudson; New York, Praeger, 1964), provides the best short survey. For the end of the period, see V. R. d'A. Desborough, *The Last Mycenaeans and Their Successors* (Oxford, Clarendon Press; New York, Oxford University Press, 1964). Other titles, involving the controversy over the relation of the Homeric poems to the Mycenaean world, are given immediately below.

THE ARCHAIC AGE

The best narrative is C. G. Starr, *The Origins of Greek Civilization, 1100–650 B.C.* (New York, Knopf, 1961; London, Jonathan Cape, 1962). For a detailed history after the Dark Age, see A. R. Burn, *The Lyric Age of Greece* (London, Arnold; New York, St. Martin's and Funk & Wagnalls (paperback) 1960).

The best balanced account of Homer and the 'Homeric problem' is G. S. Kirk, *The Songs of Homer* (Cambridge and New York, Cambridge University Press, 1962), also issued in a shortened paperback version as *Homer and the Epic* (1965).

On Troy, the basic general account of the archaeology is C. W. Blegen, *Troy and the Trojans* (London, Thames & Hudson; New York, Praeger, 1963). The present state of the debate over the historicity of the traditional account is brought into sharp focus by M. I. Finley, 'The Trojan War', with replies by J. L. Caskey, G. S. Kirk and D. L. Page, *Journal of Hellenic Studies*, 84 (1964), pp. 1–20; see also Finley, *Aspects of Antiquity*, already mentioned above. Page's views are fully developed in his *History and the Homeric Iliad* (University of California Press, 1959). *A Companion to Homer*, ed. A. J. B. Wace and F. H. Stubbings (London and New York, Macmillan, 1962), starts from the position, rejected in the present volume, that the Homeric poems are essentially a reflection of the Mycenaean world. For an attempt to reconstruct Dark Age society from the poems, see M. I. Finley, *The World of Odysseus* (New York, Viking Press, 1954, and rev. ed. (paperback) 1965; London, Chatto & Windus, 1956, reprinted with revisions Penguin, 1967).

On 'colonization', see John Boardman, *The Greeks Overseas* (London and Baltimore, Penguin; Gloucester, Mass.,

Peter Smith, 1964); T. J. Dunbabin, *The Western Greeks* (Oxford, Clarendon Press, 1948); M. I. Finley, *Ancient Sicily to the Arab Conquest* (London, Chatto & Windus; New York, Viking, 1968), ch. 1–3; J. M. Cook, 'Greek Settlement in the Eastern Aegean and Asia Minor', *CAH* 7; R. D. Barnett, 'Phrygia and the Peoples of Anatolia in the Iron Age', *CAH* 56.

A. Andrewes, *The Greek Tyrants* (London, Hutchinson; New York, Hillary and Harper & Row (paperback), 1956), the standard introduction, should be supplemented by A. Snodgrass, 'The Hoplite Reform and History', *Journal of Hellenic Studies*, 85 (1965), pp. 110–22. On Archaic Sparta and Athens, two recent works give suggestions for further reading: W. G. Forrest, *A History of Sparta 950–152 B.C.* (London, Hutchinson, 1968), and Victor Ehrenberg, *From Solon to Socrates* (London, Methuen; New York, Barnes & Noble, 1967), parts I–IV.

On various aspects of Archaic culture, the following titles are self-explanatory: H. J. Rose, *A Handbook of Greek Mythology* (6 ed., London, Methuen, 1958; New York, Dutton, 1959); H. W. Parke and D. E. W. Wormell, *The Delphic Oracle* (2 vols., Oxford, Blackwell; New York, Humanities Press, 1956); W. K. C. Guthrie, *A History of Greek Philosophy*, vol. I, *The Earlier Presocratics and the Pythagoreans* (Cambridge and New York, Cambridge University Press, 1962); G. E. R. Lloyd, *Early Greek Science: Thales to Aristotle* (London, Chatto & Windus; New York, Norton: forthcoming in the present series), ch. 1–3; A. W. H. Adkins, *Merit and Responsibility. A Study in Greek Values* (Oxford, Clarendon Press; New York, Oxford University Press, 1962). ch. 1–8; L. H. Jeffery, *The Local Scripts of Archaic Greece* (Oxford, Clarendon Press; New York, Oxford University Press, 1961); C. M. Bowra, *Greek Lyric Poetry from Alcman to Simonides* (2 ed., Oxford, Clarendon Press; New York, Oxford University Press, 1961); R. M. Cook, *Greek Painted Pottery* (rev. ed., London, Methuen; New York, Barnes & Noble, 1966); J. N. Coldstream, *Greek Geometric Pottery* (London, Methuen; New York, Barnes & Noble, 1968). Perhaps half the essays in Bruno Snell, *The Discovery of the Mind*, translated by T. G. Rosenmeyer (Oxford, Blackwell; New York, Harper & Row, 1953), deal with Archaic literature and ideas.

A note on sources: Apart from the two Homeric poems, available in a variety of editions and translations, and the poetry of Hesiod, excellently rendered into prose by H. G. Evelyn-White in the Loeb Classical Library edition (Cambridge, Mass., Harvard University Press; London, Heinemann), contemporary written sources are restricted to fragments of the poets and philosophers. The former are collected in five Loeb volumes, entitled *Lyra Graeca* and *Elegy and Iambus*, edited by J. M. Edmonds, but the reader must be warned that the editor exercised a free hand in reconstructing and rendering the fragments. For the latter, there is an excellent selection, in the original and translation, with full discussion, in G. S. Kirk and J. E. Raven, *The Presocratic Philosophers* (Cambridge and New York, Cambridge University Press, 1962).

INDEX

King Lear

William Shakespeare

Notes by Rebecca Warren

Longman

York Press

Exterior picture of the Globe Theatre reproduced by permission of the Raymond Mander and Joe Mitchenson Theatre Collection
Reconstruction of the Globe Theatre interior reprinted from Hodges: **The Globe Restored** (1968) by permission of Oxford University Press

YORK PRESS
322 Old Brompton Road, London SW5 9JH

Pearson Education Limited
Edinburgh Gate, Harlow,
Essex CM20 2JE, United Kingdom
Associated companies, branches and representatives throughout the world

First published 1998
Third impression 1999

ISBN 0-582-32921-3

Designed by Vicki Pacey, Trojan Horse, London
Phototypeset by Gem Graphics, Trenance, Mawgan Porth, Cornwall
Colour reproduction and film output by Spectrum Colour
Prodcued by Addison Wesley Longman China Limited, Hong Kong

CONTENTS

Part six

Critical history

Part seven

Broader perspectives

Introduction

How to study a play

Studying on your own requires self-discipline and a carefully thought-out work plan in order to be effective.

- Drama is a special kind of writing (the technical term is 'genre') because it needs a performance in the theatre to arrive at a full interpretation of its meaning. Try to imagine that you are a member of the audience when reading the play. Think about how it could be presented on the stage, not just about the words on the page.
- Drama is always about conflict of some sort (which may be below the surface). Identify the conflicts in the play and you will be close to identifying the large ideas or themes which bind all the parts together.
- Make careful notes on themes, character, plot and any sub-plots of the play.
- Why do you like or dislike the characters in the play? How do your feelings towards them develop and change?
- Playwrights find non-realistic ways of allowing an audience to see into the minds and motives of their characters, for example soliloquy, aside or music. Consider how such dramatic devices are used in the play you are studying.
- Think of the playwright writing the play. Why were these particular arrangements of events, characters and speeches chosen?
- Cite exact sources for all quotations, whether from the text itself or from critical commentaries. Wherever possible find your own examples from the play to back up your opinions.
- Always express your ideas in your own words.

This York Note offers an introduction to *King Lear* and cannot substitute for close reading of the text and the study of secondary sources.

Today, *King Lear* is one of Shakespeare's most frequently performed plays. It is not difficult to see why it attracts actors and directors. The story it has to tell – of an ageing patriarch who goes mad and loses everything after a fatal error of judgement – is a powerful one. We watch the agonising downfall of a man whose life is torn apart. The human issues explored in the play resonate in any age: the conflict between parents and children, sibling rivalry, the painful process of working out who and what you are. The picture we are presented with, of frail, difficult and precarious old age challenged by thrusting youth, has struck a chord with many cultures, not just our own. Many literary traditions have their own versions of the Lear story. As Goethe remarked, 'Every old man is a King Lear'. We all wonder what our twilight years will bring, and struggle to prepare ourselves for death. This play is a particularly stark examination of the ageing process. All the deaths that occur – on and off stage – are violent and brutal. *King Lear* also explores the enduringly compelling struggle between good and evil, issues about power and responsibility, and man's relationship with the universe: in particular, nature and the gods.

Literary critics have been eagerly drawn to *King Lear* too. For many this is Shakespeare's most profound **tragedy**, one of the greatest plays written in any language at any time. It throws up questions which remain as perplexing now as they were to Shakespeare's early critics. We are asked to consider a number of 'big' philosophical questions when we read this play. Is mankind cruel or kind? How do we assess human justice? What are we to make of the presentation of religion in *King Lear*? There are no easy answers to these questions, or to the many others you will find yourself asking as you study the play. *King Lear* is a disturbing read, more shocking in its mental and physical violence than any of Shakespeare's other plays. It pushes its readers, as its central character is pushed, to consider the nature of suffering and the human condition. *King Lear* also offers many opportunities to indulge in the two emotions **Aristotle** defined as necessary in tragedy: pity and fear. This play is both exhausting and exhilarating. Audiences and readers alike find its relentlessness deeply moving.

THE PLOT AND ITS SOURCES

King Lear has a double plot; a main plot and a subplot. The story of Gloucester and his sons heightens the tragedy that occurs in the main plot and provides points of comparison with the royal family. The main focus, however, is the tragic protagonist, Lear. His foolishness and suffering absorb us most. Lear is a symbolic figure who represents England. In *King Lear* Shakespeare explores what happens when the realm is plunged into crisis, focusing on the consequences of the actions of two rash patriarchs. The action unfolds swiftly. By the end of the first scene the kingdom has been divided and Lear's family harmony is shattered. Thereafter the descent into chaos gathers pace, culminating in a final scene of dramatic and violent death.

When seeking source material for his play Shakespeare probably turned to the historian Holinshed's *Chronicles of England, Scotland and Ireland* (1577), which he had used before. There were also accounts of Lear's reign in a sentimental play of the 1590s, *The True Chronicle History of King Leir*, Spenser's great poem *The Faerie Queen* and in John Higgins' *A Mirror for Magistrates. The True Chronicle History of King Leir* had a 'happy ending', with Lear restored to his throne. Shakespeare might have found his subplot in Sidney's prose romance *Arcadia.* Sidney tells the story of a blind Paphalogian king with two sons, one of whom plots against him. When he realises the truth about his evil son, the king wishes to throw himself from a cliff.

Finally, Shakespeare was probably familiar with two 'real life' Lear stories. During his early life in London a former mayor of the city, Sir William Allen, divided his property between his three daughters. His decision proved to be disastrous, for he was badly treated by all his offspring. There was also the case of Sir Brian Annesley, a gentleman pensioner of Elizabeth I. In 1603 his eldest daughter and her husband tried to have the old man certified as a senile lunatic, so that they could take control of his property. His youngest daughter Cordell saved the day by challenging her sister in court.

By considering Shakespeare's changes and additions to the Lear story and his use of the Gloucester subplot, it is possible to see where the playwright's dramatic interests lie. Lear's madness is Shakespeare's invention, as is the manner of Cordelia's death. It seems that Shakespeare is intent on producing an impression of bleakness.

SUMMARIES

It is not possible to date the composition of *King Lear* exactly, but it is thought that the play was written between late 1605 and early 1606. There was a performance of the play at court in late 1606, although it is unlikely that this was the first performance. *King Lear* probably had its first outing at The Globe Theatre, like many of Shakespeare's other plays. A greater problem exists in trying to decide which version of *King Lear* to accept as the most authentic 'Shakespearean' text. The first published version of *King Lear* appeared in 1608 (the First Quarto). There are various theories about how the Quarto text was arrived at. It has been suggested that the First Quarto was produced by a printer with the assistance of the boy actors who played Gonerill and Regan, who also had access to a rough draft of the play. Only half of Shakespeare's plays were published in the playwright's lifetime in the paperback Quarto format, and not all of these Quartos were based on authentic manuscripts. They are thus 'unauthorised' versions of Shakespeare's plays. After the playwright's death, all of Shakespeare's works were prepared for publication as the First Folio of 1623. It has been suggested that the Folio was based on a revised prompt book copy of *King Lear*. It also seems likely that this cut Folio text represents the version of the play that was performed successfully, after the play's initial performances in 1605–6.

The problem is this: the Quarto and Folio versions of *King Lear* differ quite radically in parts. The Quartos omit approximately a hundred lines which are found in the Folio, while the Folio does not include three hundred lines of the Quarto. The main omissions in the Folio include Lear's 'mock trial' of Gonerill in the hovel during Act III, the sympathetic dialogue between Cornwall's two servants following Gloucester's blinding, and all of Act IV Scene 3 where the Gentleman describes Cordelia's grief. The end of the final scene of the play, including Lear's final speech, is also different in the two texts. Stanley Wells and Gary Taylor, the editors of the Oxford *The Complete Works of Shakespeare*, feel that the mood of the revised Folio text of *King Lear* is less reflective. The Folio version is also bleaker and more pessimistic. So which is the version of the play which most closely reflects Shakespeare's dramatic intentions? It is very difficult to say. We cannot be sure that Shakespeare himself made the revisions found in the Folio – since no texts of *King Lear* survive in the playwright's handwriting.

Most modern editions of *King Lear* are based on the Folio, with the missing Quarto lines restored. However, Wells and Taylor suggest that the two versions of *King Lear* deserve consideration as separate plays, and present both the Quarto and Folio texts in their *The Complete Works*. It is certainly worth looking at both versions of *King Lear*. You should also check to see which version(s) of *King Lear* your own play text is based on.

For a more detailed discussion of the Quarto and Folio versions of *King Lear* and the differences in the Quarto and Folio texts, see Kenneth Muir's introduction to the play in the Arden edition, and Stanley Wells and Gary Taylor's *The Complete Works*. See Further Reading for information about these editions of *King Lear*.

The edition used in these Notes is the Penguin Edition of *King Lear*, edited by G.K. Hunter.

SYNOPSIS

Reaching old age and desiring a quiet life without the responsibilities and cares of state, King Lear decides to divide his kingdom between his three daughters, Gonerill, Regan and Cordelia. He devises a 'love-test' to see which daughter loves him most, expecting his favourite youngest daughter Cordelia to 'win' and claim the largest share of the kingdom. Cordelia thwarts his plan, refusing to take part in the 'love-test'. Furious, Lear casts her off and divides the kingdom between Gonerill and Regan. Cordelia marries the King of France, and leaves Britain. Gonerill and Regan decide to rid themselves of their tiresome father once and for all, and plot against Lear. They drive him out into a storm and shut the doors against him. Alone on the heath except for two faithful servants (Kent and the Fool) and a counterfeit mad beggar (Poor Tom), Lear goes mad. Meanwhile, his friend the Earl of Gloucester has also been treated treacherously by his illegitimate son Edmund, who has duped him into believing his legitimate son Edgar seeks his life. Attempting to help Lear, Gloucester incurs the wrath of Lear's daughters and is blinded as a punishment. Learning from letters of her father's plight, Cordelia returns to Britain with the French army. She intends restoring Lear to his throne. Lear and Cordelia are reunited at the French camp in Dover. The French and British armies clash in battle. The French army loses. Lear and Cordelia are imprisoned by Edmund. Gonerill and Regan have both been rivals for Edmund's love, and their lust drives the sisters to desperate behaviour. Gonerill poisons Regan and then kills herself. Meanwhile Edmund has ordered Lear and Cordelia's deaths. In spite of the efforts of Gonerill's husband Albany to save them, Cordelia is hanged in prison. Her death is too much for Lear, who has come to a greater understanding of himself and others through his madness. Lear dies a broken man, half mad.

ACT I

SCENE 1 Lear divests himself of the cares of state using a 'love-test'. Cordelia and Kent are banished for displeasing him. The kingdom is divided between Gonerill and Regan

The play opens at Lear's court. Kent and Gloucester discuss the division of the kingdom. There are rumours about King Lear's intentions towards his two sons-in-law, the dukes of Albany and Cornwall. Kent suggests that Lear has favoured the Duke of Albany up to now. Gloucester introduces his illegitimate son Edmund to Kent. We learn that Edmund has been 'out nine years, and away he / shall again' (lines 31–2). We also learn that Gloucester has another legitimate son, and that he favours both sons equally.

Lear enters with his three daughters, Gonerill, Regan and Cordelia, and Gonerill and Regan's husbands, Albany and Cornwall. He announces that he has divided his kingdom in three and intends to distribute it between his daughters. He wants to 'shake all cares and business from our age' (line 39) and pass the responsibility of ruling on to his children. However, he also wishes to retain the 'Pre-eminence, and all the large effects / That troop with majesty' (lines 131–2). In order to determine who should enjoy the largest share of the kingdom, Lear asks his daughters to take part in a ceremonial 'love-test'. The daughter who says she loves him most will be the 'winner'.

Gonerill speaks first. She says she loves her father more than 'eyesight, space, and liberty' (line 56). Regan emphasises the value of her love; she should be priced at Gonerill's 'worth'. Cordelia dislikes her sisters' 'ponderous' words and hopes that she will be able to speak of her love more honestly and simply. She refuses to take part in Lear's 'contest' and says she has 'nothing' to say, except that she loves Lear as her duty instructs her. Lear is hurt and angry. He urges Cordelia to speak again. When she refuses to obey him, he casts her off without a moment's hesitation. Kent attempts to argue with the king, accusing him of 'hideous rashness' (line 151). He also warns Lear that Gonerill and Regan are false flatterers. Further enraged, Lear banishes Kent too. He then calls for Cordelia's two suitors, France and Burgundy and invests Albany and Cornwall with power. We learn that he intends keeping one hundred knights in his service, who will accompany him as he divides his time between Gonerill and Regan.

Burgundy politely refuses to take Cordelia's hand in marriage unless Lear provides the dowry he had promised previously. France takes her – penniless and without her father's favour – for her virtues alone. He leads Cordelia away. An urgent discussion between Gonerill and Regan closes the scene. Gonerill resolves that the sisters 'must do something, and i'th'heat' (line 306). They complain about Lear's rash judgement and unpredictable behaviour and say they are worried that they will receive unfair treatment, like their sister Cordelia.

A mood of uncertainty is established in the first six lines of the play, which are typical of Elizabethan and Jacobean drama, where characters set the scene and introduce key themes and ideas. We learn that inheritance and property issues are at stake in *King Lear* when Kent and Gloucester discuss the division of the kingdom. Ideas about favouritism are also introduced in the opening exchange. Edmund's silence is significant. It is symbolic of his position as the bastard son, who has no 'voice', rights or position in society. Shakespeare keeps Edmund's true character concealed at this point, so that his opening **soliloquy** in the next scene is exciting and surprising. Edmund's polite exterior conceals his evil nature, suggesting that the difference between appearances and reality is a key theme in this play. Gloucester takes his rule of Edmund for granted, shown by the brief (some would say brutal) lines he speaks about Edmund's past and future. However, we should not assume that Gloucester is embarrassed by his illegitimate offspring. He jokes easily about Edmund's bastardy, suggesting that he has rather lax morals. Questions about family relationships are raised.

Lear's entrance is impressive, suggesting his power. But we question his use of that power almost immediately. His 'love-test' is foolish and egotistical, as is his desire to be treated as an important, royal personage after he has given away his kingdom. We should also be alarmed by Lear's intention to break up his state. His actions are not those of a responsible ruler. In I.1 Lear shows many times that he is most concerned with appearances, and does not see clearly. He is fooled by Gonerill and Regan's superficial and elegant speeches and fails to recognise Cordelia and Kent's honesty. Cordelia stands up for genuine feeling and the correct order in family life when she says that some of her love should go to her husband when she marries. Her strength of character and integrity are shown again when she scorns Burgundy and parts frostily from her sisters, telling them that she knows they are cunning and false. However, some commentators see Lear's youngest daughter as stubborn and destructive (like her father?). There is a troubling irony in the fact that it is Cordelia who rebels against Lear first. Kent is also subversive in this scene. He uses insulting language when he refers to Lear as 'thou' and 'old man' (line 146). However, we understand that Cordelia and Kent have Lear – and England's – best interests at heart. They hope to alert Lear to his false, materialistic values.

Lear behaves like a tyrant in I.1. However, we know he has lost control when he goes to strike Kent. He continues to issue orders, and speaks very cruelly to Cordelia, but his authority has been denied. It is possible to feel some sympathy for the king, in spite of his rash behaviour. He clearly loved his youngest daughter a great deal, dividing the kingdom so that she would receive the most opulent share, hoping he could rely on her 'kind nursery' (line 124) as he 'crawls' (line 41) towards death (his language here suggests the vulnerability of a baby). He is pained and humiliated by Cordelia's refusal to take part in his 'love-test'. Nonetheless, we are likely to recognise the truth of Gonerill and Regan's remarks about their father at the end of the scene. They sum up the explosive, violent

Lear we have just seen. Can we trust these two though? Perhaps Gonerill and Regan simply justify the wicked intentions they already possess when they decide to 'hit together' (line 302). By the end of this scene family and national harmony have been destroyed. One daughter has challenged her father, and two more prepare to subvert his authority. Lear's tragic fall proceeds from his misuse of power in I.1.

darker undisclosed

champains open countryside, plains

validity value, worth

intererred admitted to, joined with (giving the man who marries Cordelia an advantage in life)

Hecat Hecate, goddess of night, darkness, the underworld, and witchcraft

propinquity, property of blood close family ties, kinship

Scythian savage; Scythians who lived in an area of Russia were thought to be a barbaric, cruel people, given to cannibalism

makes his generation messes continuing the theme of barbaric cannibalism; he who feeds on his own children

th' addition honours and titles

sway control

Apollo in Roman mythology, the god of the Sun

Jupiter the Roman ruler of the gods

infirmities she owes faults or disabilities she possesses

Election makes not up in such conditions it is not possible to make a choice in these circumstances

still soliciting constantly looking for favours

tardiness in nature natural reticence

respect status

washed tearful; there is the sense that Cordelia sees clearly what her sisters are like, through 'washed eyes'

plighted concealed

SCENE 2 Edmund makes his father Gloucester believe that Edgar seeks his life

Alone on stage, Edmund offers his view of life. He refuses to submit to the patriarchal hierarchy we saw in operation in I.1. Instead, he declares that nature is his goddess. He argues that he possesses personal qualities that make him his legitimate brother's equal. Why should he be denied property and power because he is illegitimate? Edmund is determined to 'grow' and 'prosper' (line 20). Like Gonerill and Regan, he is ready to defend his own interests. He has written a letter which he intends to use to gain advantage over Edgar. At this point in the play he seeks to inherit his brother's land.

Gloucester comes in muttering, disturbed by Lear's rashness. He notices Edmund putting away his letter and asks to see it. Edmund pretends that he is reluctant to allow his father to see the letter, which is supposedly from Edgar. Gloucester is alarmed by what he reads. 'Edgar' suggests that he is unhappy because he wants to enjoy Gloucester's fortunes now, and feels frustrated by the 'idle and fond bondage' of 'aged tyranny' (line 49). He seems to be suggesting that he wishes his father dead, so that he and Edmund can enjoy half of Gloucester's revenue each. Edmund makes his father even more suspicious by telling him that he heard Edgar say that 'sons at perfect age and fathers declined, the father should be as ward to the son, and the son manage his revenue' (lines 73–5). Appalled, Gloucester demands that his legitimate son be 'apprehended' immediately. Edmund pretends to be concerned about family honour and suggests that Gloucester should wait to hear Edgar condemn himself out of his own mouth before taking action. Gloucester agrees to let Edmund 'Frame the business' (line 98) of discovering the truth about Edgar's feelings. Gloucester then reflects pessimistically on the conflict in the nation. He mentions predictions of discord, treason, friendships cooling and fathers and sons going against the 'bias of nature' (line 111). He promises Edmund that he will gain by uncovering Edgar's villainy.

Alone again, Edmund rejects his father's superstitious beliefs. He says that 'whoremaster man' (lines 126–7) is responsible for his own fortunes and actions. He sees Edgar coming and pretends to be musing on the effects of the recent eclipses. The brothers joke about Edmund's supposed fondness for astronomy. Edmund then tells Edgar that he has offended their father and advises him to keep out of Gloucester's way. Edgar is alarmed by this and fears that 'Some villain hath done me wrong' (line 162). Edmund suggests that Edgar go into hiding at his lodgings. His brother falls in with this plan.

Edmund's opening **soliloquy** at the beginning of I.2 shows the reasoning of the discontented **malcontent**. His last line also reveals his defiance: 'Now gods stand up for bastards' (line 22). However, we quickly realise that Edmund does not need the gods to help him. He is a master manipulator and a fine actor, who takes his father and brother in with disturbing ease. Cold and calculating himself, Edmund preys on the emotions of his relatives in this scene. His view that men make or mar their own fortunes seems entirely plausible at this stage in the play. In I.1 and I.2 fathers misjudge their children, precipitating their own ruin. Gloucester's swift rejection of Edgar mirrors Lear's rejection of Cordelia in the previous scene, while Edmund's villainy prepares the way for Gonerill and Regan's treachery in the next act. The subplot mirrors the Lear plot in other ways. Gloucester is taken in by false words and appearances, just as Lear was. Gloucester's family harmony is now in jeopardy, and inheritance issues are revealed as troublesome here too. Another innocent and virtuous child is cast off, while the father promises property to his unworthy offspring in return for a show of affection. Gloucester puts himself in his son Edmund's power, just as Lear resigned his authority to Gonerill and Regan. Edmund's triumphant opportunism, energy and directness when he is alone on stage mirror Gonerill and Regan's urgent plain-speaking at the end of I.1. The evil children are gaining ground.

curiosity of nations patriarchal laws or rules

lag of younger than

well compact well made or put together

generous noble

confined to exhibition given only a small allowance to live on

upon the gad suddenly, impulsively

character handwriting

wind he unto him wheedle his intentions out of him

unstate forsake my rank and fortune

bias of nature natural tendencies

Ursa Major a cluster of stars, The Great Bear (those born under it were thought to be lecherous)

catastrophe of the old comedy in old-fashioned comedies events seemed to be worked out in a mechanical way, with a convenient event or incident of some kind e.g. a timely 'catastrophe' to bring about the **denouement** The implication is that Edgar arrives at a convenient time for Edmund

diffidences mistrust

sectary astronomical follower or student of astrology

SCENE 3 Gonerill complains to her steward Oswald about Lear and his followers

A short space of time has elapsed. Lear is now staying with Gonerill. She complains to her steward Oswald about Lear and his knights. She says that Lear has continued to act erratically, setting everyone at odds. Gonerill is determined to put a stop to this, 'I'll not endure it! … I will not speak to him' (lines 6–9). Oswald hears Lear returning from hunting and Gonerill instructs him to put on a 'weary negligence' (line 13) and tell the other servants to follow suit. She wants to provoke a clash with her father. Gonerill leaves to write a letter to Regan. Presumably she will recount Lear's recent 'gross' crimes. Oswald is sent to prepare dinner.

How seriously should we take Gonerill's complaints about Lear and his knights? It depends partly on how a director chooses to portray the knights in the next scene. It is possible to suggest that they are a rabble, and that Gonerill is justified in her irritation. But equally, because we know that Gonerill and Regan have been scheming (letters have already been sent back and forth), these complaints look suspiciously empty. It is also worth considering the duties of the host when judging Gonerill's anger. As Lear's host, Gonerill has a duty to protect her father and behave graciously towards him. Instead she prepares to subvert his authority. Throughout this scene her tone is assertive and uncompromising; she insists that she is the wronged party, suggesting that the balance of power is shifting from Lear to his daughters.

checks punishments, rebukes

course lead, example

SCENE 4 Lear and Gonerill clash. Lear leaves to stay with Regan

Lear returns from hunting to find Caius (Kent in disguise), a serving man who seeks employment. He agrees to take him on if he likes him 'no worse after dinner' (line 41). As he calls for food and his Fool, Oswald wanders in and out, following Gonerill's instructions with admirable precision. Lear is enraged and sends one of his knights to bring the insolent wretch back. There is a discussion about the 'great abatement of kindness' (line 59) shown to the king. Both Lear and his followers have noticed that Gonerill's servants have started to treat them unkindly. Lear decides to 'look further into't' (line 70) and asks again for his Fool. We learn that the Fool has been pining away since Cordelia went to France. Lear snaps, 'No more of that' (line 74). He cannot bear to hear his youngest daughter's name mentioned.

When Oswald returns (of his own accord) Lear rages at him, 'Who am I, sir?' Oswald replies insolently, 'My lady's father' (lines 77–8). The king curses and strikes him and Kent trips the 'clotpoll' (line 46) up, earning the king's praise. At this point the Fool makes his first appearance. He offers Kent his coxcomb 'for taking one's part that's out of favour' (line 99). The Fool harps on Lear's folly in riddles and songs. A lot of his lines refer directly to property, the implication being that without his property Lear is helpless. The Fool also suggests that Lear has reversed the natural order. Lear threatens to have him whipped.

Gonerill comes in frowning and launches her own attack on Lear. She accuses him of encouraging quarrelsome behaviour in his knights and suggests that a remedy must be sought. Lear is incredulous. Gonerill continues her verbal assault, complaining about the knights' degeneracy. Lear tries to dismiss these insults but his eldest daughter remains firm; if Lear does not cut down his train, she will. Lear's response to Gonerill's audacious threats is to call his train together and leave. He curses Gonerill and says he still has one 'kind and comfortable' (line 303) daughter left to go to (Regan). At this point Albany enters. Lear appeals to him rather helplessly and carries on cursing Gonerill. Albany is puzzled by Lear's passion and distress. Lear kneels and calls on 'Nature' to help him. He hopes Gonerill will either be sterile or give birth to a thankless child who will torment her. He rushes out. Albany seems shocked, but Gonerill is unperturbed. Lear returns briefly, bewildered to find that that fifty of his followers have already been dismissed (there seems to be an inconsistency in the text here; there are further references to Lear's hundred knights later in this scene and in II.4). Lear threatens to take back the power he has given away. He refuses to weep and insists that Regan will help him.

After her father has gone Gonerill continues to complain about Lear's followers and how her father 'holds our lives at mercy' (line 324) all the time he retains them. Albany is uneasy but does not assert himself. He says that they should wait to see what happens. Gonerill sends Oswald to Regan with a letter, presumably describing the course she has taken with Lear and asking for her sister's support.

This is a difficult scene for Lear, who finds his expectations and beliefs thwarted at every turn. He is challenged directly by Gonerill, and his dependant state is revealed when Oswald tells him that he is now simply his mistress's father, not a royal monarch who must be obeyed. The Fool's scathing jests also suggest Lear's powerlessness. The fact that he continues to take verbal swipes at Lear after he has been threatened with whipping reinforces the idea that Lear is no longer in control, as does the king's frantic to-ing and fro-ing at the end of the scene. Lear himself begins to question his identity in this scene when he asks 'Who is there that can tell me who I am?' (line 226). His use of 'I' is at odds with the royal 'we' he invokes in his earlier question, 'Are you our daughter?' (line 214). Lear thinks – or hopes – that he is joking when he asks these questions, but the audience will recognise that these are serious concerns, that Lear is no longer omnipotent. Even servants disobey him now. These questions also reveal Lear's blindness, although there is an indication that he realises he has behaved unwisely when he says, 'Woe that too late repents' (line 254) and calls out in anguish, 'O Lear, Lear, Lear! / Beat at this gate that let thy folly in / And thy dear judgement out!' (lines 266–7).

The dismissal of Lear's knights is significant for a number of reasons. His followers are a symbol of Lear's might and importance, but they also represent real fighting power. With only the support of a few old men, Lear will not be able to assert himself or regain control of the kingdom. His threats and curses seem increasingly empty as the scene unfolds. His speeches become increasingly disjointed as he becomes more distressed, hinting at the madness to come.

Their different responses to Lear suggest that Gonerill and Albany will clash later in the play. Gonerill is more assertive than her husband at this point. Albany's feeble protestations seem inadequate, and suggest that evil will go unchecked for some time to come. Gonerill has assumed control in the main plot in the same ruthless way Edmund deals with his father and brother in the subplot.

razed disguised, changed

general dependants servants

earnest part of Kent's wage, a token payment

Lady Brach name of a female dog, bitch, who flatters the master and is allowed to sit by the fire

frontlet frown

all licensed fool who is given the freedom to say anything

redresses remedies

wholesome wear well-being of the state

discreet proceeding sensible, apt measures or actions

epicurism gluttony

at a clap in one go

untented untreated, untreatable

buzz rumour

compact strengthen

SCENE 5 Lear sends a letter to Regan. He fears he is going mad

Lear sends Kent to deliver a letter to Regan, announcing his arrival. Kent is not to tell Regan anything about the events of the previous scene. Presumably Lear wants to offer his own account of Gonerill's heartless disobedience. The Fool continues to make barbed comments about Lear's predicament. Lear says that he has wronged Cordelia. He fears that Gonerill's ingratitude is driving him mad and wonders if he can reclaim his throne by violent means. A knight informs Lear that his horses are ready.

This scene, which appropriately takes place outside, suggests Lear's growing isolation and increasingly fragile mental state. Lear is so distracted by disturbing thoughts that he hardly engages with the Fool. His recognition that he has mistreated Cordelia increases the sense of isolation. We already suspect that Regan will receive him coldly. Soon Lear will have no one to turn to; he will be isolated from all of his daughters. Perhaps he is anxious about the reception he will receive from Regan too; is this why he does not mention the events of I.4 in his letter? Lear is still blind to a number of truths, however. He does not recognise his faults as a father (in his view, his troubles are all caused by his ungrateful offspring), and we know he has little chance of reclaiming the throne now. After the tension and violent emotions of I.5, the Fool's vulgar rhyming couplet which closes the scene comes as a moment of light relief. An interval (however short) is welcome; we know that Lear's suffering has started in earnest.

kibes chilblains

slipshod wearing slippers

ACT II

SCENE 1 Edmund persuades Edgar to flee. Gloucester issues orders to have him hunted down. Regan and Cornwall arrive at Gloucester's castle

The scene now moves to the Great Hall of Gloucester's castle. Curan informs Edmund that Cornwall and Regan are expected soon. There is gossip concerning 'likely wars' (line 10) between Cornwall and Albany, suggesting further strife between brothers. Edmund determines to use Cornwall and Regan's arrival to his own advantage. He calls Edgar down from his hiding place and tells him he must escape at once. He asks Edgar whether he has spoken against Cornwall, implying that Cornwall and Regan are as enraged against him as Gloucester. Alarmed, Edgar denies abusing Cornwall. Edgar is drawn into a mock fight with Edmund, and then flees. Edmund deliberately wounds himself. He cries out for help, and Gloucester rushes in. He sends his servants to pursue Edgar.

Edmund paints a very black picture of his brother. He says that Edgar tried to involve him in a plan to murder Gloucester. He pretends that his wound was caused by Edgar. Gloucester is fooled, horrified by the idea of a son who appears to have broken all the natural bonds between father and child. He says that Edgar will be caught, no matter how far he goes. When he is caught he will be executed. Anyone who helps Edgar will also die. Edmund reports a conversation he alleges to have had with his brother. He says that Edgar mocked his bastardy; who would take the word of the illegitimate child against the legitimate one?

A trumpet announces the arrival of Cornwall and Regan. Gloucester praises Edmund as a 'loyal and natural boy' (line 83) and says he will disinherit Edgar. Cornwall and Regan have already been told the 'strange news' (line 86) of Edgar's treachery. Regan wonders whether Edgar was egged on to thoughts of patricide by Lear's riotous knights. She has received Gonerill's letter, which gives details of the knights' unruly behaviour. Like Gonerill, Regan has no intention of giving them house room (this is the real reason why she and Cornwall have come to visit Gloucester). Cornwall praises Edmund for showing his father 'a child-like office' (line 105). Regan says she wants advice about how to answer the letters she has received. Edmund promises to serve Cornwall.

In this scene we see the evil characters continue to gain ground. Edmund's plans prosper and he now aligns himself with Cornwall and Regan; plot and subplot become intertwined. Edmund's quick wits help him here. He is able to respond to events, as well as control them. His lines to Edgar at the start of the scene are full of short, sharp statements and questions, suggesting his command of circumstances. He achieves the goal he set himself in I.2 with terrifying ease, indicating how effortlessly evil begins to run riot in the kingdom. Gloucester follows Edmund's lead entirely and appears to be overwhelmed. Like Lear, he seems vulnerable, indicated by his speech to Regan; 'my old heart is cracked, it's cracked' (line 89). Thoughts of filial ingratitude distress both patriarchs now. Gloucester is also isolated in this scene. As the evil characters draw closer together, he has little to say. Regan and Cornwall are as smooth and assured as Edmund. Both assume a commanding tone. Regan's comforting and affectionate words to Gloucester are perhaps surprising. Shakespeare is leaving her true nature partially concealed, for maximum dramatic impact in II.4. However, we are likely to distrust her; she and Gonerill share the same low opinion of Lear's followers, and Regan has deliberately chosen to thwart her father's plans by coming to visit Gloucester. Essentially, she is denying her father shelter. When Edmund offers his services to Cornwall we will be alarmed; what is the bastard son hoping to gain now?

ear kissing whispered

queasy delicate, sensitive, difficult

parricides patricide; the murder of one's father
in fell motion with a hard cruel thrust
gasted scared
pight fixed, determined
unpossessing as a bastard, Edmund has no property or inheritance rights, he possesses nothing
practice intriguing, scheming
fastened firmly decided, resolute
ill affected badly disposed

SCENE 2 Kent quarrels with Oswald and challenges him to a fight. He is punished by Cornwall, who puts him in the stocks

The two messengers, Kent/Caius and Oswald, meet outside Gloucester's castle. Kent immediately quarrels with Oswald, accusing him of being a conceited coward (amongst other things). Oswald is perplexed by Kent's aggression. He fails to recognise his adversary. When Kent challenges him to fight, Oswald shows his true colours; he backs away and yells out for help. His cries bring Edmund, Cornwall, Regan, Gonerill and servants running. Edmund tries to part the combatants, but Kent is keen to give Oswald a beating. Cornwall stops the fight. When asked why he dislikes Oswald so much, Kent says his face offends him. Unable to hold his tongue, he then insults Cornwall.

Kent is placed in the stocks as a punishment for his plain-speaking. He protests that he is on the king's business, and should not be treated in this degrading fashion. Cornwall ignores him and says that Kent will be left in the stocks until noon. Regan says he should be left there all night. When Gloucester tries to plead for Kent, Cornwall sweeps his protestations aside. Gloucester stays behind to offer his condolences to Kent. He tries to excuse Cornwall. Kent is stoical and says he'll 'sleep out' (line 154) his time in the stocks. Alone on stage he reveals that he has a letter from Cordelia. She intends to put right all the wrongs that have been done to Lear since she was banished.

The audience will enjoy Kent's long list of imaginative and lively insults. Oswald is a worthy object of scorn and the quarrel at the start of the scene provides a moment of relief. Behind Kent's insults lies a serious point; the dangers of the bad servant. It is possible to argue that *King Lear* is full of bad servants, who subvert the order that they should be serving faithfully. Kent also makes a serious point when he says he does not like the faces he sees before him; unlike Lear, he is not fooled by appearances and recognises Cornwall, Regan and Oswald for what they are. He voices the concerns of the audience when he insults Cornwall. However, Kent is punished again for his goodness and honesty, as Cordelia and Edgar have been punished, in spite of their virtues. The punishment of Kent is significant for other reasons. We see that Cornwall is arrogant, Regan vindictive. It becomes clear that husband and wife operate effectively as a team and enjoy their cruelty, hinting at the horrors to come in III.7. It is also clear that power is in new hands. Gloucester is ineffectual in this scene, and Lear's representative (Kent/Caius) is treated with scorn. The old patriarchs are pushed aside as Cornwall and Regan exert their authority. The hint that Cordelia will return offers us some hope that the progress of the evil characters might be checked.

broken meats leftover food

three suited servants were given 3 suits a year in service

super serviceable unscrupulous

finical fussy, pedantic

bawd procurer, 'madam' in a brothel

pander pimp

cullionly base, low

holy cords the natural bonds of the family

halcyon kingfisher. People believed that if you hung a kingfisher up it would twist so that its beak was turned into the wind. The implication here is that fawning, false servants like Oswald will turn their thoughts and deeds to suit their masters

Sarum Plain Salisbury Plain

Camelot the legendary home of the court of King Arthur

compact in league with

dread great and heroic (Kent is being sarcastic about Oswald's prowess as a fighter)

Ajax a self important and bragging warrior who appears in Homer's Odyssey

reverend old

SCENE 3 Edgar disguises himself as the mad beggar, Poor Tom

Out in the countryside, Edgar is alone. He heard himself proclaimed a criminal, and concealed himself in a tree. His position is desperate; he cannot attempt to flee England as all the ports (seaports and town gates) are watched, and his father's men roam the countryside hunting him down. To preserve his life Edgar decides to disguise himself as a 'Bedlam beggar' (line 14). He describes what he will do to effect this disguise; knot his hair, cover himself in dirt, wear only a blanket for protection.

The audience is left in no doubt as to the difficulties Edgar will face. The fact that he chooses to disguise himself as a social outcast reveals his desperation, and the danger he is in. In Shakespeare's day 'Bedlam' (Bethlehem) hospital housed the mentally ill. When they were released Bedlam inmates were allowed to go begging for survival; this is what Edgar has been reduced to by his brother and father. As in the previous scene, we see goodness pushed aside, degraded and punished. Edgar's situation also mirrors Lear's. Edgar is now reliant on charity, his world and expectations turned upside down. We get a glimpse of what Lear will be reduced to. The contrast between life as absolute monarch and the powerless existence described here could not be more stark. Edgar's assumed madness also points towards Lear's madness in Act III.

proclaimed publicly proclaimed an outlaw

in contempt of despising, treating with contempt

elf tangle up into knots

pelting paltry

bans curses

Turlygod there is no really satisfactory explanation for the origins of this word, it is perhaps the name of a beggar

SCENE 4 Kent is found in the stocks by Lear. Lear tries to complain to Regan about Gonerill. The sisters reduce his train. Angry and distressed, Lear rushes out into the storm

Lear arrives at Gloucester's castle, wondering why Regan and Cornwall have not sent Kent/Caius back with a message explaining their movements. The sight of Kent in the stocks upsets him. The Fool mocks Kent while

Lear refuses to believe that Cornwall and Regan are responsible for his servant's 'shame'. Kent recounts his version of the events of the previous day and night. We learn that Cornwall and Regan left home immediately on receipt of Gonerill's letter. A pithy line from the Fool follows Kent's narration. The **image** of wild geese and winter suggests that there is worse to come. The Fool continues to riddle about fathers and their children, but Lear pays him no heed. He is most concerned with his own mental state. Lear fears he is becoming hysterical with sorrow. He demands to know where Regan is and decides to look for her himself. When he leaves the stage Kent asks the Fool why Lear has come with so few followers. He doesn't receive a direct answer, but gets some advice instead: don't follow a master whose power is waning. For all his wisdom on other subjects, the Fool refuses to follow his own advice. He says that he is 'no knave' and will stay loyal to Lear.

Lear is angry and incredulous when he returns with Gloucester. Regan and Cornwall have said they are sick and weary and cannot speak with him. Lear thinks that they tricking him. He packs Gloucester off to get a better answer. But even Gloucester thwarts him by trying to excuse Cornwall's behaviour. This enrages Lear further. However, he then accepts that his son-in-law might not be well and decides to be patient. This mood doesn't last long and Lear reverts to his opinion that Cornwall and Regan are deceiving him.

Lear feels himself becoming hysterical once more and tries to control himself. The Fool offers two examples of idiotic kindness. In the first, a cook tries to make an eel pie without killing the eels first because she cannot bear to harm them. In the second, her brother puts butter on his horses' hay to improve the taste.

Cornwall and Regan arrive. Kent is freed. Lear hopes Regan is glad to see him. He is so troubled by this point that he can hardly speak, ending his first speech with a pitiful plea, 'O Regan!' However, Regan employs the same sharp tone that Gonerill used so effectively in I.4. She tells her father that he should accept his age and failing powers of judgement and be led by others. Her advice is to return to Gonerill and beg her pardon. Lear is astonished. He goes down on his knees, and, in what he thinks is a satirical speech, offers a portrait of himself as a weak old man begging for clothing and shelter. Regan has little patience with these 'unsightly tricks' (line 152) and repeats her instructions. Lear carries on complaining about his eldest daughter. Regan snaps back in an accusatory way; he will curse her too 'when the rash mood is on' (line 164). Lear denies this, saying she is a more natural child. His flattering words have no effect, so Lear shifts his attention back to Kent and asks who put him in the stocks.

At this point Gonerill arrives, disconcerting Lear, who continues to ask how Kent came to be in the stocks. Cornwall smoothly admits that he was responsible for Kent's punishment. Regan's tone becomes harsher; again she tells Lear to go back to Gonerill, and to dismiss half his train. Lear stubbornly continues to refuse this course of action. Gonerill is unconcerned. Lear fears he is losing his wits and curses her. He insists he can stay with Regan and keep his knights. Regan contradicts him and then suggests a further reduction in his train. Bewildered, Lear tries to remind his daughters that he gave them everything. They are not impressed. Gradually they argue Lear out of all of his knights.

Agonised, Lear finally bursts out, 'O, reason not the need!' (line 259). He refuses to accept his daughters' way of looking at the world. Man's needs cannot be measured as Gonerill and Regan insist on doing. He points out that even beggars have more than they need. He threatens his daughters that he will be revenged on them. As the storm starts he angrily refuses to weep but then cries out in terror, 'O Fool, I shall go mad!' (line 281). He rushes out.

The sisters justify letting Lear leave because the 'house' is too small to accommodate his followers. Gloucester follows Lear out and returns with the news that the king is 'in high rage' (line 291). Gloucester is concerned about Lear's well-being and tells us that the country he has gone out into is desolate, affording little protection from the elements. Clearly, Gloucester would like his guests to call Lear back. But they insist that Lear should be left to suffer the consequences of his actions. Regan instructs Gloucester to lock the doors, still maintaining that the king's followers are dangerous. Lear is left outside in the storm.

> This scene presents Lear with a number of difficulties, which he finds insurmountable. We watch anxiously as his power and self-possession are stripped away. A number of events and speeches early in the scene point towards the stark outcome, when Lear is rejected by his elder daughters. Kent's presence in the stocks unnerves the king; it is proof that he continues to be treated with contempt, a point reinforced by

Cornwall and Regan's refusal to speak with him. Interestingly, Lear seeks Regan out himself instead of sending a servant to fetch her. He is now reduced to conveying his own requests. His powerlessness is emphasised again when his requests for information are ignored; he asks many times how Kent came to be in the stocks before receiving an answer. The pattern of entrances and exits early in the scene mirrors the close of I.4, and hints at the chaos to come in Act III. Lear's changes of mood and tone indicate his increasing mental instability. The Fool's disturbing little tales of misguided kindness also operate as a choric introduction (see **chorus**) to the 'cruel kindness' Gonerill and Regan display later in II.4. The perfunctory and frosty greeting between Lear, Cornwall and Regan suggests that Lear is foolish to pin his hopes on his second daughter's kindness. His belief that she would never 'oppose the bolt / Against my coming in' (lines 171–2) is chillingly ironic.

Gonerill's entrance proves to be the turning point for the beleaguered king. Her lack of concern about whether Lear returns to her or not proves that the sisters are oblivious to their father's agitation and suffering. Gonerill and Regan are extremely firm and authoritative when 'measuring out' Lear's knights for him. We are reminded of the dangers of measuring love in words and numbers. Lear's insistence that he will stay with the daughter who allows him to retain the greatest number of followers is as blind and foolish as his 'love-test' in I.1. Can he not see that neither of his daughters cares for him? His bargaining is desperate; as impotent as his curses and threats of revenge.

The tone of the speeches that follow Lear's exit is very telling. Gonerill, Regan and Cornwall are unmoved by Lear's agonised final speech; their cool control contrasts starkly with his wild passion. There is a cruel desire to inflict punishment on 'the old man' (line 283) (more contemptuous words). By now the audience will recognise the hypocrisy of Regan's fears about Lear's knights. This scene has proved that Gonerill and Regan are expert manipulators, ready to use any excuse to justify their own actions. When the storm starts, we know that they have 'won'. Lear's fear that he would go mad, first voiced in I.4, has been realised.

Juno Roman goddess of the Moon
a reeking post perspiring messenger
stewed soaked in sweat
meiny followers, retinue
Hysterica passio a kind of hysteria, which made the afflicted person feel as if they were being suffocated, starting in the womb ('mother'), and then moving up to the heart and throat, hence the idea of 'climbing sorrow'
fetches excuses
flying off desertion
remotion holding themselves aloof, remote from
knapped list
scant neglect, fail to fulfil
confine limit
raiment clothing
taking infectious
scant my sizes cut down my allowances
sumpter pack horse
embossed swollen, inflamed

ACT III

SCENE 1 Out on the heath, Kent and the Gentleman search for Lear

Kent asks the Gentleman where Lear has gone. We learn that the king is out on the heath, raging against the elements. The Fool is his only companion and he is trying to distract his master with jokes. The Gentleman paints a vivid picture of Lear, tearing his hair, running about unprotected, calling for the destruction of the world. Kent speaks of the recent 'division' between Albany and Cornwall. He goes on to explain that France is preparing to invade England, having already sent some of his army across secretly. Kent gives the Gentleman a ring and asks him to deliver it to Cordelia, who has landed with the French forces at Dover. They continue searching for Lear.

Act III occurs in swift short scenes to allow us to see Lear's dramatic descent into madness. We also learn what happens to Lear's mirror image, Gloucester. There is a spiralling downwards for both characters, culminating in a scene of appalling violence against

Gloucester. Lear and Gloucester are both heroic, tragic figures in Act III. III.1 sets the scene for us. The Gentleman's descriptions of Lear on the heath prepare us for the sight of the lunatic king in the next scene, and also establish the violence of the storm. Kent provides us with information about another kind of chaos; a clash between the English and French forces. The characters' anxiety about Lear reflects the concern the audience probably feels at this point in the play.

cub drawn bear a bear, hungry because she has fed her cubs
couch shelter
unbonneted unprotected, without a hat
snuffs and packings grudges or arguments and secret conspiracies
the hard rein harsh or cruel treatment
outwall outer appearance

SCENE 2 Increasingly mad, Lear rants in the storm. The Fool and Kent try to soothe him

Out on the heath, Lear rants at the elements. He hopes the tempest will obliterate the world. He wants to see 'ingrateful man' (line 9) destroyed. He ignores the Fool when he pleads with him to return to Gloucester's castle to ask Gonerill and Regan for shelter. Lear then becomes preoccupied with thoughts of his daughters' ingratitude. He offers a heart-rending self-assessment at lines 19–20. Increasingly deranged, he accuses the storm of being in league with Gonerill and Regan. The Fool sings a song and offers an epigram about female vanity and the dangers of promiscuity. Lear won't engage with the Fool's jibes, willing himself to stay calm and patient ('I will say nothing' – line 38).

Kent catches up with his master, and is concerned by what he sees. His lines are suitably gloomy; he says this storm is so hostile man is unlikely to be able to endure it. Failing to recognise Kent, Lear carries on speaking about what he hopes the storm will uncover. He says that sinners of various kinds should tremble because the gods will find out their crimes. Perhaps he mistakes Kent for one of these sinners when he exclaims 'Tremble, thou wretch' (line 51). Lear concludes that he is 'a man / More sinned against than sinning' (lines 58–9).

Kent spies a hovel nearby, and tries to persuade Lear to take shelter. He intends to return to Gloucester's castle and beg Gonerill and Regan to take their father in. We see a new side of Lear's character when he expresses concern for the Fool and identifies with his suffering. Now he recognises how precious such things as shelter are. Lear asks Kent to lead them to the hovel. Left alone on stage, the Fool makes predictions about Albion' s (Britain's) future. Like his master he speaks about the sinners of his own age; dishonest brewers, cutpurses, usurers, pimps and prostitutes. Then he seems to describe a utopia where evil will cease to exist. When criminals turn virtuous – 'that going shall be used with feet' (i.e. things will be as they should – line 94).

Lear's speeches establish and reflect the properties of the storm. They are full of anger and distress, as the mad king moves swiftly from one topic to another. The violence of the **imagery** Lear employs reflects his state of mind. Lear's isolation is shown by his lack of interaction with the other characters on stage, which also indicates that he is now engaged in an internal struggle; he is battling to preserve his wits. The storm serves as a **metaphor** for Lear – and England's – plight. Lear's obsession with justice and criminal behaviour, introduced in this scene, is maintained until the end of the play. The king has started to consider issues he took too little care of as ruler; his journey towards greater understanding of himself and the world around him has begun.

There are two ways of interpreting the Fool's prophecy. The Fool is either suggesting – optimistically – that virtue will triumph in England, or that optimism about the future is misplaced; even in these terrible days men use their feet for walking. The Fool again provides a moment of relief, a pause in the action where the audience can gather their thoughts.

cataracts heavy rainstorm
thought executing as swift as thought
Germans seeds
court holy water flattery
servile ministers willing agents
cod piece a cod piece was a piece of clothing, a case for the male genitalia, worn outside men's breeches
gallows scare

putter chaos, tumult
similar of virtue one who makes a pretence of being virtuous
Caitiff low wretch
covert concealing, deceiving
summoners a summoner was an official of the church courts
scanted limited, lacking
throngs public gatherings, crowds of people

SCENE 3 Gloucester tells Edmund he intends to help Lear. Edmund decides to betray his father to Cornwall

The mood is tense as Gloucester frets about the 'unnatural dealing' (line 2) of Cornwall, Regan and Gonerill, who have warned him against helping Lear. Believing that Edmund shares his concern, Gloucester goes on to tell his son that Albany and Cornwall are set to clash and that France has begun his invasion to restore Lear. Gloucester proposes that he and Edmund should assist Lear. He then decides Edmund should act as a decoy, while he goes to find the king. When Gloucester leaves, Edmund announces his intention to betray his father to Cornwall.

Edmund now has his sights set on his father's title. His decision to betray his father is made without a moment's hesitation, befitting Edmund's ruthless nature. In contrast, Gloucester has prevaricated and shows here that he is anxious about his decision to support Lear. Gloucester's feverish fretting mirrors the alarm the audience will feel at the end of this scene; we know Gloucester is in great danger now. Evil continues to triumph, and good intentions will again be thwarted. Gloucester's earnest desire to assist Lear seems as hopeless and doomed as Kent and the Fool's concern in the previous scene.

footed landed
incline to support, side with
privily secretly

SCENE 4 Lear continues to rant on the heath. Poor Tom is found in a hovel

Lear, Kent and the Fool reach the hovel. When Kent suggests taking shelter, Lear demurs. He explains that the storm does not affect him because he is suffering inner torment. He says that man only feels bodily complaints when the mind is 'free' (not troubled by worries). He explicitly links the storm with his mental state and returns to the theme that torments him: filial ingratitude. Lear maintains his daughters' cruelty but now seems resigned, 'Pour on; I will endure' (line 18), he says. Again Kent urges Lear to enter the hovel. Lear tells him to take shelter first himself. He seeks isolation and wants to stay out in the storm to pray. In his prayer Lear considers the fate of the homeless.

The Fool rushes out of the hovel, scared by the creature he has found there. Kent kindly takes his hand and calls the 'spirit' out. When Edgar appears as Poor Tom, Lear becomes more demented. Lear instantly recognises himself in Tom, convinced that cruel daughters must have reduced this pitiful specimen to beggary. Poor Tom describes his miserable life, hounded by the 'foul fiend' (line 44). There is a much needed moment of relief when the Fool jokes about Edgar's clothing. The scene becomes more disturbing as Lear asks Poor Tom to recount his history.

Edgar constructs an account of himself as a degenerate servant. It contains references to lechery and the dangers of female sexuality, a theme Lear dwells on in IV.6. Tom's presence has a profound effect on Lear. He begins to empathise with the dispossessed and believes that he sees humanity in its essence when he looks at Tom. Lear decides that man is really 'a poor, bare, forked animal' (line 104); he wants to know what it means to have nothing, to be nothing. In his admiration for Tom he tries to undress. Lear wants to remove the superficial trappings that stand between him and 'Unaccommodated man' (line 103). Alarmed, Kent and the Fool try to dissuade Lear from stripping.

During the confusion, Gloucester appears. This is the first time that Edgar has set eyes on his father. Perhaps Edgar fears detection; he seems to behave in a more exaggerated way, chanting and ranting. He sings a song about a female demon who suffocates her victims. As Edgar chants, Kent tries vainly to obtain a response from Lear, who fails to recognise Gloucester. The darkness seems to make the characters nervous. Kent wants to know who Gloucester is and why he has come, and Gloucester asks anxiously about the inhabitants of the hovel. Edgar then launches into an account of seven terrible years as a mad beggar.

Gloucester is dismayed to see the king in such poor company. Tom complains piteously of the cold, but Gloucester ignores him, urging Lear to go with him to a safe place. Lear continues to be most concerned with Poor Tom, believing he is a wise Greek philosopher who can teach him. Kent joins Gloucester and pleads with the king to go, but Lear is beyond their help now.

Kent urges Gloucester to leave. Gloucester tells him that Gonerill and Regan seek Lear's death. He also speaks of his own suffering; thoughts of his son's betrayal have sent him half mad with grief. When Gloucester tells Tom to go into the hovel Lear adds 'Come, let's in all' (line 167). He jealously guards the beggar when Kent tries to part them. Kent finally accepts Tom and the characters enter the hovel.

This is a scene of isolation and suffering. Each character is oppressed by his own concerns. Kent is agitated because Lear suffers, the Fool shivers in the storm. Both are helpless bystanders. Like Lear, Gloucester is preoccupied by thoughts of filial ingratitude. Edgar's breathless craziness reflects his own sufferings as an outcast and heightens our sense of the king's suffering. His speeches are erratic in a way that Lear's are not, full of terrifying descriptions of physical and mental violence. Through his interaction with Poor Tom, Lear undergoes a terrible kind of purging. In this scene the king also displays the stoicism of a true tragic hero, although his patience seems hard won. His concern for Kent, the Fool and Poor Tom suggests that he is learning compassion, reflected in his lines about the fate of the homeless: 'O, I have ta'en / Too little care of this' (lines 32–33). The pity we feel for Lear increases as he learns to pity others. We also realise that Lear has recognised the need to look beyond appearances when he tries to remove his clothing.

Edgar's description of his life as a corrupt servant can be read as a comment on Oswald's career. Other commentators see Tom's story as a parody of the seven deadly sins. His account of seven years as a beggar seems to be directed at his father, whom he will judge harshly for his adultery later in V.3. Lear and Gloucester are both forced to face up to their sins in *King Lear*; Lear has already started to confront his failings.

In spite of the madness and suffering displayed in this scene, some hope remains. The characters sympathise with one another, although

Kent is initially reluctant to allow Poor Tom to take shelter with the king. Overall, the prevailing mood is sombre. Poor Tom's references to the 'dark tower' and the Jack the giant killer story in the final lines of the scene are ominous. Gloucester's castle now houses four murderous predators (Gonerill, Regan, Cornwall, Edmund) who plot against their fathers.

looped or windowed ragged and full of holes
shake the superflux give superfluous luxuries or riches to the poor
fathom and half the term sailors use to measure the depth of water they are sailing through
halters in his pew nooses on his balcony
to course chase, hunt
star blasting malignant diseases caused by the stars
pelican daughters a medieval legend. It was believed that young pelicans turned on and killed the parent birds and drank their blood, the implication being that Gonerill and Regan are feeding on and thus killing their father
Flibberdigibbet the name of a dancing devil. The names of many of the devils that appear in Act III, and other language Edgar uses as Poor Tom are probably taken from a book, *A Declaration of Egregious Popish Impostures* by Samuel Harsnet, which appeared in 1603. In this book Harsnet, who was chaplain to the Bishop of London, wrote scathingly about fraudulent exorcisms carried out by Catholic priests. Edgar's language as Poor Tom reflects the language used by the victims of these exorcisms in Harsnet's book
aroint get away
sallets salads
three suits to his back, six shirts to his body the clothing allowance given to the class of servant Edgar is pretending Poor Tom was
Smulkin, Modo, Mahu see note on Flibberdigibbet. Modo was a name given to Satan, while Mahu was another devil
learned Theban wise Greek scholar

SCENE 5 Edmund betrays Gloucester

Cornwall has been given the letter which contains information about the French invasion and intends to punish Gloucester for his treachery. He sends Edmund to find his father. Edmund pretends to be torn between being loyal and to Cornwall and faithful to his 'blood' (line 22), but hopes that he will find his father with Lear. This will make Cornwall even more suspicious. We are left in no doubt as to Cornwall's intentions. He seeks Gloucester's death.

The first line of the scene suggests that violence is imminent. This is confirmed by Cornwall's consistently decisive and ruthless tone. Showing his customary facility with language, Edmund speaks politely and formally to Cornwall, who now acts as if he is the father of the nation. Edmund's **aside** to the audience is as vicious and cold blooded as his new patron's lines. Both evil men lust selfishly and destructively for power.

intelligent party to the advantages spy who is helping advance the French cause
apprehension arrest

SCENE 6 Inside the hovel, Lear conducts a trial of Gonerill and Regan. Gloucester brings a coach to transport Lear to safety at Dover

Gloucester and Kent help Lear into the hovel. Gloucester departs, saying he will return with provisions. Poor Tom gibbers about the devil and the Fool continues to taunt Lear with home truths. All the characters seem to be talking to themselves, at cross purposes. Lear is lost in a mad world of his own.

Lear is still preoccupied by thoughts of vengeance. He decides to 'try' his daughters (see Justice in Images and Themes for a discussion of the trials in the play). Lear calls on Poor Tom and the Fool to assist him as justices on the bench. He imagines a joint-stool is Gonerill and accuses 'her' of kicking him. In his madness Lear thinks his eldest daughter has escaped from the 'courtroom' and screams for her to be apprehended. Edgar is in tears as he listens to Lear's lunatic agony. His 'act' momentarily breaks down at 'Bless thy five wits' (line 56). Kent implores Lear to be patient. The king continues with his trial and 'anatomizes' (line 75) Regan. He wants to find out why she has such a hard heart. There is some more black humour, as Lear castigates Poor Tom about his clothes. Kent tries to soothe him again. Finally the old king agrees to rest.

Gloucester returns and says that Lear must be removed to safety immediately because there is a plot to kill him. He has prepared a litter (coach) to transport him to Dover, where he will be met by friends (the French forces).

The cold blooded discussion in III.5 contrasts sharply with the solicitous way Gloucester and Kent continue to behave towards Lear. The mock trial is a parody of the 'love-test' in I.1. Here, however, Lear's judgement is not faulty. His madness has helped him to see his daughters clearly. The Fool speaks his last line in the play, 'And I'll go to bed at noon' (line 83). This comically mad remark is an appropriate summing up of this scene. This phrase meant 'to act the fool'. Other commentators feel that the Fool is perhaps referring to an early death. Again, this is appropriate, and not simply to the Fool. It has now been confirmed that Lear's life is in danger.

Nero a corrupt, lascivious Roman emperor, reputedly insane

Frateretto another dancing devil from Harsnet

piece out add to

Bessy the subject of a popular song at the time

Hoppedance another dancing devil from Harsnet

yokefellow of equity partner in law

minikin either shrill or attractive, sweet

brach bitch

lym bloodhound

trundle-tail curly tailed dog

thy horn is dry Bedlam beggars used horns for begging drinks. The suggestion here is that Edgar is 'worn out', empty. He is exhausted by playing the part of Poor Tom and by observing Lear's distressing madness

a litter coach or portable bed

o'erskip avoid

high noises reports of goings on amongst the important people

bewray uncover, reveal oneself

Lurk, lurk stay concealed, in hiding

SCENE 7 Cornwall and Regan take out their horrible revenge on Gloucester

Cornwall tells Gonerill to return to Albany and show him Gloucester's letter (containing the news of the French invasion). He expects Albany to join forces with him. Cornwall then tells his servants to seek out Gloucester. Regan says Gloucester should be hanged immediately, while Gonerill prefers a more vicious form of torture – the plucking out of his eyes. Edmund is sent to accompany Gonerill on her journey home. We know Gloucester will suffer horribly when Cornwall says to Edmund, 'the revenges we are bound to take upon your traitorous father are not fit for your beholding' (lines 7–9). Cornwall calls Edmund 'My lord of Gloucester' (line 14), sealing the old earl's fate. Gloucester is not expected to survive his punishment. Oswald brings news that Gloucester has helped Lear escape to Dover with thirty-five or six of his loyal knights. In a reversal of the way justice should work, Cornwall proposes to pass sentence on Gloucester without trial.

Gloucester is brought in. He knows that his guests mean to harm him. Regan speaks to him venomously, and disrespectfully plucks him by the beard – a foretaste of the violence to come. Gloucester is tied to a chair, and asks fearfully, 'What will you do?' (line 41). He compares himself to a bear in the sport of bear-baiting; he is tied to a stake while the dogs savage him. He must endure. He says that he sent Lear to Dover because he could not bear to see him tortured by Gonerill and Regan. Gloucester also describes Lear's sufferings out in the 'hell-black night' (line 59) of the storm. When Gloucester says he hopes to see 'The wingèd Vengeance overtake such children' (line 65), Cornwall gouges out one of Gloucester's eyes. Regan urges her husband to pluck out his other eye.

One of Cornwall's servants steps in. Appalled by what he sees, he bids Cornwall stop. The two men draw their swords and fight and Cornwall is wounded. Regan takes a sword from another servant and runs the challenger through. In spite of his wound, Cornwall finds the strength to put out Gloucester's other eye, mocking his victim. Gloucester hopes that Edmund will revenge him. Regan taunts Gloucester, informing the old man that Edmund hates his father. Gloucester recognises that he has been deceived and calls on the gods to protect Edgar and forgive him for doubting his true son. Regan tells servants to 'thrust' Gloucester 'out at gates and let him smell / His way to Dover' (lines 92–3). She then helps her wounded husband from the stage. Two servants decide to help Gloucester and fetch some medicine to soothe his wounded eyes. They want to take him to Poor Tom, who can act as his guide.

This scene contains one of the most shocking acts of physical violence in any of Shakespeare's plays. The physical torture here matches the mental agony Lear has endured in Act III. There are many references to eyes and sight that increase the tension we feel and prepare us for Gloucester's blinding, beginning with Gonerill's 'Pluck out his eyes' (line 5). Even though she does not take part in Gloucester's maiming, her suggestion implicates Gonerill in this crime. Like Lear, Gloucester achieves heroism through suffering. Like Kent, he suffers because he has tried to help Lear. In this scene, which contains some of his most powerful speeches in the play, Gloucester is eloquent, brave and determined as he defends himself and castigates Cornwall and Regan for their cruelty to the king. The Earl becomes the voice of the audience, describing their outrage. Like Lear, Gloucester learns the truth about his children in a particularly brutal way. He also shares Lear's agony when he discovers that he has been taken in by outward appearances. The barbarism of the whole scene is summed up by Regan's final callous order to the servants.

The cruelty of this scene indicates that the world has been turned upside down in *King Lear*. A woman suggests a method of torture, another woman relishes inflicting pain, egging her husband on to further cruelty before killing a man herself. There is another miscarriage of justice. A servant turns on his master. This act of heroism prepares us for the kindness the servants show Gloucester at the end of the scene. Although the play has reached its lowest point before the tragic final scene, the generous actions of the servants in III.7 indicate that there is some kind of justice at work.

festinate swift

hot questrists followers, who are seeking Lear urgently

quicken bind by the arms

anointed flesh this is a reference to Lear's status as God's deputy on earth, who rules by divine right (a Christian idea which is at odds with the pagan setting of the play). At the coronation monarchs were anointed with holy oil, reconfirming their sacred status

dern awful, dreadful

All cruels else subscribe there are different interpretations of this line. It might mean that Gonerill and Regan would have allowed any cruel or wild beast into the castle on such a stormy night, but not Lear (emphasising their cruelty). Or perhaps the line suggests that on this terrible night any other cruel creature would have pitied Lear and given him shelter, but not his barbaric daughters

flax a plant grown for its textile fibre which could be spun into linen thread, used here to make a poultice or covering for Gloucester's wounds

ACT IV

SCENE 1 Edgar comes across his blind, suicidal father and starts to lead him to Dover

Edgar considers the merits of being a poor, despised outcast. At least a beggar has nothing to lose or fear – he cannot sink any lower. Gloucester is led on by an old man, and Edgar's fragile optimism is shattered.

Gloucester suffers deeply. He tells the old man to leave, concerned that he will be punished for helping him. Gloucester says he has lost his way in life and wishes to 'see' Edgar again, so that he can ask for his forgiveness. This moves Edgar, whose lines reflect the despair his father feels. Gloucester offers a dark view of the world and those who rule man's fate, 'As flies to wanton boys are we to the gods; / They kill us for their sport' (lines 36–7).

The old man calls to Edgar/ Poor Tom to assist Gloucester. Edgar is torn between continuing with his disguise and revealing his identity. Gloucester begs the old man to fetch some clothes for Poor Tom. The old man is doubtful about leaving Gloucester alone with Tom, but Gloucester says that it is appropriate for a lunatic to lead a blind man. He asks Tom to lead him to Dover, and gives him money for his services. Edgar is still distressed and has difficulty in maintaining his disguise.

Like Lear, Gloucester is preoccupied by thoughts of justice. He hopes the rich man, who has too much and 'will not see / Because he does not feel' (lines 67–8), will have his eyes opened by the gods. He suggests that man needs to be stripped of his excess wealth in order to see clearly. He says that wealth should be distributed more evenly so that 'each man have enough' (line 70). Gloucester's final speech conveys his desire to die. He promises Edgar further financial reward if he leads him 'to the very brim' (line 74) of the cliff. We understand that he intends to attempt suicide.

At the start of the scene Edgar seems to feel positive; his experiences have taught him to withstand the 'blasts' (line 9) of Fortune. Like Gloucester and Lear, he is learning to endure. Gloucester's stoicism is severely tested in IV.1. His view of the sadistic gods shows us clearly that he has been pushed to the limits of endurance. Are we to accept Gloucester's verdict as an accurate description of the world of *King Lear*? Or is his pessimism a reflection of his current state of mind? At his most desolate, Gloucester acts generously towards others, speaking graciously to the old man and Poor Tom. He seems more concerned with their fortunes than his own. If the gods are cruel, this scene proves again that man can be kind. Gloucester's interest in social justice reflects Lear's, and proves that the patriarchs have learned to see the world clearly. As Gloucester says so aptly; he 'stumbled' (line 19) when he saw. For Gloucester, clarity of vision brings despair. Edgar's role in this scene is to guide our responses to his father's misery.

Mutations changes
daub cover up, pretend
Obdicut, Hobbididence more demons, probably from Harsnet
ordinance will or divine rule

SCENE 2 Gonerill and Edmund return to Gonerill's residence. Albany accuses Gonerill of cruelty to her father. He also learns of the blinding of Gloucester

Gonerill and Edmund have returned from Gloucester's castle. Gonerill is surprised that her husband has not come out to greet them. Oswald tells her that Albany has undergone a radical change of heart. He is glad of the French invasion and appalled by Edmund's treachery to his father. Gonerill says her husband is a coward. She tells Edmund to return to Cornwall to help with the preparations for battle. Gonerill offers herself to Edmund.

She says that she will shortly command him as his mistress. Edmund pledges his loyalty to her.

Albany appears and Gonerill greets him sarcastically. In return, Albany is eloquent in his denigration of Gonerill. She is a devil. The sisters have behaved like 'Tigers not daughters' (line 40). Gonerill coolly disregards these insults. Albany's language becomes more violent as he describes how he would like to tear Gonerill limb from limb. A messenger arrives with the news that Cornwall has died. Albany says this is just and shows sympathy for Gloucester. The messenger also has a letter for Gonerill, from Regan. Gonerill is suspicious of her sister. She is concerned that Regan will seek to marry Edmund. The sisters are now rivals for Edmund's love. In spite of her concerns, Gonerill does not seem unduly alarmed. She leaves to read and answer Regan's letter.

Albany is still thinking about Gloucester. He asks the messenger where Edmund was when Gloucester was tortured. On learning the truth he resolves to revenge Gloucester and support Lear's cause.

> The change in Albany suggests that the influence of the evil characters will no longer go unchecked. Albany becomes a figure of justice and morality in this scene, voicing the audience's concerns about his wife. Gonerill continues to assume authority, disregarding her husband and wooing Edmund. Her desires and actions are subversive and immoral. We are presented with a clash between good (Albany) and evil (Gonerill), which points towards the battle between the French and British forces at the end of Act IV.

Musters calling together or recruiting troops of soldiers
conduct lead, head
distaff the stick used to spin wool (a female pursuit. Gonerill implies she's more a man than her husband: he is only fit for woman's work)
head-lugged a bear pulled along by its head
self-covered disguised
tart bitter (in the sense of bad tasting)

SCENE 3 Kent and the Gentleman speak of Cordelia, and how Lear is too ashamed to see her

Kent asks a Gentleman why the King of France has returned home. We learn that he had urgent state business to attend to. Kent asks the

Gentleman how Cordelia reacted when she read his letters (describing Lear's treatment at the hands of Gonerill and Regan). We are told that 'holy water' fell from her 'heavenly eyes' (line 30) as she lamented Lear's plight. Kent reports Lear's arrival in Dover. The king is now sometimes 'in his better tune' (line 39) but so ashamed of his 'unkindness' (line 42) to Cordelia that he will not see her. The Gentleman says that Albany and Cornwall's forces are 'afoot' (line 49). Kent takes him to attend on Lear.

This scene prepares us for Cordelia's return. Lear's youngest daughter is now the epitome of graceful, Christian femininity, described as compassionate and loving. We know that the reconciliation between Lear and Cordelia will be painful and poignant. Lear has started to regain his wits, but clarity of vision brings with it distress and regret. Father and daughter now share the same emotion: sorrow.

clamour, moistened there are two possible meanings: either that Cordelia is so overcome her speech is stopped by her tears, or that she was crying while she spoke

better tune in his right mind

casualties chances (Cordelia was left to take her chance abroad in France when Lear rejected her)

afoot marching on their way

SCENE 4 Cordelia sends her soldiers to search for Lear, who is still wandering around outside. She expresses deep concern for her father

Cordelia describes how Lear has been seen, mad and singing, wearing a crown of flowers and weeds. She sends one hundred soldiers out to find Lear and calls on the earth to help restore him. A messenger informs her that the British army is drawing closer. To allay any fears the audience might have of a foreign invasion, Cordelia insists that she has come to defend Lear's rights; she is motivated by love, not political ambition. She hopes fervently that she will soon see and hear Lear.

Lear's crown of weeds has symbolic significance. The king is now associated with nature rather than the world of the court, which is fitting given his interest in justice and the human condition.

In keeping with the descriptions of her in the previous scene, Cordelia shows great compassion for her father. He is her sole concern. Like Edgar, she actively assists the parent who rejected her so cruelly.

fumiter fumitory (a weed)
furrow-weeds the weeds that grow in fields that have been ploughed. All the weeds Lear is wearing are poisonous or bitter tasting. Weeds are also destructive. They are appropriate to his current state
importuned appears as 'important' in the Quarto, beseeching

SCENE 5 Regan interrogates Oswald about a letter he is carrying from Gonerill to Edmund

Regan asks Oswald why Gonerill has written to Edmund. She tries to persuade him to show her the letter he is carrying. She tells Oswald that Edmund has ridden away to finish off Gloucester and find out how strong the French forces are. Regan also admits that it was a mistake to let Gloucester live: people who have heard of his cruel treatment have turned against her. She tries to prevent Oswald's departure, saying 'the ways are dangerous' (line 27). However, Oswald is as diligent as ever and insists that he must go. Regan asks again to see the letter and then adopts a threatening tone. She and Edmund have talked, and agreed on marriage. Gonerill must be warned off. Regan gives Oswald a letter or gift for Edmund and asks him to deliver it. She casually mentions the fact that there is a reward for anyone who kills Gloucester.

Regan's preoccupation with her own selfish lust contrasts sharply with Cordelia's generosity in the previous scene. Throughout Act IV Lear's daughters are juxtaposed, scene by scene. We watch the progress of both good and evil. The language Regan uses to describe her liaison with Edmund is entirely in keeping with the materialistic desires of the evil characters; Edmund is 'more convenient' (line 31) for her than Gonerill. It seems that Gonerill and Regan are now divided by their rivalry in love, while the good characters share the same aims and appear to be gathering strength. The fact that people are appalled by Gloucester's blinding suggests that we might be justified in hoping that evil might be vanquished.

nighted darkened
descry discover, find out
oeillades loving looks

Scene 6 Gloucester tries to commit suicide at Dover. Lear and Gloucester meet for the last time. Edgar saves Gloucester's life when Oswald threatens him

Edgar leads Gloucester to Dover. He pretends they are labouring up a steep hill to the cliff top and asks Gloucester if he can hear the sea. Gloucester's other senses are more acute now that he is blind; he thinks he is walking on even ground and has also noticed that Edgar speaks differently. Edgar dismisses these ideas. He describes the view from the cliff top. Pretending to feel dizzy, Edgar says they are so high up it is impossible to hear the sea. Gloucester asks to be moved to the edge of the cliff. He gives his peasant guide a jewel as payment for his services. Edgar informs us that he has deceived Gloucester in order to 'cure' (line 34) his despair. Kneeling, Gloucester announces to the gods that he intends to kill himself. The pain he feels is too much for him. His final generous thoughts are of his son Edgar and the beggar who has helped him. There follows the extraordinary sight of Gloucester throwing himself off the imaginary cliff and falling on the ground. Edgar worries that Gloucester's desire to kill himself might actually have caused his death.

When Gloucester revives he is still suicidal. Pretending to be a passerby on the beach, Edgar now tries to chase away his father's gloomy thoughts. He tells him his life must have been preserved by a miracle. Gloucester is wretched when he hears Edgar's description of his 'fall'; he has been unable to find comfort in death and feels the gods have thwarted him. Edgar persists. He urges Gloucester to stand and helps him up. He describes the strange creature on the cliff top, implying that a devil drove his father to attempt suicide. Edgar tries desperately to convince his father that the kind gods have saved him. This explanation seems to forge a change of heart in Gloucester, who now declares that he will endure life until life itself gives up on him.

Lear enters, wearing his crown of weeds. Edgar is appalled to see that his mind is still ravaged. Lear speaks in a disjointed way, about money, justice and archery. He insists that he is 'the King himself' (line 84) and declares he will defend himself against anyone, even a giant. Gloucester recognises Lear's voice and a strange, cruel exchange ensues. Lear mistakes Gloucester for Gonerill 'with a white beard' (line 96) and launches into a tirade against female sexuality. Lear's fear of monstrous femininity also leads him to introduce the topic of Gloucester's adultery. Perhaps one part of his fevered brain recognises his old friend. There is a cruel irony in Lear's lines about Gloucester's 'kind' bastard son. The cruelty continues as Lear seems to mock the old Earl's blindness, talking about blind Cupid and asking Gloucester to read a summons he has drawn up. Gloucester responds to Lear with pity and reverence. As Lear taunts him he begs to be allowed to kiss the king's hand.

Lear is obsessed with social and moral justice. He talks about how thieves are condemned by corrupt justices of the peace. But with a bribe the justice will let the thief off, so who is the real thief? Authority is a sham: even a dog is obeyed in office because of his status. Lear then seems to see hypocrites appearing before him; a beadle who whips a prostitute but lusts after her himself, a money lender who hangs a petty cheat. Lear disparages rich sinners who are able to break the 'strong lance of justice' (line 167), while beggars cannot escape punishment for their crimes because they have no money to make bribes. Lear seems to have reached radical conclusions about human justice. He wants to defend the poor and give them power.

Lear offers Gloucester something to 'seal th'accuser's lips' (line 171). Perhaps he wants Gloucester to bribe a justice to look leniently on one of the poor sinners he has described. He then advises Gloucester to get glasses so that he can act like a cunning politician, who conjures up intrigues to justify his actions. Lear asks Gloucester to pull off his boots. He acknowledges his friend in two lines of perfect sense, telling him to be patient. Lear then offers a pessimistic assessment of the human condition: it is man's lot to suffer and endure.

At this point Cordelia's attendants arrive. Lear seems to see them as hostile figures and runs off. The attendants pursue him while the Gentleman remains behind. Edgar asks him for news of the battle that is expected between the French and British forces. Gloucester's encounter with Lear seems to have driven away thoughts of suicide. Lear's appalling condition has made him realise that his own suffering is not so unendurable. Edgar says he will lead Gloucester to a safe place.

As they prepare to leave, Oswald comes upon Edgar and Gloucester. He is delighted because he will now be able to claim Regan's reward. Gloucester welcomes Oswald's sword. Assuming the accent of a country bumpkin, Edgar challenges Oswald, who is fatally wounded in the fight. In his dying speech Oswald asks Edgar to take the letters he is carrying to Edmund. Regretting that he had to act as Oswald's 'deathsman' (line 258), Edgar sums up the self-seeking servant neatly as the corrupt follower of an evil mistress. He reads the letters and discovers Gonerill's plot against Albany's life. Shocked, he decides to inform Albany of the contents of the letter when the time is right. He drags Oswald's body offstage for burial. Meanwhile Gloucester is preoccupied by thoughts of Lear's lunacy. He wishes he could be mad like Lear, believing that madness would distract him from his agony. In spite of the stoicism he has shown in Act IV, Gloucester finds it very difficult to maintain cheerful thoughts. Edgar returns to escort his father to safety at the French camp. A drum roll suggests the battle is imminent.

Edgar's description of the view from the cliff top serves two purposes; to convince his father that he stands on the edge of the cliff and to show Gloucester's desperation. His **aside** at line 42 hints at the terror created by Gloucester's attempted suicide, which can seem both tragic and absurd in performance. As previously, he guides our responses to Gloucester. Edgar says very little when Lear is on stage, offering brief asides. His words emphasise the **pathos** of the exchange between Lear and Gloucester. Both patriarchs seem worn out, but they 'see how this world / goes' (line 148–9) now. They have achieved understanding and wisdom through suffering. Lear's lines about adultery might be read as an attempt to come to terms with his own sexual union with his daughters' mother – did he cause those hard hearts? Lear also seems to be playing the same role for Gloucester that the Fool played for him. He is a cruel commentator in this scene. His obsession with justice fits in with his earlier concern for 'unaccommodated man' (III.4.103).

At the end of the scene Edgar takes on a more active role when he defends his father. He will play the role of revenger again in V.3. His energetic goodness offers us hope. It seems that Gloucester and Lear's pessimism about the human condition is not entirely justified.

choughs crows
sampire samphire, a plant that grows on cliffs, used by Elizabethans as a vegetable and in pickles
snuff the wick of a burnt out candle
gossamer a light fine silk
welked twisted
press money the money paid to new recruits, who had probably been press-ganged into the army
i' the clout on target
sweet marjoram a herb that was used for treating diseases of the brain
forks legs
fitchen polecat (also a slang term for a prostitute)
centaurs a mythical creature, half man, half horse, which had a reputation for lust
civet a strong musky perfume
beadle a parish constable
cozener cheat
costard apple (meaning Oswald's head here)
ballow stick, cudgel
foins the thrusts of Oswald's weapon

SCENE 7 Cordelia and Lear are reunited and reconciled

Lear has been brought to the French camp near Dover. Cordelia thanks Kent for his services. Modest as ever, Kent says he does not need repayment. Cordelia urges him to put aside his disguise but he says he still needs it. We learn that Lear is asleep. Cordelia prays to 'the kind gods' (line 14) to restore her father's senses. The Doctor says it is time to wake Lear, who has been dressed in fresh garments while sleeping. The old king is carried on in a chair and all the characters on stage prostrate themselves before him. The Doctor calls for music. Before Lear wakes Cordelia kneels by his chair, hoping that her kiss will make up for some of the 'violent harms' (line 28) done by her sisters.

Lear wakes up. He is bewildered and thinks he is in hell, 'bound / Upon a wheel of fire' (lines 47–8). He does not seem to recognise his daughter, who asks for his blessing. Lear falls on his knees before her, showing that he regrets wronging Cordelia. He sees himself clearly as 'a very foolish fond old man' (line 60). Cordelia denies that she has any reason to feel bitter towards her father. She asks Lear if he would like to walk with her. Father and daughter leave the stage together. Kent and the Gentleman remain behind to discuss the battle. Edmund has been put in charge of Cornwall's men. A bloody confrontation is expected.

This is a scene of **pathos** and renewal. Sleep and music were understood to have powerful healing properties. Our sense of restoration is heightened when the characters kneel before Lear, who is treated as a powerful monarch. All the words addressed to him are respectful and he sits 'above' his subjects once more. However, we quickly realise that Lear is not the towering figure he once was. His speeches are hesitant, and he humbles himself before Cordelia. He no longer speaks of himself as the royal 'we'. Lear understands that he sinned against his youngest daughter and wishes to honour her. He does not accept responsibility for Gonerill and Regan, however. They are now identified (in Cordelia's lines before Lear awakes) as the sole cause of the king's suffering. We are expected to view Lear as a victim now. Certainly, this is the view Lear holds himself. His lines are full of self-pity. This scene comes as an immense relief after the chaos and darkness of Acts III and IV, although news of the battle suggests the harmony that is achieved here is already under threat.

weeds clothes
perdu lost one
arbitrament outcome of the battle

ACT V

SCENE 1 Regan questions Edmund about his feelings for Gonerill. Edgar gives Albany the letter disclosing Edmund and Gonerill's plot against his life. Edmund says he will show Lear and Cordelia no mercy after the battle

Act V opens with preparations for the clash between the British and French armies. Edmund begins decisively, complaining to Regan that Albany keeps changing his plans. Regan fears that something has happened to Oswald. She asks Edmund if he loves Gonerill. Albany and Gonerill arrive with Albany's forces. Seeing Regan and Edmund together, Gonerill says she would rather lose the battle than Edmund. Albany speaks sympathetically about the reasons for the French invasion but Gonerill insists that they must all unite against the enemy now. Albany agrees and says that they must consult 'th'ancient of war' (experienced campaigners – line 32) about the best way to proceed in battle. Edmund agrees to discuss strategy in Albany's tent. Regan asks Gonerill to accompany them. She refuses. Gonerill realises Regan is concerned about leaving her alone with Edmund. But then she changes her mind and goes with the others. As Albany makes to leave, Edgar (still disguised) appears and asks to speak with him. He gives Albany the letter he found on Oswald and tells him to open it before going into battle. He asks Albany to have a trumpet sounded if Britain wins the battle, so that a champion may appear to prove the truth of the contents of the letter.

Edmund returns with the news that the French are approaching. Left alone on stage he muses about his predicament. He has sworn his love to both Gonerill and Regan, and cannot decide which one to 'take' (line 57). He knows the sisters are so jealous that one will have to die in order for him to 'enjoy' the other. Edmund decides to wait and see what happens in the battle. He informs us that Albany intends to show mercy to Lear and Cordelia if the British win. But Edmund has other plans for them. They must die.

This is a scene of uneasiness and some urgency. Gonerill and Regan's feud over Edmund continues, Gonerill and Albany are at odds, and Albany and Edmund clearly share different intentions about the battle and its outcome. Edmund's brief responses to Regan suggest his impatience or discomfort with love talk. In his first **soliloquy** he reveals his callous approach to matrimony, which matches the ruthlessness he has shown in all his dealings with others in *King Lear*. His only loyalty is to himself. His last three lines suggest that Edmund revels in his newly exalted position and power. We fear the outcome of the battle and wonder how the rivalry between Gonerill and Regan will be resolved.

forfended forbidden
conjunct intimate with
bosomed with embraced by
broils arguments, quarrel

SCENE 2 The French forces are defeated in battle. Edgar leads Gloucester to safety for the last time

Cordelia, Lear and the French forces march across the stage, and Edgar leads Gloucester on, bringing him to a safe place while the battle rages. He leaves briefly and then returns with the news that the French have lost. Lear and Cordelia have been captured. Overcome by pessimistic thoughts, Gloucester refuses to leave with Edgar, who chides him. He implies that man should not sit and 'rot' as Gloucester says he wishes to. He must prepare himself for death and await the moment chosen for him. Gloucester allows himself to be led away.

The battle is dealt with perfunctorily. Shakespeare is most interested in its consequences. We get an indication of what is to occur in the final scene when Edgar says, 'Men must endure / Their going hence even as their coming hither;/ Ripeness is all' (lines 9–11). Gloucester still wishes to die, and we know that Lear (now a prisoner) is in great danger. Both old men have endured more than enough. The tragic stoicism of these lines prepares us for the outcome of V.3.

Ripeness readiness

SCENE 3 Lear and Cordelia are sent away to prison. Edmund sends a death warrant after them. Albany accuses Gonerill and Edmund of treason and Edgar appears to challenge Edmund. Edmund is fatally wounded in the fight. Gonerill poisons Regan, and stabs herself. Lear carries on the dead body of Cordelia and dies, mourning her

Signalling the triumph of evil, Edmund leads on his prisoners to the sound of drums. He orders officers to take Lear and Cordelia away. Cordelia expresses her dismay at being captured, but couches it in terms of compassion for Lear. She asks Edmund whether she and Lear will see Gonerill and Regan. Lear is horrified; he cannot bear the idea of setting eyes on his eldest daughters again. Instead he says he would be pleased to go to prison with Cordelia. He imagines imprisonment as a time of happiness away from the superficial cares of the court. He embraces Cordelia protectively. She is his only concern, as he is hers. Cordelia is crying. Lear tells her to wipe away her tears, and offers a defiant view of his new bond with his daughter.

Lear and Cordelia are escorted to prison. Edmund orders a captain to follow them and gives him a death warrant. It seems that Edmund is now aiming at the crown. However, he has underestimated Albany, who now enters with Gonerill, Regan and officers. After briefly praising Edmund's courage in battle, Albany demands to see the prisoners. Edmund hedges. Lear and Cordelia will be ready to appear for judgement in two or three days. For once, his eloquence fails him. Albany interrupts icily with a rebuke, telling Edmund he is his subject, not his 'brother' (equal) and should be ruled by him. This annoys Regan, who defends Edmund. The sisters start to squabble. Gonerill says Edmund's personal merits 'exalt' (line 61) him; he doesn't need any title Regan can confer on him to make him worthy. Regan announces her intention of marrying Edmund. Albany insults Edmund as 'Half-blooded' (line 81) and arrests him for treason.

Albany then sounds the trumpet to call Edmund's accuser. He announces his own willingness to challenge Edmund. We now learn that Gonerill has poisoned Regan, who complains of feeling increasingly unwell. Edmund remains defiant. He declares his intention to 'maintain / My truth and honour firmly' '(lines 101–2). Regan is carried away sick. On the third trumpet Edgar appears, armed. He accuses Edmund of betraying Albany, 'thy gods, thy brother, and thy father' (line 132). Edmund is impressed by Edgar's 'fair and warlike' (line 140) exterior, and agrees to fight. He is wounded. Dismayed, Gonerill says the fight was unlawful. Albany confronts her with her letter to Edmund. Gonerill tries to tear it up; like her paramour, she is defiant to the last. She tries a last desperate attempt at asserting her power before running off.

As he lies dying, Edmund confesses his crimes. He says he will forgive his adversary if he is a nobleman. Edgar puts aside his disguise. He judges Edmund and his father harshly. Edmund admits the justice of Edgar's remarks and stoically accepts his own death. Albany embraces Edgar. Edgar then recounts his own history since the play began, including his attempts to keep Gloucester from despair. He regrets remaining in disguise so long. He is particularly distressed when he describes Gloucester's death. It seems that his reunion with Edgar was too much for Gloucester, whose heart, ''Twixt two extremes of passion, joy and grief, / Burst smilingly' (lines 196–7). Albany is overwhelmed by this tale of woe, but Edmund says it has moved him, 'and shall perchance do good' (line 198).

The final movement of the play begins when the Gentleman enters carrying a bloody knife. Gonerill has killed herself and Regan too is dead. Kent comes to 'bid my King and master aye good night' (line 233). Kent's words bring Albany to a stark realisation – he has forgotten all about Lear. He urgently asks Edmund where he sent Lear and Cordelia. Gonerill and Regan's bodies are dragged on to the stage. A moment of panic ensues as Albany and Edmund try to establish how to repeal the death warrant, but it is much too late.

As Edmund is carried off to die, Lear comes in with Cordelia's body in his arms. He is distraught and asks for a feather to place on Cordelia's lips. He hopes that his daughter still breathes. Kent asks in horror, 'Is this the promised end?' (line 261). Lear calls all those around him murderers and traitors for allowing Cordelia to die. We learn that he committed one last act of heroism in his daughter's defence: he killed her hangman. Lear then seems to tumble into madness again; his eyesight fails him, all his senses give up the fight to live. Kent tells Lear of Gonerill and Regan's deaths, but this has no effect on the grieving man. A messenger brings news that Edmund has died.

Albany says that he intends resigning his power to Lear. He also says that Edgar and Kent will receive back their rights as earls, and be rewarded with new honours. Lear continues to grieve over Cordelia's corpse. Choking, he asks someone to undo his button. Edgar rushes to his aid but Kent tells him to let be; Lear will welcome death after the sufferings of his life. Sorrowfully, he adds that he too expects to die soon. He brushes off Albany's suggestions about sharing power and ruling Britain. Lear dies, perhaps believing that Cordelia still lives. Albany and Edgar are left to sustain the 'gored' (line 318) state. Edgar calls on everyone to speak plainly and honestly and acknowledge their grief. He also says the survivors 'Shall never see so much nor live so long' (line 324), suggesting that lives of those who remain have been shattered by the events of V.3.

Events occur swiftly in this tragic final scene, which is dominated by violent deaths. There is a brief moment of hope when Lear describes his life with Cordelia in prison, but his dreams are revealed as an illusion almost immediately. Thereafter, sorrow and pain are emphasised, even though the evil characters' plots are uncovered and Albany and Edgar insist on justice. The final devastating effects of

Edmund's evil influence are felt in this scene. It is possible to argue that he is responsible for the deaths of the whole royal family, as well as his father's fate. His own death is, as Edgar seems to suggest, richly deserved. The same can be said of Gonerill and Regan's deaths.

It is hard to feel that justice is served when Cordelia's corpse is carried on, however. The good characters may have drawn together and asserted themselves, but they are unable to restore order in the way that they wish. Albany's offer to resign power might be seen as an ill-timed and futile gesture, a distraction from Lear's grief. In spite of his valour, Edgar has been unable to preserve his father's life. The final doleful lines of the play do not provide a sense of hope for the future. We are left exhausted and numb, like the characters.

As usual, Kent's tone is appropriate to the occasion. His sorrowful stoicism strikes the right note. Kent has no desire to live after his master has lost the battle, and when Lear appears himself, we know that optimism of any kind is out of place. The agony of Lear's first words, 'Howl, howl, howl! O, you are men of stones!' (line 255) expresses the misery of all the characters on stage. The repetition in Lear's lines reveals the extent of his grief and suggests that Cordelia's death is an unendurable blow. We must agree with Kent's assessment that Lear will find release in death. Like Gloucester, he dies feeling both joy and pain. We may feel that the outcome of *King Lear* is not entirely just, but it is in many ways appropriate. All those who have sinned have certainly been punished.

gilded butterflies Lear is referring to superficial courtiers
attaint accused by
banns wedding banns, read publicly in church to announce a forthcoming marriage
canker-bit worm eaten
cope face, fight
maugre despite
An interlude! How entertaining! (An interlude was a short, comic play performed in the period before Shakespeare was writing)
falchion sword

PART THREE

CRITICAL APPROACHES

CHARACTERISATION

Although characters are presented as individuals it is important to remember that some are based on familiar dramatic types from Renaissance drama. Edmund is partly **malcontent**, **Machiavellian** villain, the Fool is 'all-licensed' jester, whose role it is to comment on the action. Because of the functions they serve in the plot, characters sometimes appear to act inconsistently. For example, Edmund decides to do good at the end of the play. Why? He says he is moved by Edgar's description of Gloucester's death. But we must not forget that Shakespeare needs Edmund to act virtuously in order to increase dramatic tension – will Cordelia and Lear be spared?

Shakespeare is not primarily concerned with motives; he is more interested in the effects of characters' decisions and natures. In *King Lear* he focuses on the tragic consequences of two fathers' actions, and how events shape their characters. During the course of the play the other characters also change and grow; some are good and become better, others are bad and become more depraved. Lear and Gloucester are exceptions. Neither is good or bad in a straightforward way. Lear's **characterisation** is particularly complex. He is not a tragic hero with a single tragic flaw which causes his downfall. Nor is his growth a simple movement from ignorance to knowledge. When he emerges from his madness Lear may have learned a great deal, but doubts remain about the depth of his understanding. Our responses to Lear are complex too. He is infuriating in Act I Scene 1, becoming increasingly sympathetic as he suffers.

It is also worth remembering that interpretations of character cannot be set in stone. Each age sees the characters through its own eyes, and each time *King Lear* is performed on stage, directors and actors bring their own ideas to the text. Thus it is possible to have a range of Lears, Cordelias, Edmunds. As a reader you need to focus on what characters say, the language they use, and how they interact.

LEAR

As suggested above, Lear is a complex tragic hero, who excites a variety of responses. Watching his disastrous actions of I.1 it is hard not to feel that Lear deserves punishment for his folly. He displays many traits designed to alienate an audience. Quick to vituperative anger when displeased and too arrogant to take advice, Lear is blind and irresponsible as father and ruler. His 'darker purpose' would have alarmed the Jacobean audience, who would remember how the taxing question of the succession had loomed large during the reign of Elizabeth I. Lear attempts to divide power from responsibility. He is preoccupied with appearances. If he can retain the trappings of majesty without the 'cares and business' of ruling he is content. We realise early how false his values are. It is also possible to see his desire to rely on Cordelia's 'kind nursery' (I.1.124) as selfish. He intends marrying her off in I.1 but expects to be nursed while he crawls 'unburdened' (I.1.41) towards death. Lear is both tyrannical patriarch and demanding child at the start of the play.

And yet we sympathise with this egotistical autocrat. In Act II Lear's better qualities are revealed. His hiring of Kent/Caius is a sign that Lear inspires loyalty, and his interaction with the Fool shows a more tolerant side to his nature. It also becomes clear that Lear is trying to remain calm even when he feels he is being wronged (I.4.56–70). In the next scene Lear recognises that he has behaved foolishly and treated Cordelia unkindly (I.5.24). As his insight and troubles grow, so does our concern. We begin to share his outrage as Gonerill and Regan become more repugnant. There is desperation as well as egotism in his confrontation with his 'dog-hearted' (IV.3.00) daughters in II.4. Gradually Lear's rages become signs of impotence, not authority. By the time he rushes out into the storm our sympathies are likely to lie – and remain – with the beleaguered king.

Many critics see Lear's insanity as a learning process. Lear needs to suffer to improve his understanding of himself and the society in which he lives. Certainly he considers a number of topics he paid little attention to: the wretched condition of the poor, the corrupt justice system, true necessity. He learns to distinguish between appearances and reality and considers the sufferings of those close to him. Lear also becomes much more self-critical. He emerges from his torment a more humble, loving and attractive character.

However, other commentators suggest that Lear remains self-obsessed and vengeful. His philosophical enquiries on the heath are punctuated by thoughts of punishing Gonerill and Regan. Again and again he returns to the crimes committed against him. He struggles to accept responsibility for his elder daughters' cruel natures and never fully acknowledges the folly of his actions of I.1.

We are not allowed to remain too critical though. His reconciliation with Cordelia shows the best of Lear. Ashamed of his former unkindness, he humbles himself before his youngest daughter, acknowledging her superiority. We can forgive him now focusing on the way he has been abused. At the end of the play Lear seems to move beyond himself. He has certainly accepted his powerless, diminished status and now sees himself primarily as Cordelia's father. His language reflects his progress. Gone is the royal 'we'. Now Lear uses the first person when he speaks of himself and his feelings. Cordelia is reclaimed lovingly as 'my Cordelia' (V.3.20). In Act V Lear clings to his 'best object' (I.1.214) protectively. He revenges her death by killing the 'slave' responsible for hanging her. In all of his speeches in V.3 the dying king focuses on Cordelia and the overwhelming grief he feels at her passing. Lear's love for and defence of Cordelia go a long way to redeeming him from charges of egotism. Lear has clearly learned the value of true emotion. His recognition of the injustice of Cordelia's death suggests that his judgement has been restored (V.3.304–5). But wisdom comes too late. Watching the final bleak moments of the play it is easy to feel that Lear's sufferings have been in vain.

GONERILL AND REGAN

Lear's elder daughters are very subversive figures. Initially, Gonerill seems to be the dominant sister. She decides that something must be done to ensure that Lear's rough treatment of Cordelia does not extend to Regan and herself. It is also Gonerill who raises the issue of Lear's knights and provokes the first confrontation with her father in I.4. Up to this point Regan seems happy to follow Gonerill's course of action. But we get hints of her particular brand of sadism in II.2 when she urges Cornwall to inflict further punishment on Kent. And then in II.4 she leads the onslaught against Lear. The sisters are now vicious equals. Both participate in what is for many the most horrific scene in the play, the blinding of Gloucester.

Gonerill suggests the method of torture, 'Pluck out his … eyes!' (III.7.56), and then Regan assaults Gloucester, egging her husband on to further cruelty.

Gonerill and Regan share many character traits. Both are threatening and autocratic, cold and ambitious. Both lust after Edmund in a predatory and unfeminine way. They are masculine in other ways. Gonerill denies Albany's authority and arrogantly asserts her own power when she says, 'the laws are mine, not thine' (V.3.156). Regan may not be an adulteress, but she is a murderess, like her sister. She does man's work when she runs the servant through in III.7. Gonerill and Regan's vindictive assertiveness would have been particularly shocking to a Jacobean audience. Renaissance models of femininity required women to be quiet and submissive. Lear's daughters subvert all the accepted codes of feminine behaviour. They set out to destroy the family and the state. They are agents of chaos and misrule. The terror the sisters inspire is emphasised by the animal **imagery** in the play and by the abhorrence of female sexuality exhibited, especially by Lear. Ultimately we are supposed to reject Gonerill and Regan utterly. We might recognise the validity of their complaints about Lear in I.1; we might momentarily sympathise with them because they are not Lear's favourites, but we still abhor them. Even Edmund comments on their bad natures. Jealous, treacherous, immoral; these two display all the most distressing features of inhumanity, murdering and maiming without remorse. The best that can be said for Gonerill and Regan is that they are energetic in their pursuit of self-gratification. There is a horrible fascination in watching them at work.

CORDELIA

Lear's favourite daughter is possibly more problematical for audiences today than she would have been for the Jacobean theatregoer. She can seem infuriatingly pious. Why does she refuse to take part in Lear's love-test, when she knows how evil Gonerill and Regan are? Can we blame her for the violence and cruelty of her sisters' reign? These are awkward questions. And what of Cordelia's subversion of Lear's authority? Some critics interpret her refusal to speak flattering words to Lear and her acceptance of France as acts of defiance; she is in direct conflict with patriarchy on both occasions, refusing to submit to her father's will. Her stubborn 'Nothing'

(I.1.87) leads the way for Gonerill and Regan's rebellion. If we follow these arguments through it is possible to interpret Cordelia's death as a reward for her early disobedience. These, however, are extreme views, which do not really fit in with the portrayal of Cordelia's character in Acts IV and V, or with the consistently high esteem in which Cordelia is held by the good characters. Remember, France takes her for her virtues alone.

It is also necessary to look at Cordelia's motives in I.1. She is seeking to alert Lear to his poor judgement. Her refusal to participate in a glib public-speaking contest can be seen as a sign of her integrity. As the play progresses we learn to distrust all the characters who have an easy way with words. Cordelia's 'Nothing' (I.1.87) looks increasingly honest and worthy. When she returns in Act IV Cordelia is anything but subversive. In the Quarto we are prepared for her reappearance by Kent and the Gentleman, who stress her feminine beauty and modesty and the pain she feels when hearing about Lear's sufferings. We are presented with a perfect daughter who will act as redeemer. In IV.7 she is solicitous and respectful towards her father, restored as Lear's 'best object' (I.1.214). It is probably this Cordelia we remember; the selfless daughter, full of pity and love. When Lear carries on her corpse, yelling in agony, we are appalled. Like Lear we want to know why 'a dog, a horse, a rat have life / And thou no breath at all?' (V.3.304–5).

Cordelia's death has troubled critics and audiences since the play was first performed. There are various ways of explaining it. Shakespeare needs a final cruel blow to bring about Lear's death. Perhaps Cordelia's death is an expression of the playwright's tragic vision. It might also be a final example of man's inhumanity to man in the world of *King Lear*. Shakespeare perhaps wants to show the full horror of the consequences of Lear's folly. For some, Cordelia's death is the real **tragedy** of *King Lear*.

Our assessment of Cordelia should probably conclude that although she is as stubborn as the rest of her family, she is a paragon in comparison with her sisters. In two telling lines Lear says 'Her voice was ever soft / Gentle and low – an excellent thing in a woman' (V.3.270–1). It is impossible to imagine Lear's other two 'dog-hearted' (IV.3.45) daughters ever being described in this way. Cordelia's **characterisation** goes some way to counteract the vicious, masculine cruelty of Gonerill and Regan, and the abhorrence of the female so prevalent in the play. We would probably agree that her death is worth avenging.

Gloucester

Gloucester has some individual features – his superstition, his adultery – but his character is determined largely by the parallel role he plays. Like Lear, he is a complacent father, used to assuming authority. Like Lear, Gloucester acts rashly and ruthlessly when he believes that his son Edgar has rebelled against him, putting himself in his evil son's power. Like Lear, Gloucester fails to 'keep his house in order' – his adultery might be seen as a failure to take his patriarchal responsibilities seriously. He is as blind as his ruler.

Gloucester seems to lack resolution for much of Act II. He tries vainly to keep the peace between Lear and his daughters and it is difficult not to judge him harshly when his doors are shut against the king. All he can offer are faint-hearted protests (II.4.295–7). But Gloucester also displays more positive qualities. When he takes action he is brave and determined. He helps Lear on the heath, providing a litter to transport him to safety. Gloucester is heroic in III.7, denouncing Gonerill and Regan ferociously. He proves that he can be stoical in the face of monstrous cruelty. When he learns the truth about Edmund his tormented desire to be reconciled with Edgar redeems him. Like Lear, Gloucester becomes increasingly generous as he suffers. He expresses great pity for Lear in Act IV and is genuinely concerned about the dangers the old man and Poor Tom face when helping him. His concern for social justice mirrors Lear's.

Gloucester's pain and despair reflect Lear's. While the lunatic king raves about his daughters Gloucester confesses sadly that he is 'almost mad' (III.4.159) himself, thinking about Edgar's supposed treachery. Even after his 'fall' at Dover cliff and his agreement to 'bear / Affliction till it do cry out itself / "Enough, enough", and die' (IV.6.75–7) Gloucester remains suicidal. He welcomes Oswald's sword and is still deeply depressed as late as V.2. His dark thoughts play a key role in establishing and maintaining the bleak atmosphere of the second half of the play. Gloucester's pessimistic lines often seem prophetic: 'This great world / Shall so wear out to naught' (IV.6.135–6). His willingness to die perhaps points towards the carnage of V.3, preparing us for the final tragic outcome. His death can be seen as a 'dry run' for Lear's. Some critics see Lear's passing as a mirror image of Gloucester's. The old earl dies when his 'flawed heart – / Alack, too weak the conflict to support – / 'Twixt two extremes of passion, joy and grief, / Burst smilingly' (V.3.194–7). The reconciliation with Edgar is too much to bear.

Gloucester is punished very harshly for his misjudgements of character. Edgar's verdict, that he dies for adultery, is not easily accepted. For all his faults, Gloucester will probably be viewed by most audiences as a character more sinned against than sinning.

EDGAR

Many critics feel dissatisfied with Edgar. He plays so many roles and performs such a wide range of functions; is he simply a plot device? Shakespeare does not spend much time establishing Edgar's virtues before having him disguise himself as Poor Tom. Gloucester's legitimate son starts the play a passive, credulous dupe upon whom Edmund's devious practices ride easy. In Act I he shows none of the heroism he displays later in the play. So how are we to view his lightning changes?

It is possible to detect progression in Edgar's **characterisation** as he moves from one role to another. He grows in stature through his use of disguises. He is forced to assume the garb of a madman to preserve his life, but his final disguise – masked avenger – enables him to take command of his own fate. Those who complain of Edgar's weak gullibility also forget that Jacobean audiences would have understood that good characters were easy to fool. Villains were accepted as being so cunning that their evil intentions were impossible to detect. Edgar's willingness to be guided by Edmund might be seen as proof of his worthiness.

On the heath the role of lunatic beggar pushes Edgar centre stage. Many critics have noticed how the presence of the fake madman helps Lear. As he interacts with Poor Tom, Lear's humanity and understanding increase. Edgar also comments on Lear and Gloucester's suffering, guiding audience responses to the two patriarchs in Acts III and IV. He is actively generous too. In Act IV Edgar guides Gloucester and tries to chase away his gloomy thoughts. Like Cordelia, Edgar feels only sympathy for the father who rejected him so brutally. At the end of IV.6 Edgar's role-playing enables him to defend Gloucester when Oswald threatens him. To preserve Edgar's moral character (revengers in Jacobean drama often have sinister motives) Shakespeare shows us his remorse. His valour awakened,

Edgar is now ready to challenge Edmund. His facility with language has been used to protect himself and others. His deceptions are essentially honest.

In Act V Edgar becomes an agent of justice. He helps to restore the old order. It is possible to view Edgar as the only character unsullied enough to rule after Lear's death. He has committed no crime against his family or the state. He has never questioned the authority of his elders. He took action when necessary. The worst we can accuse Edgar of is leaving it very late to reveal himself to Gloucester, and he is heartily sorry for this. Edgar has endured appalling privation and shown mercy and strength. When he speaks of his journey through the play as a 'pilgrimage' (V.3.194) we understand the serious sense of purpose behind Edgar's role-playing. Surely he has proved himself many times over? When he unassumingly takes charge we have some justification for feeling that his succession is acceptable.

Some doubts remain. His uncompromising judgement of his father's 'crimes' is disturbing. What has happened to his Christian pity? His belief that the gods are just looks decidedly suspect when Cordelia dies. In comparison with the titanic Lear, Edgar can also seem lacklustre. Our reception of his character depends heavily upon how he is played on stage. In performance Edgar's heroic qualities can be stressed, and his disparate parts can be forged into a more or less satisfactory whole.

EDMUND

Like many villains in Jacobean drama, Edmund seethes with frustration about the 'plague of custom' (I.2.3) that keeps him on the fringes of society. His **Machiavellian** qualities include his political ambition and willingness to use unscrupulous methods to achieve his aims. As Edmund says himself, he is adaptable and ready to manipulate events to serve his turn; 'all with me's meet / that I can fashion fit' (I.2.180). His ability to adopt the right tone in any situation helps him in his progress towards power.

But does Edmund really set himself up against the society he operates in, as some critics suggest? Certainly he sneers at its values, as his toying with the words 'base' and 'legitimate' shows (see I.2.10 and I.2.18–19). Edmund seems to subscribe to a savage code: survival of the fittest. His goddess, Nature, is a brutal, anarchic force. Edmund never apologises for his wickedness; he revels in it right up to the final scene. All the beliefs he outlines in I.2 suggest he rejects the hierarchy that has made his father and brother so prosperous. But his own ambitions are worldly; really, he wants to succeed in society's terms. He aims first at Edgar's inheritance, then at Gloucester's title and finally at the throne of England. Surely Edmund cannot therefore be viewed as an anti-establishment figure?

Yet Edmund is subversive. The alacrity of his rise is an indication of this. He is very successful in Gonerill and Regan's cruel world. He is responsible for the deaths of three princesses, as well as the cruel maiming of his father. His progress is halted too late to save Lear. By the end of the final scene Edmund has proved himself to be formidably destructive. He almost obtains everything he wants.

However, we come to loathe everything Edmund stands for. We may admire his tenacity and quick wits, enjoy his energetic acting out of roles and the way he takes us into his confidence through his use of **soliloquies**; but we must reject him, as we reject Gonerill and Regan. In V.3 Edmund is defeated when Albany and Edgar reassert the values of the old order. Now Edmund is forced to reject his code and submit. His fall is as meteoric as his rise. We know his subversion has failed when we hear him say he will forgive his deathsman if he is of noble blood. His dying desire to do good also seems to cancel out his earlier delight in his own villainy. Edmund's strange last line, 'Yet Edmund was beloved' (V.3.237) might be read as confirming the virtuous characters' insistence throughout the play that caring and loyalty are important. Few will regret the defiant bastard son's demise.

THE FOOL

The Fool plays a number of roles: voice of conscience, social commentator, truth-teller, representative of Cordelia, vehicle for **pathos**, Lear's alter-ego, dramatic **chorus**. His songs, riddles and epigrams also provide comic relief. The flippant remark about Poor Tom's clothing is a good example of the Fool lightening the tone of a distressing scene (III.4.60–1). Many of the Fool's other speeches can be played for comic effect, but it is possible to stress the 'bitter' rather than the witty fool. When he first appears in the play the Fool is extremely critical of Lear: 'Dost thou call me fool, boy? / All thy other titles thou hast given away; that thou wast born with'

(I.4.146–8). These lines are typical of the Fool's interaction with Lear. His sarcasm is blunt and hard hitting. The Fool's bitterness can partly be understood by considering his role as Cordelia's representative. A truth-teller, like Lear's youngest daughter, he pines away when she goes to France. Many of the Fool's early cutting speeches are designed to alert Lear to his daughters' true characters. However, unlike Cordelia, the Fool is never punished for his truth telling. He is 'all-licensed' (I.4.196). Jesters were often kept by the monarch to provide witty analysis of contemporary behaviour and to remind the sovereign of his humanity. Certainly Lear's Fool fulfils these functions for his master. He also enjoys a close and affectionate relationship with 'nuncle' Lear (II.4.117). It is the Fool Lear calls out to when he fears he is going mad. On the heath the king considers his servant's sufferings alongside his own. In return the Fool remains steadfastly loyal. In a play where family relationships are disastrously bad, the Fool seems to play the role of good son.

The Fool's role as social commentator has been linked to the prophecy he makes at the end of Act III Scene 2. In this speech the Fool comments on the injustices and corruption of Lear's reign (III.2.79–96) and perhaps predicts a better time to come. Throughout the play he draws attention to the chaos Lear has caused in the kingdom by making his daughters his mothers. The implication of many of his speeches is that Lear has wronged the country as well as himself.

Some critics wonder whether the Fool's relentless harping drives Lear mad. Most prefer to believe that the Fool serves a positive function when he criticises his master. He pushes Lear towards the truth and then tries to 'out-jest' his injuries, supporting the king as he makes his terrible journey through Act III. So why does the Fool disappear? Some commentators suggest Jacobean audiences would not have been disconcerted by the disappearance of a character half way through the play. Other critics think that the Fool is dropped when he is no longer needed. The Fool's role was to help Lear see more clearly and when his job is completed, he vanishes. Other critics suggest it would be inappropriate to have a comic character (however dark his humour) in the bleak final acts of the play. Finally, it is possible that the same actor played the Fool and Cordelia, and therefore they could not be on stage at the same time.

During this century, the interpretation and presentation of the Fool have become increasingly important to critics and directors alike. He has been played by women (though not always as female), as a music hall clown, as a waif in ragged clothes, as a worn out old man, as a young drag queen. In each case, the director seems to be choosing to emphasise a particular aspect of the relationship between Lear and his Fool, and something of his or her vision of the world of *King Lear*. Which version of the Fool do you feel adds most to your understanding of King Lear, the man, and *King Lear*, the play?

KENT

Kent's most notable characteristics are his loyalty and bluntness. It is the former that motivates him and the latter which causes him trouble. Kent speaks up immediately when he sees Lear acting with 'hideous rashness' (I.1.151). He only resorts to blunt language – 'What wouldst thou do, old man?' (I.1.145) – when his respectful interjections are ignored. Thereafter he reverts to his usual reverence, addressing Lear as 'my lord' and 'my liege'. His dogged determination to stick to the 'old language' of Lear's court can be seen as a measure of his loyalty. It might also indicate that Kent is a conservative, backward-looking figure. There is other evidence that points in this direction. During Lear's madness Kent is reluctant to allow Poor Tom to accompany his master, failing to recognise the beggar's suffering and appalled that the king has 'no better company' (III.4.135). Is this moral blindness? Kent is a representative of the hierarchy that Lear destroyed when he gave away his power, an anachronism. It does not come as a surprise to hear him say he expects and hopes to die in V.3. The world has moved on and Kent has no place in it now.

Does this seem harsh? Most critics would suggest that Kent is a wholly positive figure. His judgement and advice in I.1 are absolutely sound, and his warnings are all justified by the events of the play. We can trust him. Kent accepts banishment without a grudge and immediately assumes a disguise so that he can continue to follow Lear. He suffers punishment stoically in Act II. Out in the storm he thinks only of his master's comfort. He is constantly active in Lear's service. His faithful perseverance is admirable. We can also admire Kent's anger. It always seems justified. Some critics argue that Kent's anger mars Lear's cause, but it is a relief to see a character take on Gonerill, Regan, Cornwall and Oswald. Kent voices the audience's concerns and opinions when he says: 'I have seen better faces in my time / Than stands on any shoulder that I see / Before me at this instant' (II.2.91–3).

Kent keeps us informed about important developments in the plot and acts as Cordelia's champion. However, in spite of his constancy, he begins to seem worn down in the second half of the play. He endures as long as his master needs him but his tone becomes increasingly melancholy when Cordelia reappears. His rhyming couplet at the end of IV.7 is downbeat: 'My point and period will be throughly wrought / Or well or ill, as this day's battle's fought' (IV.7.96–7). Perhaps Shakespeare is using Kent to hint at Lear's death. Does Kent see that he will not be needed for much longer? Kent's lines in V.3 are weary too. His heavily **alliterated** description of Gonerill and Regan's deaths is like a bell tolling for Lear. Kent then comments sorrowfully on his master's passing, 'Vex not his ghost. O, let him pass. He hates him / That would upon the rack of this tough world / Stretch him out longer' (V.3.311–13). It is appropriate that the dependable Kent sums up his master's pain in this distressing scene. He can usually be relied on to hit the right note and will be seen by most audiences of most productions as a reliable guide to the characters and moods of the play. The world of *King Lear* would be considerably darker without Kent's diligence.

ALBANY AND CORNWALL

It is hard to judge the characters of Albany and Cornwall when they first appear on stage. They do not play any real part in the first scene, appearing only as consorts to their wives, Gonerill and Regan. Perhaps Shakespeare gives us a hint that Albany is to be trusted in the opening lines of the play when Kent tells us that Lear seems to favour him, but our attention is not focused on these two characters until later.

Albany can seem problematic. The audience is suspicious of Gonerill long before her husband recognises her inhumanity, and his interjections in the first scene in which he plays any significant part (Act I Scene 4) seem weak. Admittedly, he has missed much of Gonerill's hectoring of Lear, but 'What's the matter, sir?' (I.4.292) is surely inadequate. Are we to assume that Albany is so good himself that he has been taken in by Gonerill? After Lear takes himself off in high dudgeon, Albany wants to wait and see what happens. At this stage he certainly lacks Gonerill's force and decisiveness.

It is easy to be critical of Albany's inaction and lack of foresight, but they are both necessary to the plot. If he attempted to check his wife's progress now, it would distract from the main business of the play at this point – Lear's deteriorating relationship with his daughters.

Albany's rectitude also contrasts neatly with Cornwall's increasing ruthlessness. In Act II Scene 1 we see how Regan's unpleasant husband is drawn to Edmund ('Natures of such deep trust we shall much need; / You we first seize on' – lines 114–15). This is a sure sign that Cornwall is morally dubious. We also quickly realise that unlike Albany, Cornwall is ready to assume command and join his wife and sister-in-law in their campaign against Lear. His tone is habitually authoritarian. He conducts the investigation into Kent and Oswald's altercation, and announces Kent's punishment in an angry tone that suggests 'the fiery quality of the Duke' (II.4.88). In III.7 Cornwall's contempt for any authority other than his own is made horribly clear. He aspires to the crown and acts as if he were the law. Cornwall is responsible for the most shocking act of physical violence in *King Lear* – the blinding of Gloucester. This makes him utterly repugnant.

Having demonstrated the vile depths that humanity can sink to, Shakespeare has no further need of Cornwall. His death at the end of Act III enables Shakespeare to set up the sisters' rivalry for Edmund more effectively, and there is also the point made by the way Cornwall meets his end. His own servant turns on him, just as he turned on his host and his king. This is **poetic justice**. Cornwall's corruption is counterbalanced by his brother-in-law's increasing moral strength. Albany is absent from the play for two acts, and speaks with a new energy and decisiveness when he reappears. He also appears to have altered his opinion of his wife quite radically. His abuse of Gonerill when he accuses her of mistreating Lear indicates that we can now trust Albany (IV.2). What we need from him, however, is action, not words. Albany rises to the occasion in V.3. He denounces and arrests Edmund, offers to challenge him and then presides over the duel between Gloucester's two sons. After the fight, he continues to play an authoritarian role. He asks Edgar to tell the story of his miserable existence in hiding, enabling the audience to hear of Gloucester's death. It is also Albany who delivers a stern epitaph for Gonerill and Regan. Shakespeare now wants us to see him as an agent of justice and correct morality. When Lear appears Albany gracefully resigns the 'absolute power' he has briefly assumed as leader of the British forces. But his virtue is hopeless now. In the final moments of the play his words seem inadequate again. Albany's brief final lines suggest that language cannot express the distress and pity the characters feel at the end of the play.

Edgar's last speech is attributed to Albany in the Quarto, reinforcing his authority. But it remains difficult to believe in Albany. He is always too late, so often a bystander. One line in particular seems to undermine his good intentions completely. As Cordelia's body is carried on to the stage he calls out in alarm, 'The gods defend her' (V.3.254). We are forced to conclude that Albany is out of his depth in the world of *King Lear*.

Oswald

Oswald is a minor character but he serves a number of useful functions. His most important role is as Gonerill's servant. He carries out orders diligently and faithfully and delivers a number of significant letters that move the action of the play on. He is Gonerill's agent in corruption and his bad qualities mirror his mistress's warped nature. Oswald is an insolent, cowardly liar and as self-seeking as the other evil characters. Keen to receive a financial reward, he is only too ready to kill Gloucester when he comes across him in Act IV. His selfish opportunism reflects Gonerill's ambitious rapacity. Oswald also provides a parallel with Kent (the honest plain-speaking servant) and awakens Edgar's valour.

Images and themes

These two aspects of the play are covered in the same section, since ideas are often developed through the patterns of images Shakespeare creates. Through a consideration of the **imagery** you will come to a fuller understanding of the play and its meanings. One of the most intriguing and rewarding aspects of studying *King Lear* is the fact that some of the images and themes remain perplexing. These notes are not exhaustive, and you will find it useful to work through the play yourself, tracing the development of images and considering your own responses to them.

NOTHING

'Nothing' and 'Nothingness' are important concepts in *King Lear*. As he loses everything – his status, his family, his mind – Lear learns the value of Cordelia's 'Nothing, my lord' (I.1.87). Her refusal to participate in the love-test sets off the whole disastrous chain of events. Thereafter, other characters help Lear to come to terms with his 'nothingness', using **imagery** that echoes Cordelia's words. In Act I Scene 4 the Fool taunts Lear with the word 'nothing' (I.4.129–33 and I.4.187–90), and then in Act III the sight of Poor Tom pushes Lear to ask 'Is man no more than this?' (III.4.99–100). Finally Lear learns how empty Gonerill and Regan's words were and finds he has moved closer to Cordelia's true values: 'I know not what to say' he murmurs (IV.7.54).

'Nothing' causes Gloucester the same trouble in the subplot. Like Gonerill and Regan, Edmund uses false words to gain everything. Edmund pretends that his fake letter is 'Nothing, my lord', copying Cordelia's reply in an ironic and alarming way (I.2.32). Gloucester too loses everything, and learns to see more clearly. A very troublesome word, 'nothing'.

CLOTHING

References to clothing are closely linked to ideas about appearance and reality. Outward appearances are often deceptive in *King Lear*. When Lear stoops to blind folly it seems that honesty has to hide itself. Virtuous characters assume disguises in order to survive, continuing to do good in their new lowly roles. The apparel of Lear's closest companions on the heath – the Fool, Kent and Edgar – is significant. All three are humbly dressed; the Fool in his motley, Kent as a man servant and Edgar in the garb of the social outcast. In spite of their inferior status – signified by their clothing – servants are frequently the source of hope, charity and justice in *King Lear*.

Ceremonial garments and the clothing of the court are deeply suspect. They conceal the truth. Lear cannot see beyond the trappings of majesty and assumes his crown makes him 'ague-proof' (IV.6.104–5). Gonerill, Regan and Edmund cover up their depravity with attractive exteriors. When Lear is forced to face reality he decides to remove his kingly garments, 'Off off! You lendings' (III.4.105). His clothing is proof of his folly and inappropriate, for two reasons. Firstly, Lear no longer has any power, and secondly, he has started to look beyond appearances. He needs to rid himself of the trappings of majesty so that he can learn. In Act IV we know that Lear has gained wisdom when he says astutely 'furred gowns hide all' (IV.6.166). He has recognised the truth about himself and his daughters. When his sanity is restored Lear is ready to be put in fresh clothes. He no longer needs his crown of poisonous and bitter weeds, a symbol of his jarred senses. Appropriately, it is Cordelia – his truthful daughter – who instructs her servants to dress Lear in more fitting garments.

There are other references to clothing that help us understand the play. Like Poor Tom, Edgar warns against vanity, 'set not thy sweet heart on proud array' (III.4.79). Lear would have done well to heed this advice early in the play. Edgar also creates a history for Poor Tom as a lustful serving man who had 'three suits to his back, six shirts to his body' (III.4.129–30), linking clothing with corruption.

ANIMALS

There is a wealth of animal **imagery** in *King Lear*. The most important recurring references are to savage creatures, which are associated with Gonerill and Regan. The sisters are also likened to fiends and monsters. Gonerill is 'sharp-toothed, like a vulture', with a 'wolfish visage' (I.5.305). Lear curses her as a 'detested kite' (I.4.259) and tells Regan she 'looked black … most serpent like' upon him (I.4.156–7). Gloucester says the sisters possess 'boarish fangs' (III.7.57) and Albany eventually sees them as 'Tigers not daughters' (IV.2.40), who behave like 'monsters of the deep' (IV.2.49). Even Edmund, who is presumably attracted to the sisters, and described himself as a 'toad-spotted traitor', speaks of them using animal imagery (V.3.136). They are jealous as 'the stung / Are of the adder' (V.1.56–7). Their sexuality is as abhorrent as their cruelty. Lear describes women as living 'centaurs' (IV.6.124). The implications of all these references are clear: Gonerill and Regan are cruel predators, 'pelican daughters' who want to see their father bleed (III.4.72). Their inhumanity is reconfirmed when Gloucester and Cordelia describe how a wild beast would have been allowed shelter in the storm, but not Lear (III.7.61–4 and IV.7.36–40). Appropriately, Gonerill and Regan are destroyed by their animal instincts.

There are other references to animals which help us understand Lear's plight. The Fool uses telling **imagery** when he says to Lear 'the hedge-sparrow fed the cuckoo so long / That its had it head bit off by it young' (I.4.211–12). The image of Lear as a hedge-sparrow emphasises his vulnerability. Like Poor Tom, Edgar dwells on the way he is stalked by devils, recalling the way Lear is treated by Gonerill and Regan. Reduced to an abject state on the heath, Lear recognises that man is 'a poor bare forked animal' (III.4.104). His identification with Poor Tom again suggests Lear's helplessness. How could a 'poor bare forked animal' cope with the powerful predators linked to Gonerill and Regan? Lear's vulnerability is emphasised at the start of the final scene when the king pictures life in prison, where he and Cordelia will 'sing like birds in a cage' (V.3.9). For the first time we are presented with an attractive animal image. However, song-birds are passive, tame creatures. This image hints that Lear's visions of happiness are deluded.

SIGHT AND BLINDNESS

The importance of seeing yourself and the world clearly is one of the key themes in *King Lear*. It is reflected in the many images of sight and blindness, light and dark, eyes and weeping. One of the earliest references to eyes comes in Act I Scene 1, after Lear has explained his 'darker purpose' (I.1.36) and failed to see the truth about his three daughters. Kent tries to warn the king that he is behaving foolishly, 'see better, Lear' (I.1.158). He begs his master to let him remain 'The true blank of thine eye' (I.1.159). His reward is an angry dismissal, 'Out of my sight' (I.1.157). Unable to see anyone's merits or faults clearly, Lear refuses to look on those who have offended him. However, Lear has another critic who forces him to consider his actions more closely. The Fool sums up Lear's folly neatly with a **metaphor**, 'So out went the candle and we were left darkling' (I.4.213). This line serves as a prediction for the end of Act II, when Lear is overwhelmed by dark thoughts and shut out in the storm. We might also see Lear as the candle. As monarch he is the source of light and life in the kingdom. When he burns 'out' (is out of favour) all the characters associated with Lear are 'left darkling'.

After the storm, Lear's ability to see more clearly is apparent when he meets Gloucester. In IV.6 the black humour of the references to sight heightens the **pathos** of the old men's suffering. But it also comes as something of a relief. There is reason in Lear's madness now:

> LEAR: No eyes in your head, nor no money in your purse? Your eyes are in a heavy case, your purse in a light; yet you see how this world goes.
>
> GLOUCESTER: I see it feelingly
>
> LEAR: What, art mad? A man may see how this world goes with no eyes. Look with thine ears. (IV.6.146–52)

Some critics find Lear's puns about eyes desperately cruel. But Gloucester and Lear do now 'see how the world goes'. They both 'stumbled' when they saw. Gloucester's blinding is the physical manifestation of the mental torture Lear endured on the heath. We were prepared for it by a series references to sight, which built up tension effectively. In I.2 Gloucester asked Edmund to 'look into' Edgar's treachery and then in III.7 the references to eyes come thick and fast, starting with Gonerill's 'Pluck out his eyes!' (III.7.5).

Until Cordelia returns, like Gloucester, we feel that all is 'dark and comfortless' (III.7.84). Cordelia is associated with healing tears and radiant light. Throughout his confrontations with Gonerill and Regan and during his descent into madness Lear refused to weep. 'Old fond eyes … I'll pluck ye out' he declared vehemently (I.4.298–9). His desperate struggle against weeping can be seen as proof of Lear's determination not to be vanquished by his pelican daughters. However, he cries when he is reunited with Cordelia. Is this a sign of weakness or an indication that he sees himself and his daughter more clearly? In Act V Lear is defiant again: he and Cordelia will not weep in prison. When she is hanged, Lear finally gives in to his grief, 'Howl, howl, howl! / O, you are men of stones! / Had I your tongues and eyes I'd use them so / That heaven's vault should crack' (V.3.255–7). His eyes fail him as he mourns the loss of his 'best object' (I.1.214).

MADNESS

Unlike other Renaissance dramatists, who used 'mad scenes' for comic effect, Shakespeare seems intent on a serious portrayal of madness in *King Lear.* There are different types of madness in the play. Lear's rash actions of I.1 might be viewed as political insanity. The bloodlust exhibited by

Gonerill, Regan and Cornwall is another abhorrent kind of madness. So how are we to view the king's descent into madness? Does insanity cure Lear's moral blindness? Lear compares his madness to the torments of hell and struggles frantically to retain his wits, 'O let me not be mad, not mad, sweet heaven!' (I.5.43). The other characters are horrified by his loss of reason and try desperately to keep him sane. The storm – which reflects Lear's madness – is appallingly destructive, almost too much for man to endure. It is particularly difficult to see Lear's madness as beneficial in V.3. Having regained his wits and judgement, Lear is tormented again when Cordelia dies. In his final moments he is deluded once more, believing that his daughter still breathes.

There are other types of madness that shed a sombre light on Lear's insanity: the Fool's professional madness (his clowning), Edgar's fake madness and Gloucester's half-crazed pity. The madness of the Fool and Edgar might be intended to provide comic relief. The Fool's jests often lighten the tone and some of Edgar's antics as Poor Tom can seem amusing. The Elizabethans visited Bedlam (Bethlehem) Hospital for entertainment, to enjoy the spectacle of the mad beggars, so it is possible that Shakespeare intended the audience to laugh at Poor Tom. However, Edgar's craziness also seems designed to heighten the **pathos** of Act III; certainly, his descriptions of being driven close to suicide by devils are anything but funny. The same is true of the craziest scene in the play, the mock trial, which can be very disturbing on stage. Ultimately, the madness of *King Lear* is deeply distressing. It develops from and points back to the king's instability.

SUFFERING

The suffering in *King Lear* is intense, violent and relentless. Many of the characters are driven almost beyond the limits of endurance, reflected in the **imagery** of the play. Lear speaks of his daughters – especially Gonerill – attacking him physically. He tells Regan that her sister has 'struck' (II.4.155) him with her tongue and 'tied, sharp tooth'd unkindness' (II.4.000) around his heart. His daughters are 'a disease that's in my flesh … a boil / A plague-sore, or embossed carbuncle, / In my corrupted blood' (II.4.216–20). Gonerill and Regan have wounded Lear and now eat away at his flesh. His 'frame of nature' is 'wrenched' from 'the fixed place'

(I.4.265–6). As Lear's heart breaks 'into a hundred thousand flaws' his mind disintegrates (II.4.280). He is 'bound / Upon a wheel of fire', 'scalded' by his own tears (IV.7.45–8). Lear also employs images of the torments of hell when he rages against female sexuality in IV.6. Femininity is closely linked to suffering in this play. Even when his senses are restored Lear continues to suffer. He has been 'cut to the brains' and finds it impossible to recover from his daughters' assault (IV.6.194). 'Burning shame' keeps him from Cordelia (IV.3.46). Guilt about his former unkindness stings his mind so 'venomously' that he cannot face her (IV.3.46).

The **imagery** that other characters use when commenting on Lear's pain echoes the king's words. Gloucester describes Lear as 'O ruined piece of nature!' (IV.6.135), for Edgar he is a 'side-piercing sight' (IV.6.85). The violence of so many of Edgar's frantic speeches as Poor Tom intensifies the sense of suffering on the heath. 'The foul fiend bites my back' (III.6.17) he wails, telling horrifying stories of being whipped, of knives in his bed and nooses on his balcony. Gloucester and Lear are overwhelmed by their suffering, in spite of their companions' efforts to alleviate their woes. Gloucester dies of a broken heart, while Lear's moment of greatest agony comes when Cordelia dies. He seems to choke to death, asking for a button to be unfastened. By now Kent welcomes death too. His line 'Break heart, I prithee break' might refer to Lear's suffering or his own (V.3.310). It is appropriate to both characters.

At this point we need to consider what causes the intense suffering in *King Lear*. Gloucester thinks that the gods are sadistic, while Lear wants to know why nature has given him two malignant daughters. However, it is hard to blame the gods or nature for the violence in the play. The audience might feel that all the agony experienced can be traced back to human acts of unkindness. Characters suffer for their own sins or because they are sinned against. This seems harsh on the innocents, Cordelia and Edgar, but Gloucester and Lear hardly deserve the extreme torment they endure either. And it is not only the characters who suffer. At the end of the play the state is in disarray, signified by the word 'gored' (V.3.318). The storm serves as a **metaphor** for England's suffering as well as Lear's. The worst torments in *King Lear* are caused and perpetuated by the characters themselves.

But what is learned through suffering? Our understanding of the suffering in the play needs to include an assessment of its benefits. The good endure and help each other. Lear and Gloucester become more compassionate, reassessing themselves and the society they live in. Edgar becomes stronger and fit to rule. Through suffering these three male characters achieve heroism. It seems that the best natures can absorb pain and learn. In *King Lear* Shakespeare seems to suggest that it is man's fate to suffer. Lear says this very plainly in Act IV, 'When we are born we cry that we are come / To this great stage of fools' (IV.6.183–4).

NATURE

On the heath Lear tries to find answers to two questions. Why do his daughters have such hard hearts and what is the cause of thunder? His assumptions about what is natural have been challenged. He wants to know whether nature is responsible for his turmoil. The play does not provide straightforward answers to Lear's queries. We are presented with conflicting views of nature and what is natural. The dominance of the evil characters might lead us to feel that nature is a cruel force in *King Lear*. Edmund suggests that nature is a malevolent goddess who provides him with the bad nature necessary to challenge the status quo. Therefore his badness is natural. Gonerill and Regan's careers seem to confirm Edmund's view. Cruelty comes naturally to them and they delight in it. For these characters there is no natural order; they seek to create their own selfish universe.

But the good characters see this trio as unnatural. We are told that Gonerill and Regan behave monstrously, in a way that shames nature. So there is another kind of nature to consider: benign nature. Cordelia calls on the 'unpublished virtues of the earth' to restore Lear and displays the virtues of a good nature (IV.4.16). For Kent, the Fool, Edgar and Cordelia it is natural to be loving, trusting and loyal. Watching these characters it is possible to conclude that human nature is good. This group also believes in a natural order, which they struggle to restore. Yet they suffer.

We need to look to Lear for answers to these puzzles. The king represents the natural order. At the start of the play he presides over a harmonious hierarchy. Lear transgresses against the natural order when he fails to recognise Cordelia's worthiness, falsely calling her 'a wretch whom nature is ashamed / Almost t' acknowledge hers' (I.1.212–13). He compounds his mistake when he gives Gonerill and Regan power over him.

Lear's unnatural dealing leads to unnatural dealing in others. Gloucester errs in a similar fashion, disinheriting his legitimate heir in favour of the bastard, whom he mistakes for a 'Loyal and natural boy' (II.1.83). Lear and Gloucester's errors are disastrous. Lear finds that his 'frame of nature' has been wrenched 'From the fixed place' (I.4.265–6). This **image** suggests the seriousness of Lear's crimes against the natural order. An enormous struggle ensues, as nature tries to reassert herself. The storm can be seen as both punishment and protest.

And yet, at the close of Act V, it is difficult to believe that nature is benevolent or that the natural order has really 'won'. Cordelia's death presents a problem for those who wish to see the end of *King Lear* as a triumph for nature and the hierarchy. Lear seems to suggest that nature is barbaric when he asks, 'Why should a dog, a horse, a rat have life, / And thou no breath at all?' (V.3.304–5). Perhaps we are meant to see Cordelia's death as the final punishment for Lear's transgression against nature. And Edgar may be a worthy monarch in the making, but his succession is hardly a triumph for the natural order.

Do we have answers to Lear's questions? We probably accept that Gonerill and Regan are naturally evil. There is no obvious reason why they have hard hearts. But it is Lear who causes the thunder; he allows the hard hearts a free reign. Our conclusion must be that nature reflects the mistakes of man in *King Lear*. And when man stoops to folly, the natural order is easily destroyed.

JUSTICE

Throughout *King Lear* characters judge and put each other on trial. Gloucester and Lear both misjudge their children, who seem to possess better judgement. Cordelia has the measure of her sisters and Gonerill and Regan's assessment of their father is acute and accurate. Edmund knows exactly how to take in his gullible relatives. It seems that good judgement is not the preserve of those with good intentions.

The workings of human justice reflect Lear and Gloucester's faults. The 'trials' that occur in the play are all flawed. Lear's 'love-test' is ill-conceived and has disastrous consequences. In Act II the trial of Kent for plain-speaking is an excuse for Cornwall and Regan to exercise power in an arrogant way. Lear's mock trial of Gonerill and Regan is presided over by a lunatic and attended by a fake madman and a court jester. The defendant is a joint-stool. This trial is a parody of the love-test. It highlights the absurdity of Lear's actions in I.1. It also undermines all the other trials carried out by authority figures in *King Lear*. Gloucester's blinding is an appalling example of human injustice. Cornwall and Regan pervert the law to satisfy their own craving for revenge. It is possible to see the battle between the French and English forces as another trial which has dire consequences. Cordelia is hanged in prison and Lear dies. Some see Cordelia's death as the greatest injustice in the play. Human judgement and the justice system look extremely fallible when the curtain goes down on Act V.

This point is reinforced by the examples of natural or **poetic justice** that we see in the play. In V.3 Edgar takes the law into his own hands when he challenges Edmund. This is 'wild justice' at work. However, we accept the outcome of the duel as appropriate. Edmund deserves to die. We see poetic justice at work elsewhere; Cornwall is turned on and killed by his own servant, Gonerill and Regan are destroyed by their jealous lust and Oswald meets a sticky end.

The thorniest question about justice concerns Gloucester and Lear. Do they deserve to suffer and die? Some critics would say that a rather harsh kind of justice is at work here. Edgar suggests this when he says to Edmund, 'The dark and vicious place where thee he got / Cost him his eyes' (V.3.170–1). Gloucester pays very dearly for his sins (although some Elizabethans believed that blinding was the appropriate punishment for adultery). Lear also pays for his sins. Cordelia is taken from him immediately after he recognises her merits. Although his judgement has been restored, it is too late for Lear.

King Lear is also concerned with social justice. Lear and Gloucester both consider this topic carefully and seem to reach radical conclusions. Gloucester calls on the heavens to distribute wealth more evenly, while Lear considers the lives of the 'Poor naked wretches' he paid so little attention to (III.4.28–36). In Act IV Lear rages against corrupt members of the judiciary and seems to sneer at himself and all those who presume to rule and judge others when he says, 'a dog's obeyed in office' (IV.6.159–60).

At the end of the play we are presented with two new agents of justice, Albany and Edgar. We accept the justice of their actions in V.3. But human judgement still looks faulty. Albany has almost been overwhelmed by events and Edgar's bitter words about Gloucester's death seem callous.

Surely no one in *King Lear* is morally impeccable? Perhaps Shakespeare wants us to remain uncomfortable about justice.

THE GODS

There are many references to the pagan and Christian deities in *King Lear*. The characters appeal to them in times of crisis, hoping for divine assistance. Their attitudes towards the gods reflect their natures. Ideas about the gods can also be linked to the theme of justice. Are the gods just, indifferent or destructive? We hear conflicting views from the characters. At the start of the play Lear believes that the gods are on his side. He expects them to punish Gonerill and Regan for their ingratitude. Later, however, Lear worries that the heavens are hostile; perhaps they stir 'these daughters' hearts / Against their father' (II.4.269–70). His paranoia reflects his egotism and instability. By Act V he seems to have rediscovered his faith. We see the strength of Lear's love when he says it will take 'a brand from heaven' to part him and Cordelia (V.3.23). There is a terrible irony in the fact that it is a mere mortal, Edmund, who deprives Lear of his beloved daughter. Lear makes no mention of the gods when he asks why Cordelia has been killed. His silence might be read as proof that we are to blame man for the carnage of Act V.

Other characters' attitudes to the gods make the issue of faith thornier still. What are we to make of Cordelia and Edgar, who behave with Christian fortitude and the virtues of patience, pity and benevolence? The religious **imagery** used to describe Cordelia in IV.6 clearly identifies her as an example of Christian goodness. Cordelia sees the gods as kindly and helpful, calling on them to restore Lear's senses. But she is sacrificed. How can we believe the gods are just when her body is carried on to the stage directly after Albany's line 'The gods defend her' (V.3.254)? At this moment we are likely to agree with Gloucester's pessimistic assessment of the gods; they seem capricious and sadistic. Edgar's faith presents problems too. His statement, 'The gods are just, and of our pleasant vices / Make instruments to plague us' does not ring true when Cordelia is hanged (V.3.168–9). It is hard to reconcile Edgar's belief in the justice of divine retribution with his description of his journey through the play as a 'pilgrimage' (V.3.194). And does his father really deserve to die for adultery?

So, is Shakespeare making a case for atheism? Does Cordelia's death undermine every positive statement made about the gods in *King Lear*? We need to consider Edmund, who professes to worship nature but shows little respect for any religion. When he does refer to the gods Edmund speaks ironically. In II.1 he mocks his father when he pretends to believe in 'the revenging gods / 'Gainst parricides' (II.1.44–5). Even when he pants for life and decides to do good in Act V Scene 3, Edmund never suggests that his change of heart comes about because he suddenly believes in divine retribution. The alacrity of Edmund's rise and the fact that the faithless, worldly bastard is responsible for Cordelia's death suggest man is as powerful and cruel as any force above. However, Edmund's progress is eventually stopped by two god-fearing characters. The atheist is not allowed to defeat the faithful. Shakespeare refuses to provide us with any straightforward answers to the many questions we have about religion in *King Lear*.

THE FAMILY AND FEUDALISM

The Jacobean age was a time of social and religious change. The feudal, medieval view of the world was under scrutiny and traditional assumptions about gender and class were being questioned by many. With its focus on the king and his family, many contemporary critics believe that *King Lear* reflects the anxieties of the period. The play charts the breakdown – not just of a character – but of a whole way of life. Albany and Kent's opening lines hint that we are in a world of political uncertainty.

In I.1 Lear behaves like a medieval monarch. He is used to wielding his power with absolute authority and expects meek obedience. When Kent challenges him he is outraged, 'On thine allegiance' he rages (I.1.167). He dismisses Cordelia with words which reflect his power, 'Better thou had not been born than not t' have pleased me better' (I.1.232–3), and 'begone / Without our grace, our love, our benison!' (I.2.264–5). When she is disinherited Cordelia becomes a nonentity. She can only regain a position in the world when she is chosen in marriage by another man, who takes her without that symbol of her father's power, her dowry. Lear's medieval absolutism is already being undermined.

When he rejects Cordelia, Lear plunges his family and community into crisis. He allows a new breed of opportunists to undermine the hierarchy. It is a measure of the strength of the new breed that they get as far as they do. Gonerill, Regan and Edmund will not accept the roles allotted to them. Gonerill and Regan refuse to behave like good, submissive Renaissance women should. Edmund will not be marginalised. All three grasp at and enjoy exercising power. They show no respect for the family or the state. Even when Gonerill, Regan and Edmund are vanquished in Act V, the restored hierarchy looks shaky. The first family lies dead on the stage. The survivors are all numb, hardly ready to sustain the 'gored' state (V.3.228). Lear's family procession at the start of Act I was perhaps the final ceremony of an anachronistic code.

LANGUAGE

King Lear is written in **blank verse** and prose. Blank verse consists of unrhymed iambic pentameters, with five stressed syllables and five unstressed syllables to each line. You will notice that Shakespeare does not stick to the rules of blank verse rigidly. He uses shorter lines for emphasis (you will find many examples of this, especially during tense moments or scenes of chaos). Longer lines are used to avoid the comic sing-song or monotonous effect of repeated iambic pentameters. At the end of scenes Shakespeare sometimes uses rhyming couplets to provide a sense of **closure**. Rhyme is also used to draw attention to particular thoughts or ideas. The Fool's songs and proverbs are an example of this.

'Low' or comic characters generally speak in prose in Elizabethan and Jacobean drama. Traditionally, scenes of madness were also written in prose. Shakespeare obeys these conventions in *King Lear*, but you will notice that prose is used on other occasions too. Sometimes scenes contain both verse and prose. We would expect Lear to speak in verse because he is a king. However, as his wits desert him, he shifts from verse to prose and back again, signifying the disruption in his mind. You will also notice that Lear uses the third person (the royal 'we') early in the play, but adopts the more humble first person ('I', 'methinks') when he recognises that he is powerless. This change reflects his change in status, from king to 'a foolish old man'. You might want to consider the dramatic effects of other language choices. For example, why does Gloucester enter in I.2 muttering in prose? Perhaps Shakespeare wants to show how troubled Gloucester is as he feverishly considers recent events. The swift moving prose also perhaps anticipates Gloucester's hasty decision-making later in the scene.

The language of *King Lear* – especially the final scene – is direct and simple, with the exception of Edgar's mad talk and the Fool's riddles. This simplicity is an integral part of the play's dramatic power, as are two other conventions. Characters use **asides** and **soliloquies** to inform the audience about their feelings and intentions, drawing us into their world. Characters also have their own personal 'styles', reflecting their roles, emotions and natures. For example, Gonerill and Regan use clipped commands, which demonstrate their craving for power. The patterns of **images** and **metaphors** Shakespeare uses add to our understanding of the play and its characters enormously and should be considered alongside style and punctuation in any analysis of Shakespeare's use of language in *King Lear* (see Images and Themes).

PART FOUR

TEXTUAL ANALYSIS

TEXT 1 (II.4.212–81)

GONERILL: At your choice, sir.

LEAR: I prithee, daughter, do not make me mad.
I will not trouble thee, my child. Farewell.
We'll no more meet, no more see one another.
But yet thou art my flesh, my blood, my daughter –
Or rather a disease that's in my flesh,
Which I must needs call mine. Thou art a boil,
A plague-sore, or embossed carbuncle,
In my corrupted blood. But I'll not chide thee.
Let shame come when it will, I do not call it.
I do not bid the thunder-bearer shoot,
Nor tell tales of thee to high-judging Jove.
Mend when thou canst, be better at thy leisure;
I can be patient, I can stay with Regan,
I and my hundred knights.

REGAN: Not altogether so.
I looked not for you yet, nor am provided
For your fit welcome. Give ear, sir, to my sister;
For those that mingle reason with your passion
Must be content to think you old, and so –
But she knows what she does.

LEAR: Is this well spoken?

REGAN: I dare avouch it, sir. What, fifty followers?
Is it not well? What should you need of more?
Yea, or so many, sith that both charge and danger
Speak 'gainst so great a number? How in one house
Should many people under two commands
Hold amity? 'Tis hard, almost impossible.

GONERILL: Why might not you, my lord, receive attendance
From those that she calls servants, or from mine?

REGAN: Why not, my lord? If then they chanced to slack ye,
We could control them. If you will come to me,
For now I spy a danger, I entreat you
To bring but five-and-twenty; to no more
Will I give place or notice.

LEAR: I gave you all –

REGAN: And in good time you gave it.

LEAR: Made you my guardians, my depositaries;
But kept a reservation to be followed
With such a number. What, must I come to you
With five-and-twenty – Regan, said you so?

REGAN: And speak't again, my lord, No more with me.

LEAR: Those wicked creatures yet do look well-favoured
When others are more wicked. Not being the worst
Stands in some rank of praise. [*To* GONERILL] I'll go with thee.
Thy fifty yet doth double five-and-twenty,
And thou art twice her love.

GONERILL: Hear me, my lord;
What need you five-and-twenty, ten, or five
To follow, in a house where twice so many
Have a command to tend you?

REGAN: What need one?

LEAR: O, reason not the need! Our basest beggars
Are in the poorest thing superfluous.
Allow not nature more than nature needs –
Man's life is cheap as beast's. Thou art a lady;
If only to go warm were gorgeous,
Why, nature needs not what thou gorgeous wear'st,
Which scarcely keeps thee warm. But for true need –
You heavens, give me that patience, patience I need!

You see me here, you gods, a poor old man,
As full of grief as age, wretched in both;
If it be you that stirs these daughters' hearts
Against their father, fool me not so much
To bear it tamely; touch me with noble anger,
And let not women's weapons, water drops,
Stain my man's cheeks. No, you unnatural hags,
I will have such revenges on you both
That all the world shall – I will do such things –
What they are yet I know not; but they shall be
The terrors of the earth. You think I'll weep.
No, I'll not weep.
I have full cause of weeping;

[*storm and tempest*]

but this heart
Shall break into a hundred thousand flaws
Or ere I'll weep. O Fool, I shall go mad!

This extract is a turning point for Lear. After the confrontation with Gonerill and Regan in II.4, he is driven out into the storm and goes mad. Prior to the discussion about his knights, this scene has already proved difficult for the old king. He has been treated insolently by Regan and Cornwall and his authority has been challenged. Not only has Kent been found in the stocks, but Lear's questions about his servant's punishment have also been disregarded. By the time Gonerill arrives, Lear has become an increasingly impotent figure.

We know that Lear can expect further trouble when Regan takes Gonerill's hand, greeting her warmly. The sisters are united and ready to strike. The subject of Lear's followers proves to be his undoing, as we suspected it might be when Gonerill complained about them in Act I Scene 4. Regan introduces the topic here, telling Lear repeatedly to return to Gonerill and reduce his train. To the beleaguered king his followers represent himself: his status, dignity, authority. In other words, they represent Lear as he was. By reducing their number, Gonerill and Regan show their father that he no longer has a role to play: he is nothing.

Gonerill and Regan's reduction of Lear's followers is a masterpiece of orchestrated cruelty. The sisters use a variety of hypocritical excuses to dismiss Lear's men. Regan tells Lear that 'both charge and danger / Speak 'gainst so great a number' (lines 234–5). It would be impossible for 'two commands' in one household to 'Hold amity.' She adds that if Lear had fewer followers, they would be easier to command (but note who is to do the commanding – the new royal 'we' – Gonerill and Regan). Finally Gonerill suggests that Lear needs no one to attend him since she already has plenty of servants with 'a command to tend you' (line 258). Here we see Gonerill and Regan at their most brutally efficient. Not a word is wasted. Their (rhetorical) questions are direct and purposeful and their statements firm:

> LEAR: Regan, said you so?
>
> REGAN: And speak't again, my lord. No more with me. (II.4.249–50)

Impatient to get their work done, the sisters cut Lear off when he is speaking. At the end of their swift 'discussion' Regan finishes her elder sister's train of thought with a stark, short question. Their tone has been hectoring and authoritarian throughout. This is exactly what we would have expected from the sisters, having witnessed their resentful conversation at the end of Act I Scene 1. Regan is particularly vicious. Her 'And in good time you gave it' (line 245) is as mean-spirited and chilling as her brazen question, 'What need one?' Regan's role as 'leader' in this scene ensures that Lear's annihilation is merciless. During I.4 we realised Gonerill was ferocious. Now the other daughter proves herself to be every bit as callous. But what an impressive instrument of torture these two make; there is a horrible fascination in watching them at work in this scene.

At first, Lear cannot quite believe what is happening. He struggles to maintain his dignity. His opening lines to Gonerill show his desperation: 'I prithee, daughter, do not make me mad / I will not trouble thee my child. Farewell' (lines 213–14). His politeness is pitiful. Two lines later Lear is angry again. He calls Gonerill 'a disease that's in my flesh, … a boil / A plague-sore, or embossed carbuncle' (lines 217–19). The **imagery** of disease is apt. It accompanies the images of predatory animals used to describe Gonerill and Regan and emphasises how Lear is being assaulted by his own flesh and blood. These images are followed by thoughts of vengeance, although Lear again tries to be patient:

> ... But I'll not chide thee.
> Let shame come when it will, I do not call it.
> I do not bid the thunder-bearer shoot,
> Nor tell tales of thee to high-judging Jove. (lines 220–3)

Lear hopes – understandably – that the gods will punish his ungrateful daughter. However, his insistence that he will 'tell tales' seems childish. And his tolerance is revealed as blindness when he says 'I can be patient, I can stay with Regan, / I and my hundred knights' (lines 225–6). How little Lear has learned. He cannot shake off the idea that love is a commodity that can be bought, pleading feebly, 'I gave you all' (line 245). Lear blindly links love with money when he reminds Gonerill and Regan that he made them his 'guardians' as well as his 'depositories'. Like Edgar in the previous scene, Lear is reduced to a state of beggary, reliant on a hostile world for charity. He seems to realise this at line 259. Lear begins to speak like the helpless dependant he is:

> You heavens, give me that patience, patience I need!
> You see me here, you gods, a poor old man,
> As full of grief as age, wretched in both;
> If it be you that stirs these daughters' hearts
> Against their father, fool me not so much
> To bear it tamely (II.4.266–71)

'A poor old man', Lear now has to beg for assistance. He is overwhelmed by wretchedness, terrified that his 'daughters' hearts' will defeat him. In this speech Lear also starts to consider what a man is, what true necessity means, ideas that will preoccupy him in Act III.

But how much truth does Lear really face? His description of himself may be accurate, but he is full of self-pity, and still egotistical. He moves so quickly from considering what man needs to his own 'true need'. He sees only the sins of others. Some see Lear's request to be touched by 'noble anger' and his furious refusal to weep as signs that he is still blindly clinging trying to his regal persona. However, it is impossible not to pity Lear here. His struggle not to bear cruel treatment 'tamely' is impressive. Stoicism may not restore his power, but Lear's pride and fortitude can be seen as the qualities of a true tragic hero.

Lear's last speech shows the mixture of courage and fear Lear has displayed throughout II.4. His incomplete threats, 'That all the world shall – I will do such things' (line 275) are signs that Lear no longer has any control over his daughters, or his mind. But his desire for vengeance will strike a chord with the audience: Gonerill and Regan deserve to be punished. Our sympathy increases with Lear's dramatic and agonised exit, 'O Fool! I shall go mad' (line 281). The stage directions (storm and tempest) also provide an ominous warning of the suffering to come.

In this extract there has been an unrelenting march towards a vicious new world, where only the fittest will survive. Our fears about Gonerill and Regan have been confirmed. Regardless of the reservations we may feel about Lear and his actions, we will not be able to avoid appreciating the **pathos** of the king's situation. He has been forced to confront the truth about his daughters in a very cruel way. This extract is significant because it shows Gonerill and Regan ruthlessly in control, their energy undiminished. What new atrocities can we expect from them in Act III? There has been no sign of anything or anyone halting the progress of the evil characters, who have gained ground dramatically in Act II. This scene marks the triumph of duplicity and barbarism. As the storm starts our alarm grows.

TEXT 2 (III.2.1–73)

LEAR: Blow, winds, and crack your cheeks! Rage! Blow!
You cataracts and hurricanoes, spout
Till you have drenched our steeples, drowned the cocks!
You sulphurous and thought-executing fires,
Vaunt-curriers of oak-cleaving thunderbolts,
Singe my white head! And thou all-shaking thunder,
Strike flat the thick rotundity o'the world,
Crack Nature's moulds, all germens spill at once
That makes ingrateful man!

FOOL: O, nuncle, court holy-water in a dry house is better than this rain-water out o'door. Good nuncle, in; ask thy daughters' blessing. Here's a night pities neither wise men nor fools.

LEAR: Rumble thy bellyful! Spit, fire! Spout, rain!
Nor rain, wind, thunder, fire are my daughters.

I tax not you, you elements, with unkindness;
I never gave you kingdom, called you children.
You owe me no subscription; then let fall
Your horrible pleasure. Here I stand, your slave,
A poor, infirm, weak and despised old man.
But yet I call you servile ministers,
that will with two pernicious daughters join
Your high-engendered battles 'gainst a head
So old and white as this. O, ho! 'Tis foul!

FOOL: He that has a house to put's head in has a good head-piece:

The cod-piece that will house
Before the head has any,
The head and he shall louse;
So beggars marry many.
The man that makes his toe
What he his heart should make,
Shall of a corn cry woe,
And turn his sleep to wake.
For there was never yet fair woman but she made mouths in a glass.

[*Enter* KENT]

LEAR: No, I will be the pattern of all patience.
I will say nothing.

KENT: Who's there?

FOOL: Marry, here's grace and a cod-piece – that's a wise man and a fool.

KENT: Alas, sir, are you here? Things that love night
Love not such nights as these. The wrathful skies
Gallow the very wanderers of the dark
And make them keep their caves. Since I was man,
Such sheets of fire, such bursts of horrid thunder,
Such groans of roaring wind and rain I never
Remember to have heard. Man's nature cannot carry
Th'affliction not the fear.

LEAR: Let the great gods
That keep this dreadful pudder o'er our heads
Find out their enemies now. Tremble, thou wretch

That hast within thee undivulgèd crimes
Unwhipped of justice. Hide thee, thou bloody hand,
Thou perjured, and thou simular of virtue
That art incestuous. Caitiff, to pieces shake,
That under covert and convenient seeming
Has practised on man's life. Close pent-up guilts,
Rive your concealing continents, and cry
These dreadful summoners grace. I am a man
More sinned against than sinning.

KENT: Alack, bare-headed?
Gracious my lord, hard by here is a hovel;
Some friendship will it lend you 'gainst the tempest.
Repose you there while I to this hard house –
More harder than the stones whereof 'tis raised;
Which even but now, demanding after you,
Denied me to come in – return and force
Their scanted courtesy.

LEAR: My wits begin to turn.
Come on, my boy. How dost my boy? Art cold?
I am cold myself. Where is the straw, my fellow?
The art of our necessities is strange
And can make vile things precious. Come, your hovel.
Poor fool and knave, I have one part in my heart
That's sorry yet for thee.

In this scene the style and structure of Lear's speeches convey the king's confused and violent state of mind. We see anger, a desire for revenge, egotism, and more positively, humility and a recognition of previous mistakes. Lear's speeches also reflect the movements of the storm. Lear's opening line, 'Blow, winds ... Rage, blow' is like a crack of thunder, suggesting that Shakespeare is using Lear's language to create the effects of the storm for the audience. Lear *is* the storm. His actions have led to misrule in the kingdom, and nature reflects that chaos. Lear has made others suffer, now the storm makes him suffer.

Lear wants to see the world destroyed by 'cataracts and hurricanoes' (line 2) because of the treachery of 'ingrateful man' (line 9). These last two words indicate that Lear blames Gonerill and Regan for his suffering. But he also seems to welcome his own destruction when he yells, 'Singe my white head!' (line 6). Perhaps this is an acknowledgement of his sins, a desire to be punished for his folly. However, Lear continues to act out the role of mighty monarch. His first speech is a long list of commands. He expects the tempest to do his bidding. Has Lear really woken up to his errors? Lear's second speech is less explosive, but still full of rage:

> I tax not you, you elements, with unkindness;
> I never gave you kingdom, called you children.
> You owe me no subscription; then let fall
> Your horrible pleasure. (III.2.16–19)

Now Lear recognises that he cannot rule the elements. He says – with crazy egotism – that they owe him 'no subscription'. These lines continue the theme of 'ingrateful man' and sum up the lunatic king's version of events so far. Lear's words convey the self-pity he feels: 'Here I stand, your slave, / A poor, infirm, weak, and despised old man' (lines 19–20). This description might be seen as the accurate self-assessment of a man who is beginning to see himself more clearly. All the adjectives are bleak, with a particularly stark final choice: despised. Lear's reference to himself as a 'slave' is significant too. In II.4 he said he would rather work as Oswald's slave than return to Gonerill. Now he begins to see that he has – indeed is – nothing. His paranoid delusion that the storm is in league with his 'pernicious daughters' (line 22) seems to confirm his arrogant vulnerability.

The violence of the storm and his daughters' treachery push Lear into considering other violent or unnatural criminals who remain 'Unwhipped of justice' (line 53). He starts to look at the lives of those he was responsible for as ruler through new eyes, struggling to understand the world that has been revealed to him. However, Lear returns to himself again in the final lines of this speech: 'I am a man / More sinned against than sinning' (lines 58–9). This statement needs careful consideration. Is it true? Given the events of the final moments of the play, the judgement is likely to go in Lear's favour.

While Lear welcomes the storm, Kent and the Fool show us how dreadful its effects are and guide our responses to Lear. Kent is aghast when he finds his master 'bare-headed' (line 60). The fact that Lear runs about 'unbonneted' indicates how weak he is, and shows how far he has fallen since the start of Act I, when he had his crown and all the other trappings of majesty to protect him. Now Lear is mentally and physically exposed. When Lear tries to remove his clothing in Act III Scene 4 he deliberately chooses to humble himself further and moves closer to empathising with the plight of 'unaccommodated man'. Kent's speech at lines 42–9 serves two purposes. His descriptions of the storm, with its 'sheets of fire', 'horrid thunder' and 'groans of roaring wind and rain' bring the tempest more vividly to life for the audience and reinforce its dangers. We are told that 'Man's nature cannot carry / Th'affliction nor the fear' of nights like these. The Fool, who finds the storm very hard to bear, urges Lear to return and 'ask thy daughters' blessing' (lines 11–12). For the Fool to ask Lear to submit to his daughters, things must indeed be desperate on the heath. This desperation is forced home when Kent seems to suggest the same course of action at line 63. The Fool's vulnerability also heightens and reflects Lear's. He shows us an attractive side of Lear's character. The king now finds time to feel for another, 'Come on, my boy. How dost my boy? Art cold? … Poor fool and knave, I have one part in my heart / That's sorry yet for thee' (lines 68–73). These lines will impress the audience, although Lear is still obviously caught up in his own sufferings (only 'one part' of his heart feels sorry for the Fool). But who can blame Lear for focusing on his own agony here ? It is clear that he is increasingly isolated in his madness. He hardly acknowledges his companions on the heath until he speaks to the Fool at line 68.

This scene is significant for several reasons. It shows us Lear in the first stages of his madness and we see the outcome we expected at the end of II.4. We learn that Lear is preoccupied by thoughts about filial ingratitude but also considers broader questions as he struggles to retain his wits. We see him start to move towards greater self-awareness in spite of his continued egotism. Lear becomes more generous. The storm reflects the terrible state England is now in, ruled by cruel monsters. The hostile setting and violent **imagery** increase our fears about events to come and make us fear for Lear's safety. How will the king survive this night, which seems so unendurable? This scene also offers us a faint glimmer of hope about human nature. The Fool and Kent stick by their master, the Fool calling Lear by the affectionate name 'nuncle' and Kent insisting on addressing Lear respectfully as 'my lord'. These flashes of compassion are vital in Act III, which closes with an act of appalling inhumanity.

TEXT 3 (IV.7.30–84)

CORDELIA: Had you not been their father, these white flakes
Did challenge pity of them. Was this a face
To be opposed against the jarring winds?
To stand against the deep dread-bolted thunder,
In the most terrible and nimble stroke
Of quick cross lightning? To watch, poor perdu,
With this thin helm? Mine enemy's dog,
Though he had bit me, should have stood that night
Against my fire; and wast thou fain, poor father,
To hovel thee with swine and rogues forlorn
In short and musty straw? Alack, alack!
'Tis wonder that thy life and wits at once
Had not concluded all. – He wakes! Speak to him.

DOCTOR: Madam, do you; 'tis fittest.

CORDELIA: How does my royal lord? How fares your majesty?

LEAR: You do me wrong to take me out o'the grave.
Thou art a soul in bliss; but I am bound
Upon a wheel of fire, that mine own tears
Do scald like molten lead.

CORDELIA: Sir, do you know me?

LEAR: You are a spirit, I know. Where did you die?

CORDELIA: Still, still far wide!

DOCTOR: He's scarce awake. Let him alone awhile.

LEAR: Where have I been? Where am I? Fair daylight?
I am mightily abused. I should even die with pity
To see another thus. I know not what to say.
I will not swear these are my hands. Let's see.
I feel this pin-prick. Would I were assured
Of my condition.

CORDELIA: O look upon me, sir,
And hold your hand in benediction o'er me.

[LEAR *falls to his knees*]
No, sir, you must not kneel.

LEAR: Pray do not mock me.
I am a very foolish fond old man,
Four score and upward, not an hour more nor less,
And, to deal plainly,
I fear I am not in my perfect mind.
Methinks I should know you, and know this man;
Yet I am doubtful; for I am mainly ignorant
What this place is; and all the skill I have
Remembers not these garments; nor I know not
Where I did lodge last night. Do not laugh at me,
For, as I am a man, I think this lady
To be my child Cordelia.

CORDELIA: [*weeping*] And so I am, I am.

LEAR: Be your tears wet? Yes, faith! I pray, weep not.
If you have poison for me I will drink it.
I know you do not love me, for your sisters
Have, as I do remember, done me wrong.
You have some cause; they have not.

CORDELIA: No cause, no cause.

LEAR: Am I in France?

KENT: In your own kingdom, sir.

LEAR: Do not abuse me.

DOCTOR: Be comforted, good madam. The great rage,
You see, is killed in him; and yet it is danger
To make him even o'er the time he has lost.
Desire him to go in; trouble him no more
Till further settling.

CORDELIA: Will't please your highness walk?

LEAR: You must bear with me. Pray you now, forget and forgive. I am old and foolish.

This quiet and moving scene comes as a relief after the violent struggles of Act III, and the harsh comedy of Gloucester and Lear's final meeting in Act IV Scene 6. We are prepared for a scene of reconciliation by Kent's conversation with the Gentleman in Act IV Scene 3. Here we learned that Lear was so ashamed of 'his own unkindness' that he would not see Cordelia (IV.3.42–5). Other dramatic devices also point towards restoration. Music is being played, and as Lear is carried in wearing fresh garments, all the characters on stage fall to their knees, reaffirming Lear's status as king. Cordelia kneels at her father's side and kisses his hand. This gesture of love and pity sets the tone for the scene to come.

Cordelia's speech at line 30 is her last long speech in the play. Her sole concern is Lear. As she describes Lear's sufferings in the storm we are reminded of Gonerill and Regan's cruelty. When Cordelia asks 'Was this a face / To be opposed against the jarring winds?' (lines 31–2) we will share her outrage. Finally, we are reminded how far the 'poor perdu' has fallen when Cordelia laments the way her father had to 'hovel thee … / In short and musty straw' (lines 39–40). These sorrowful descriptions highlight Lear's vulnerability and reaffirm Cordelia's virtuous nature. Her warmth and compassion contrast sharply with her sisters' cold vindictiveness. Cordelia's modesty is shown when she asks the Doctor to speak to Lear first. She seems as reluctant to speak now as she was in Act I Scene 1. Are we to assume that Cordelia still finds it hard to express her love? Perhaps she shrinks from speaking because she is nervous about how her 'child-changed' father will react when he sees her. Cordelia's request to the Doctor provides a last moment of tension before the reconciliation.

When Lear wakes up Cordelia's anxious questions, 'How does my royal lord? How fares your majesty?' (line 44) indicate that she now submits to her father's authority. The formal distance of these words is softened by the possessive 'my', which suggests Cordelia's desire to re-establish a close relationship with Lear. She urgently wants to be recognised and is upset when she realises her father is 'Still, still far wide' (line 50). She continues to seem choked for the rest of the scene; falling to her knees and begging for Lear's blessing, and then weeping during Lear's hesitant self-appraisal at line 60. After this she is so overwrought that she can only offer a brief 'No cause, no cause' (line 75) and ask gently if her father will take a walk with her (but only if it pleases him). In IV.7 Cordelia seems to be the perfect, doting daughter. Her submissiveness suggests to some modern critics that Shakespeare has started to rehabilitate and reaffirm the patriarchal hierarchy in the final scenes of the play. Cordelia's insistence that she has no reason to hate Lear confirms, perhaps, that the authority he exercised over in Act I Scene 1 has now been accepted as just. Alternatively, we might see her gentle pity as redemptive, and her 'No cause, no cause' as the natural response of a caring daughter.

Lear's lines indicate that the king is now a figure of **pathos**. His first speech shows his relentless suffering:

> You do me wrong to take me out o' the grave.
> Thou are a soul in bliss; but I am bound
> Upon a wheel of fire, that mine own tears
> Do scald like molten lead. (IV.7.45–8)

Life is torturous for Lear. He has finally given in to weeping and is utterly bewildered by what he sees. He says that he cannot piece together the events of the previous twenty four hours and murmurs helplessly, 'I know not what to say' (line 54). Perhaps Lear has learned the lesson that Cordelia was trying to teach him in I.1, that language cannot express emotions truly. He is humbled. This humility is continued in other lines. Although Lear continues to speak largely about himself in a self-pitying tone, he looks outwards too. He says that he would hate 'To see another thus' (line 54) and expresses doubts about his senses. He sums himself up with devastating simplicity; he is 'a very foolish, fond old man … not in my perfect mind' (lines 60–3). Most significantly, he attempts to kneel before Cordelia and recognises that she has 'some cause' (line 75) for hating him. It might also be argued that Lear's use of first person pronouns, 'methinks' and 'I', suggests greater humility. Gone is the earlier use of the omnipotent third person, the royal 'we'. Lear seems to have accepted his diminished status. When he offers to drink poison even the most hard hearted spectator will be moved to tears. Lear's self-pity seems acceptable now – he has suffered so deeply.

Lear's view of himself is altogether more realistic than the version of Lear Cordelia responds to. The simplicity of the king's language reflects his diminished status. Lear shuns anything that smacks of regality, denying that he has any authority:

LEAR: Am I in France?

KENT: In your own kingdom, sir.

LEAR: Do not abuse me.

It is too late. Fresh garments cannot restore Lear to his former glory. Lear is now more concerned with 'my child Cordelia' (line 70). We are being prepared for V.3, when Lear acts out the role of protective father.

We are pulled in two ways in this scene. Cordelia and Lear express the same emotions: pain, humility, concern. Their mutual caring is shown by the way they finish off each other's lines (Cordelia constantly tries to reassure her father, as at line 75). When they leave the stage together it seems that the reconciliation is complete. Lear has finally achieved his heart's desire; he can now rely on Cordelia's 'kind nursery'. This outcome provides us with a sense of relief. But we also doubt that Lear will survive long. He no longer speaks or acts like a mighty king. Every line he delivers confirms his weakness. Cordelia's reverence is ultimately rather hopeless.

This scene is significant because we see a fragile family harmony restored when Cordelia is reclaimed. Lear no longer holds false values. He recognises love and goodness accurately. We welcome his increased wisdom and humility. Act IV Scene 7 also provides an outlet for the pity we have felt for the old king since the end of Act II. Cordelia's tears guide our responses and foreshadow Lear's agonised mourning of Act V Scene 3. Finally, this scene points towards the restoration of the hierarchy that occurs at the end of *King Lear*. As the play moves into Act V we wait anxiously to see whether Cordelia's virtues or Gonerill and Regan's vices will triumph.

Part five

Background

William shakespeare's life

There are no personal records of Shakespeare's life. Official documents and occasional references to him by contemporary dramatists enable us to draw the main outline of his public life, but his private life remains hidden. Although not at all unusual for a writer of his time, this lack of first-hand evidence has tempted many to read his plays as personal records and to look in them for clues to his character and convictions. The results are unconvincing, partly because Renaissance art was not subjective or designed primarily to express its creator's personality, and partly because the drama of any period is very difficult to read biographically. Except when plays are written by committed dramatists to promote social or political causes (as by Shaw or Brecht), it is all but impossible to decide who amongst the variety of fictional characters in a drama represents the dramatist, or which of the various and often conflicting points of view expressed is authorial.

What we do know can be quickly summarised. Shakespeare was born into a well-to-do family in the market town of Stratford-upon-Avon in Warwickshire, where he was baptised, in Holy Trinity Church, on 26 April 1564. His father, John Shakespeare, was a prosperous glover and leather merchant who became a person of some importance in the town: in 1565 he was elected an alderman, and in 1568 he became high bailiff (or mayor) of Stratford. In 1557 he had married Mary Arden. Their third child (of eight) and eldest son, William, learned to read and write at the primary (or 'petty') school in Stratford and then, it seems probable, attended the local grammar school, where he would have studied Latin, history, logic and rhetoric. In November 1582 William, then aged eighteen, married Anne Hathaway, who was twenty-six years old. They had a daughter, Susanna, in May 1583, and twins, Hamnet and Judith, in 1585.

Shakespeare next appears in the historical record in 1592 when he was mentioned as a London actor and playwright in a pamphlet by the dramatist Robert Greene. These 'lost years' 1585–92 have been the subject of much speculation, but how they were occupied remains as much a mystery as when Shakespeare left Stratford, and why. In his pamphlet,

THE GLOBE THEATRE.

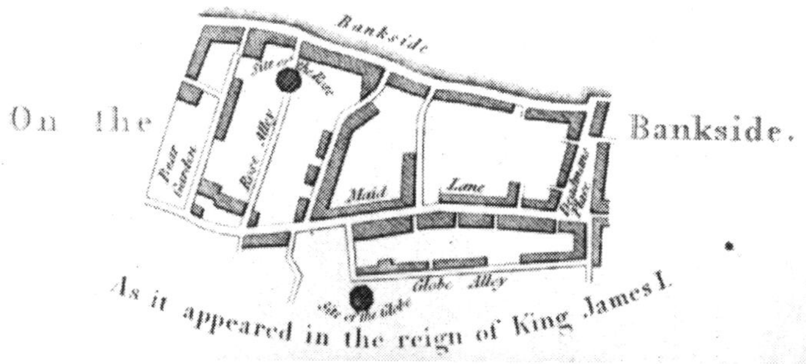

On the Bankside.

As it appeared in the reign of King James I.

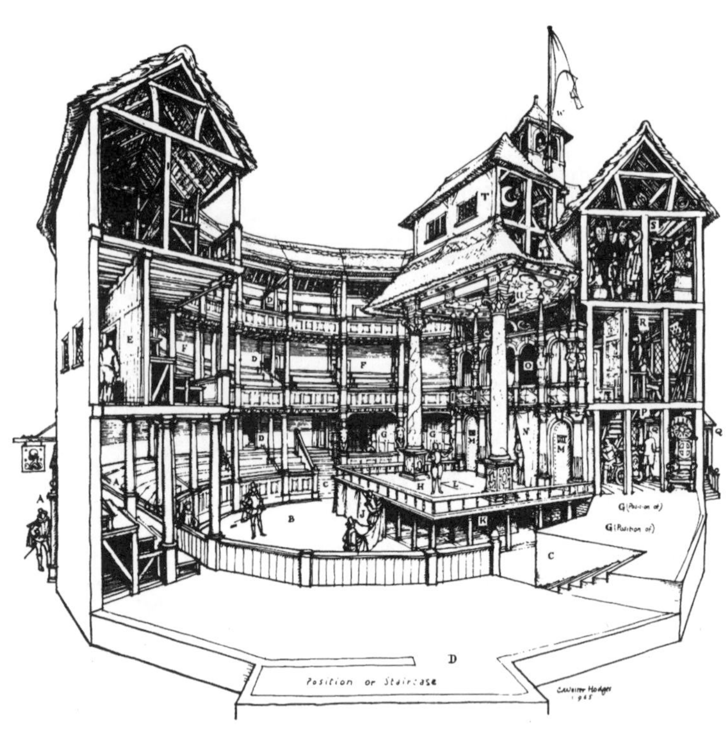

A CONJECTURAL RECONSTRUCTION OF THE INTERIOR OF THE GLOBE PLAYHOUSE

AA Main entrance
B The Yard
CC Entrances to lowest galleries
D Entrance to staircase and upper galleries
E Corridor serving the different sections of the middle gallery
F Middle gallery ('Twopenny Rooms')
G 'Gentlemen's Rooms or Lords Rooms'
H The stage
J The hanging being put up round the stage
K The 'Hell' under the stage
L The stage trap, leading down to the Hell
MM Stage doorsN Curtained 'place behind
N Curtained 'place behind the stage'
O Gallery above the stage, used as required sometimes by musicians, sometimes by spectators, and often as part of the play
P Back-stage area (the tiring-house)
Q Tiring-house door
R Dressing-rooms
S Wardrobe and storage
T The hut housing the machine for lowering enthroned gods, etc., to the stage
U The 'Heavens'
W Hoisting the playhouse flag

Greene's Groatsworth of Wit, Greene expresses to his fellow dramatists his outrage that the 'upstart crow' Shakespeare has the impudence to believe he 'is as well able to bombast out a **blank verse** as the best of you'. To have aroused this hostility from a rival, Shakespeare must, by 1592, have been long enough in London to have made a name for himself as a playwright. We may conjecture that he had left Stratford in 1586 or 1587.

During the next twenty years, Shakespeare continued to live in London, regularly visiting his wife and family in Stratford. He continued to act, but his chief fame was as a dramatist. From 1594 he wrote exclusively for the Lord Chamberlain's Men, which rapidly became the leading dramatic company and from 1603 enjoyed the patronage of James I as the King's Men. His plays were extremely popular and he became a shareholder in his theatre company. He was able to buy lands around Stratford and a large house in the town, to which he retired about 1611. He died there on 23 April 1616 and was buried in Holy Trinity Church on 25 April.

Shakespeare's dramatic career

Between the late 1580s and 1613 Shakespeare wrote thirty-seven plays, and contributed to some by other dramatists. This was by no means an exceptional number for a professional playwright of the times. The exact date of the composition of individual plays is a matter of debate – for only a few plays is the date of their first performance known – but the broad outlines of Shakespeare's dramatic career have been established. He began in the late 1580s and early 1590s by rewriting earlier plays and working with plotlines inspired by the Classics. He concentrated on comedies (such as *The Comedy of Errors*, 1590–4, which derived from the Latin playwright Plautus) and plays dealing with English history (such as the three parts of *Henry VI*, 1589–92), though he also tried his hand at bloodthirsty revenge **tragedy** (*Titus Andronicus*, 1592–3, indebted to both Ovid and Seneca). During the 1590s Shakespeare developed his expertise in these kinds of play to write such comic masterpieces such as *A Midsummer Night's Dream* (1594–5) and *As You Like It* (1599–1600) and history plays such as *Henry IV* (1596–8) and *Henry V* (1598–9).

As the new century begins a new note is detectable. Plays such as *Troilus and Cressida* (1601–2) and *Measure for Measure* (1603–4), poised between comedy and **tragedy**, evoke complex responses. Because of their generic uncertainty and ambivalent tone such works are sometimes referred to as 'problem plays', but it is tragedy which comes to dominate the extra-ordinary sequence of masterpieces: *Hamlet* (1600–1), *Othello* (1602–4), *King Lear* (1605–6), *Macbeth* (1605–6) and *Antony and Cleopatra* (1606).

In the last years of his dramatic career, Shakespeare wrote a group of plays of a quite different kind. These 'romances', as they are often called, are in many ways the most remarkable of all his plays. The group comprises *Pericles* (1608), *Cymbeline* (1609–11), *The Winter's Tale* (1610–11) and *The Tempest* (1610–11). These plays (particularly *Cymbeline*) reprise many of the situations and themes of the earlier dramas but in fantastical and exotic dramatic designs which, set in distant lands, covering large tracts of time and involving music, mime, dance and tableaux, have something of the qualities of masques and pageants. The situations which in the tragedies had led to disaster are here resolved: the great theme is restoration and reconciliation. Where in the tragedies Ophelia, Desdemona and Cordelia died, the daughters of these plays – Marina, Imogen, Perdita, Miranda – survive and are reunited with their parents and lovers.

THE TEXTS OF SHAKESPEARE'S PLAYS

Nineteen of Shakespeare's plays were printed during his lifetime in what are called 'quartos' (books, each containing one play, and made up of sheets of paper each folded twice to make four leaves). Shakespeare, however, did not supervise their publication. This was not unusual. When a playwright had sold a play to a dramatic company he sold his rights in it: copyright belonged to whoever had possession of an actual copy of the text, and so consequently authors had no control over what happened to their work. Anyone who could get hold of the text of a play might publish it if they wished. Hence, what found its way into print might be the author's copy, but it might be an actor's copy or prompt copy, perhaps cut or altered for performance; sometimes, actors (or even members of the audience) might publish what they could remember of the text. Printers, working without the benefit of the author's oversight, introduced their own errors, through misreading the manuscript for example, and by 'correcting' what seemed to them not to make sense.

In 1623 John Heminges and Henry Condell, two actors in Shakespeare's company, collected together texts of thirty-six of Shakespeare's plays (*Pericles* was omitted) and published them in a large folio (a book in which each sheet of paper is folded once in half, to give two leaves). This, the First Folio, was followed by later editions in 1632, 1663 and 1685. Despite its appearance of authority, however, the texts in the First Folio still present many difficulties, for there are printing errors and confused passages in the plays, and its texts often differ significantly from those of the earlier quartos, when these exist.

Shakespeare's texts have, then, been through a number of intermediaries. We do not have his authority for any one of his plays, and hence we cannot know exactly what it was that he wrote. Bibliographers, textual critics and editors have spent a great deal of effort on endeavouring to get behind the errors, uncertainties and contradictions in the available texts to recover the plays as Shakespeare originally wrote them. What we read is the result of these efforts. Modern texts are what editors have constructed from the available evidence: they correspond to no sixteenth- or seventeenth-century editions, and to no early performance of a Shakespeare play. Furthermore, these composite texts differ from each other, for different editors read the early texts differently and come to different conclusions. A Shakespeare text is an unstable and a contrived thing.

Often, of course, its judgements embody, if not the personal prejudices of the editor, then the cultural preferences of the time in which he or she was working. Growing awareness of this has led recent scholars to distrust the whole editorial enterprise and to repudiate the attempt to construct a 'perfect' text. Stanley Wells and Gary Taylor, the editors of the Oxford edition of *The Complete Works* (1988), point out that almost certainly the texts of Shakespeare's plays were altered in performance, and from one performance to another, so that there may never have been a single version. They note, too, that Shakespeare probably revised and rewrote some plays. They do not claim to print a definitive text of any play, but prefer what seems to them the 'more theatrical' version, and when there is a great difference between available versions, as with *King Lear*, they print two texts (see A Note on the Text).

Shakespeare arrived in London at the very time that the Elizabethan period was poised to become the 'golden age' of English literature. Although Elizabeth reigned as queen from 1558 to 1603, the term 'Elizabethan' is used very loosely in a literary sense to refer to the period 1580 to 1625, when the great works of the age were produced. (Sometimes the later part of this period is distinguished as 'Jacobean', from the Latin form of the name of the king who succeeded Elizabeth, James I of England and VI of Scotland, who reigned from 1603 to 1625.) The poet Edmund Spenser heralded this new age with his pastoral poem *The Shepheardes Calender* (1579) and in his essay *An Apologie for Poetrie* (written about 1580, although not published until 1595) his friend Sir Philip Sidney championed the imaginative power of the 'speaking picture of poesy', famously declaring that 'Nature never set forth the earth in so rich a tapestry as divers poets have done … Her world is brazen, the poet's only deliver a golden'.

Spenser and Sidney were part of that rejuvenating movement in European culture which since the nineteenth century has been known by the term *Renaissance*. Meaning literally *rebirth* it denotes a revival and redirection of artistic and intellectual endeavour which began in Italy in the fourteenth century in the poetry of Petrarch. It spread gradually northwards across Europe, and is first detectable in England in the early sixteenth century in the writings of the scholar and statesman Sir Thomas More and in the poetry of Sir Thomas Wyatt and Henry Howard, Earl of Surrey. Its keynote was a curiosity in thought which challenged old assumptions and traditions. To the innovative spirit of the Renaissance, the preceding ages appeared dully unoriginal and conformist.

That spirit was fuelled by the rediscovery of many Classical texts and the culture of Greece and Rome. This fostered a confidence in human reason and in human potential which, in every sphere, challenged old convictions. The discovery of America and its peoples (Columbus had sailed in 1492) demonstrated that the world was a larger and stranger place than had been thought. The cosmological speculation of Copernicus (later confirmed by Galileo) that the sun, not the earth was the centre of our planetary system challenged the centuries-old belief that the earth and human beings were at the centre of the cosmos. The pragmatic political philosophy of **Machiavelli** seemed to cut politics free from its traditional link with morality by permitting to statesmen any means which secured the desired end. And the religious movements we know collectively as the Reformation broke with the Church of Rome and set the individual conscience, not ecclesiastical authority, at the centre of the religious life. Nothing, it seemed, was beyond questioning, nothing impossible.

Shakespeare's drama is innovative and challenging in exactly the way of the Renaissance. It questions the beliefs, assumptions and politics upon which Elizabethan society was founded. And although the plays always conclude in a restoration of order and stability, many critics are inclined to argue that their imaginative energy goes into subverting, rather than reinforcing, traditional values. Convention, audience expectation and censorship all required the *status quo* to be endorsed by the plots' conclusions, but the dramas find ways to allow alternative sentiments to be expressed. Frequently, figures of authority are undercut by some comic or parodic figure. Despairing, critical, dissident, disillusioned, unbalanced, rebellious, mocking voices are repeatedly to be heard in the plays, rejecting, resenting, defying the established order. They belong always to marginal, socially unacceptable figures, 'licensed', as it were, by their situations to say what would be unacceptable from socially privileged or responsible citizens. The question is: are such characters – like The Fool in *King Lear* – given these views to discredit them, or were they the only ones through whom a voice could be given to radical and dissident ideas? Is Shakespeare a conservative or a revolutionary? (See Critical History for a range of views about the radicalism of Lear.)

Renaissance culture was intensely nationalistic. With the break-up of the internationalism of the Middle Ages the evolving nation states which still mark the map of Europe began for the first time to acquire distinctive cultural identities. There was intense rivalry among them as they sought to achieve in their own vernacular languages a culture which could equal that of Greece and Rome. Spenser's great allegorical epic poem *The Faerie Queene*, which began to appear from 1590, celebrated Elizabeth and was intended to outdo the poetic achievements of France and Italy and to stand beside works of Virgil and Homer. Shakespeare is equally preoccupied with national identity. His history plays tell an epic story which examines how modern England came into being through the conflicts of the fifteenth-century Wars of the Roses which brought the Tudors to the throne. He is fascinated, too, by the related subject of politics and the exercise of power. With the collapse of medieval feudalism and the authority of local barons, the royal court in the Renaissance came to assume a new status as the centre of power and patronage. It was here that the destiny of a country was shaped. Courts, and how to succeed in them, consequently fascinated the Renaissance; and they fascinated Shakespeare and his audience. *King Lear* is set initially at court, and shows what happens when power is given away and the King displaced.

But the dramatic gaze is not merely admiring; through a variety of devices, a critical perspective is brought to bear. The court may be paralleled by a very different world, revealing uncomfortable similarities (for example, Henry's court and the Boar's Head tavern, ruled over by Falstaff in *Henry IV*). Its hypocrisy may be bitterly denounced (for example, in the diatribes of the mad Lear) and its self-seeking ambition represented disturbingly in the figure of a **Machiavellian** villain (such as Edmund in *Lear*) or a **malcontent** (such as Iago in *Othello*). Shakespeare is fond of displacing the court to another context, the better to examine its assumptions and pretensions and to offer alternatives to the courtly life (for example, in the pastoral setting of the forest of Arden in *As You Like It* or Prospero's island in *The Tempest*). Courtiers are frequently figures of fun whose unmanly sophistication ('neat and trimly dressed, / Fresh as a bridegroom … perfumed like a milliner', says Hotspur of such a man in *Henry IV*, I.3.33–6) is contrasted with plain-speaking integrity: Oswald is set against Kent in *King Lear*.

(When thinking of these matters, we should remember that stage plays were subject to censorship, and any criticism had therefore to be muted or oblique: direct criticism of the monarch or contemporary English court would not be tolerated. This has something to do with why Shakespeare's plays are always set either in the past, or abroad.)

The nationalism of the English Renaissance was reinforced by Protestantism. Henry VIII had broken with Rome in the 1530s and in Shakespeare's time there was an independent Protestant state church. Because the Pope in Rome had excommunicated Queen Elizabeth as a heretic and relieved the English of their allegiance to the Crown, there was deep suspicion of Roman Catholics as potential traitors. This was enforced by the attempted invasion of the Spanish Armada in 1588. This was a religiously inspired crusade to overthrow Elizabeth and restore England to Roman Catholic allegiance. Roman Catholicism was hence easily identified with hostility to England. Its association with disloyalty and treachery was enforced by the Gunpowder Plot of 1605, a Roman Catholic attempt to destroy the government of England.

Shakespeare's plays are remarkably free from direct religious sentiment, but their emphases are Protestant. Young women, for example, are destined for marriage, not for nunneries (precisely what Isabella appears to escape at the end of *Measure for Measure*; friars are dubious characters, full of schemes and deceptions, if with benign intentions, as in *Much Ado About Nothing* or *Romeo and Juliet*. (We should add, though, that Puritans, extreme Protestants, are even less kindly treated: think of Malvolio in *Twelfth Night*!). *King Lear* is set in pagan times, but still informed by Christian teaching. For a discussion of the religion in the play, see Images and Themes.

The central figures of the plays are frequently individuals beset by temptation, by the lure of evil – Angelo in *Measure for Measure*, Othello, Lear, Macbeth – and not only in tragedies: Falstaff is described as 'that old white-bearded Satan' (*1 Henry IV*, II.4.454). We follow their inner struggles. Shakespeare's heroes have the preoccupation with self and the introspective tendencies encouraged by Protestantism: his tragic heroes are haunted by their consciences, seeking their true selves, agonising over what course of action to take as they follow what can often be understood as a kind of spiritual progress towards heaven or hell.

Shakespeare's theatre

The theatre for which the plays were written was one of the most remarkable innovations of the Renaissance. There had been no theatres or acting companies during the medieval period. Performed on carts and in open spaces at Christian festivals, plays had been almost exclusively religious. Such professional actors as there were wandered the country putting on a variety of entertainments in the yards of inns, on makeshift stages in market squares, or anywhere else suitable. They did not perform full-length plays, but mimes, juggling and comedy acts. Such actors were regarded by officialdom and polite society as little better than vagabonds and layabouts.

Just before Shakespeare went to London all this began to change. A number of young men who had been to the universities of Oxford and

Cambridge came to London in the 1580s and began to write plays which made use of what they had learned about the Classical drama of ancient Greece and Rome. Plays such as John Lyly's *Alexander and Campaspe* (1584), Christopher Marlowe's *Tamburlaine the Great* (about 1587) and Thomas Kyd's *The Spanish Tragedy* (1588–9) were unlike anything that had been written in English before. They were full-length plays on secular subjects, taking their plots from history and legend, adopting many of the devices of Classical drama, and offering a range of **characterisation** and situation hitherto unattempted in English drama. With the exception of Lyly's prose dramas, they were in **blank verse** (unrhymed iambic pentameters) which the Earl of Surrey had introduced into English earlier in the sixteenth century. This was a freer and more expressive medium than the rhymed verse of medieval drama. It was the drama of these 'university wits' which Shakespeare challenged when he came to London. Greene was one of them, and we have heard how little he liked this Shakespeare setting himself up as a dramatist.

The most significant change of all, however, was that these dramatists wrote for the professional theatre. In 1576 James Burbage built the first permanent theatre in England, in Shoreditch, just beyond London's northern boundary. It was called simply 'The Theatre'. Others soon followed. Thus, when Shakespeare came to London, there was a flourishing drama, theatres and companies of actors waiting for him, such as there had never been before in England. His company performed at James Burbage's Theatre until 1596, and used the Swan and Curtain until they moved into their own new theatre, the Globe, in 1599. It was burned down in 1613 when a cannon was fired during a performance of Shakespeare's *Henry VIII.*

With the completion in 1996 of Sam Wanamaker's project to construct in London a replica of The Globe, and with productions now running there, a version of Shakespeare's theatre can be experienced at first hand. It is very different to the usual modern experience of drama. The form of the Elizabethan theatre derived from the inn yards and animal baiting rings in which actors had been accustomed to perform in the past. They were circular wooden buildings with a paved courtyard in the middle open to the sky. A rectangular stage jutted out into the middle of this yard. Some of the audience stood in the yard (or 'pit') to watch the play. They were thus on three sides of the stage, close up to it and on a level with it.

These 'groundlings' paid only a penny to get in, but for wealthier spectators there were seats in three covered tiers or galleries between the inner and outer walls of the building, extending round most of the auditorium and overlooking the pit and the stage. Such a theatre could hold about 3,000 spectators. The yards were about 80ft in diameter and the rectangular stage approximately 40ft by 30ft and 5ft 6in high. Shakespeare aptly called such a theatre a 'wooden O' in the Prologue to *Henry V* (line 13).

The stage itself was partially covered by a roof or canopy which projected from the wall at the rear of the stage and was supported by two posts at the front. This protected the stage and performers from inclement weather, and to it were secured winches and other machinery for stage effects. On either side at the back of the stage was a door. These led into the dressing room (or 'tiring house') and it was by means of these doors that actors entered and left the stage. Between these doors was a small recess or alcove which was curtained off. Such a 'discovery place' served, for example, for Juliet's bedroom when in Act IV Scene 4 of *Romeo and Juliet* the Nurse went to the back of the stage and drew the curtain to find, or 'discover' in Elizabethan English, Juliet apparently dead on her bed. Above the discovery place was a balcony, used for the famous balcony scenes of *Romeo and Juliet* (II.2 and III.5), or for the battlements of Richard's castle when he is confronted by Bolingbroke in *Richard II* (III.3). Actors (all parts in the Elizabethan theatre were taken by boys or men) had access to the area beneath the stage; from here, in the 'cellarage', would have come the voice of the ghost of Hamlet's father (*Hamlet*, II.1.150–82).

On these stages there was very little in the way of scenery or props – there was nowhere to store them (there were no wings in this theatre) nor any way to set them up (no tabs across the stage), and, anyway, productions had to be transportable for performance at court or at noble houses. The stage was bare, which is why characters often tell us where they are: there was nothing on the stage to indicate location. It is also why location is so rarely topographical, and much more often symbolic. It suggests a dramatic mood or situation, rather than a place: Lear's barren heath reflects his destitute state, as the storm his emotional turmoil.

None of the plays printed in Shakespeare's lifetime marks Act or scene divisions. These have been introduced by later editors, but they should not mislead us into supposing that there was any break in Elizabethan performances such as might happen today while the curtains are closed and the set is changed. The staging of Elizabethan plays was continuous, with the many short 'scenes' of which Shakespeare's plays are often constructed following one after another in quick succession. We have to think of a more fluid and much faster production than we are generally used to: in the prologues to *Romeo and Juliet* (line 12) and *Henry VIII* (line 13) Shakespeare speaks of only two hours as the playing time. It is because plays were staged continuously that exits and entrances are written in as part of the script: characters speak as they enter or leave the stage because otherwise there would be a silence while, in full view, they took up their positions. (This is also why dead bodies are carried off: they cannot get up and walk off.)

In 1608 Shakespeare's company, the King's Men, acquired the Blackfriars Theatre, a smaller, rectangular indoor theatre, holding about 700 people, with seats for all the members of the audience, facilities for elaborate stage effects and, because it was enclosed, artificial lighting. It has been suggested that the plays written for this 'private' theatre differed from those written for the Globe, since, as it cost more to go to a private theatre, the audience came from a higher social stratum and demanded the more elaborate and courtly entertainment which Shakespeare's romances provide. However, the King's Men continued to play in the Globe in the summer, using Blackfriars in the winter, and it is not certain that Shakespeare's last plays were written specifically for the Blackfriars Theatre, or first performed there.

Reading shakespeare

Shakespeare's plays were written for this stage, but there is also a sense in which they were written *by* this stage. The material and physical circumstances of their production in such theatres had a profound effect upon the nature of Elizabethan plays. Unless we bear this in mind, we are likely to find them very strange, for we will read with expectations shaped by our own familiarity with modern fiction and modern drama. This is, by and large, realistic; it seeks to persuade us that what we are reading or watching is really happening. This is quite foreign to Shakespeare. If we try to read him like this, we shall find ourselves irritated by the improbabilities of his plot, confused by his chronology, puzzled by locations, frustrated by unanswered questions and dissatisfied by the motivation of the action. The absurd ease with which disguised persons pass through Shakespeare's plays is a case in point: why does no one recognise people they know so well? There is a great deal of psychological accuracy in Shakespeare's plays, but we are far from any attempt at realism. In *King Lear* Edgar and Kent spend four Acts in disguise; we are to accept their disguises as a theatrical given.

The reason is that in Shakespeare's theatre it was impossible to pretend that the audience was not watching a contrived performance. In a modern theatre, the audience is encouraged to forget itself as it becomes absorbed by the action on stage. The worlds of the spectators and of the actors are sharply distinguished by the lighting: in the dark auditorium the audience is passive, silent, anonymous, receptive and attentive; on the lighted stage the actors are active, vocal, demonstrative and dramatic. (The distinction is, of course, still more marked in the cinema.) There is no communication between the two worlds: for the audience to speak would be interruptive; for the actors to address the audience would be to break the illusion of the play. In the Elizabethan theatre, this distinction did not exist, and for two reasons: first, performances took place in the open air and in daylight which illuminated everyone equally; secondly, the spectators were all around the stage (and wealthier spectators actually on it), and were dressed no differently to the actors, who wore contemporary dress. In such a theatre, spectators would be as aware of each other as of the actors; they could not lose their identity in a corporate group, nor could they ever forget that they were spectators at a performance. There was no chance that they could believe 'this is really happening'.

This, then, was communal theatre, not only in the sense that it was going on in the middle of a crowd but in the sense that the crowd joined in. Elizabethan audiences had none of our deference: they did not keep quiet, or arrive on time, or remain for the whole performance. They joined in, interrupted, even getting on the stage. And plays were preceded and followed by jigs and clowning. It was all much more like our experience of a pantomime, and at a pantomime we are fully aware, and are meant to be aware, that we are watching games being played with reality. The conventions of pantomime revel in their own artificiality: the fishnet tights are to signal that the handsome prince is a woman, the Dame's monstrous false breasts signal that 'she' is a man.

Something very similar is the case with Elizabethan theatre: it utilised its very theatricality. Instead of trying to persuade spectators that they are not in a theatre watching a performance, Elizabethan plays acknowledge the presence of the audience. It is addressed not only by prologues, epilogues and **choruses**, but in **soliloquies**. There is no realistic reason why characters should suddenly explain themselves to empty rooms, but, of course, it is not an empty room. The actor is surrounded by people. Soliloquies are not addressed to the world of the play: they are for the audience's benefit. And that audience's complicity is assumed: when a character like Prospero declares himself to be invisible, it is accepted that he is. Disguises are taken to be impenetrable, however improbable, and we are to accept impossibly contrived situations, such as barely hidden characters remaining undetected (indeed, on the Elizabethan stage there was nowhere at all they could hide).

These, then, are plays which are aware of themselves as dramas; in critical terminology, they are self-reflexive, commenting upon themselves as dramatic pieces and prompting the audience to think about the theatrical experience. They do this not only through their direct address to the audience but through their fondness for the play-within-a-play (which reminds the audience that the encompassing play is also a play) and their constant use of images from, and allusions to, the theatre. They are fascinated by role playing, by acting, appearance and reality. Things are rarely what they seem, either in comedy (for example, in *A Midsummer Night's Dream*) or **tragedy** (*Romeo and Juliet*). This offers one way to think about those disguises: they are thematic rather than realistic. Kent's disguise in *Lear* reveals his true, loyal self, while Edmund, who is not disguised, hides his true self. In *As You Like It*, Rosalind is more truly herself disguised as a man than when dressed as a woman.

The effect of all this is to confuse the distinction we would make between 'real life' and 'acting'. The case of Rosalind, for example, raises searching questions about gender roles, about how far it is 'natural' to be womanly or manly: how does the stage, on which a man can play a woman playing a man (and have a man fall in love with him/her), differ from life, in which we assume the roles we think appropriate to masculine and feminine behaviour? Gonerill and Regan's masculinity forces us to reassess gender roles in *King Lear*. The same is true of political roles: when a Richard II or Lear is so aware of the regal part he is performing, of the trappings and rituals of kingship, their plays raise the uncomfortable possibility that the answer to the question, what constitutes a successful king, is simply: a good actor. Indeed, human life generally is repeatedly rendered through the **imagery** of the stage, from Lear's 'When we are born we cry that we are come / To this great stage of fools …' (IV.6.183–4) to Prospero's paralleling of human life to a performance which, like the globe (both world and theatre) will end (IV.I.146–58). When life is a fiction, like this play, or this play is a fiction like life, what is the difference? 'All the world's a stage …' (*As You Like It*, II.7.139).

Part six

Critical history

King Lear has enjoyed a rich critical history. This section offers an overview of some of the ideas that have exercised the minds of writers and scholars over the past three centuries.

Seventeenth-century criticism

During Shakespeare's lifetime *King Lear* does not appear to have been as successful as *Hamlet* or *Macbeth*. We can presume the play was well received, however, because it was performed at court for James I. Thereafter, for the rest of the seventeenth century, it seems to have been ignored. After the Restoration, *King Lear* was rewritten by Nahum Tate in 1681. Tate felt that the ending was far too gloomy. He also felt that the structure of the play was disorganised. His version of *King Lear* includes a happy ending (Lear does not die) and a romance between Edgar and Cordelia.

Eighteenth-century criticism

Two noteworthy eighteenth-century critics agreed with Tate's assessment of *King Lear* as faulty. In 1753 Joseph Wharton objected to the Gloucester subplot as unlikely and distracting, and reckoned Gloucester's blinding too horrid to be exhibited on the stage. Wharton also found Gonerill and Regan's savagery too diabolical to be credible. While he accepted the way in which 'the wicked prosper and the virtuous miscarry' because it was 'a just representation of the common events of human life', Samuel Johnson (1768) took Shakespeare to task for the lack of justice at the end of *King Lear*. He found Cordelia's death deeply shocking. These early critics were on sound territory; scholars are still arguing about the savagery in *King Lear*, and whether or not justice exists in the world of the play.

NINETEENTH-CENTURY CRITICISM

Moving on to the nineteenth century, we find a range of views, although critics agreed that the play was harsh. Charles Lamb (1811) thought *King Lear* unactable. August Wilhelm Schlegel (1808) saw a drama in which 'the science of compassion is exhausted': 'humanity is stripped of all external and internal advantages, and given up prey to naked helplessness'. William Hazlitt (1817) noted the 'giddy anarchy' of *King Lear*, and the way in which the unnatural comes to dominate. However, Hazlitt also believed that Shakespeare showed a 'firm faith in filial piety'. Again, all these ideas have been taken up by contemporary critics; suffering, anarchy, bleakness, faith, and the topic that obsesses Lear so much – the behaviour of children.

At the end of the century the poet Swinburne (1880) was struck by the dark fatalism of Shakespeare's vision. 'Requital, redemption, amends, equity, pity and mercy are words without a meaning here'. Other Victorian critics saw grandeur and strength in the play, and Lear continued to trouble and move them. *King Lear* was now recognised as a great literary achievement. For George Brandes (1895), Cordelia was 'the living emblem of womanly dignity', while the play as a whole portrayed 'the titanic **tragedy** of human life; there rings forth from it a chorus of passionate jeering, wildly yearning, and desperate wailing voices'. The sense of despair Brandes identifies here continues to be important to twentieth-century critics.

EARLY TWENTIETH-CENTURY CRITICISM

There have been many movements in literary criticism during this century, with each new discipline rejecting or reworking the ideas of previous critics. We now have a range of conflicting views of *King Lear*. A major development in Shakespearean criticism came with the publication of A.C. Bradley's *Shakespearean Tragedy* in 1905. Bradley believed that it was possible to understand a text and the playwright's intentions through close reading. He focused on character and motivation. For Bradley a Shakespearean tragedy is the tragedy of an individual who suffers as he comes to terms with his personality. Bradley made many criticisms of *King Lear*, commenting on careless inconsistencies, the loose, episodic structure and the unwieldy subplot. However, he also conceded that the play was 'one of the world's greatest poems'. For him Lear was a great, superior figure, whose suffering is heart-rending. Bradley also felt that this solemn tragedy was essentially unfathomable. Although Bradley's emphasis on character has been rejected by recent critics, many would agree that *King Lear* remains impossible to pin down.

In 1930, G. Wilson Knight's *The Wheel of Fire* was published. In '*King Lear* and the Comedy of the Grotesque', Wilson Knight explored the absurd cruelty in the play. 'The tragedy is most poignant in that it is purposeless, unreasonable. It [*King Lear*] is the most fearless artistic facing of the ultimate cruelty of things in our literature. That cruelty would be less were there not this element of comedy ... Mankind is, as it were, deliberately or comically tormented by "the gods". He is not even allowed to die tragically'. This view of the play marks a departure from previous accounts of *King Lear*. Up to now, there had been very little emphasis on the (horrible) comedy of the play, even though the cruelty and absurdity had been noted before.

The question of whether or not *King Lear* can be interpreted as a 'Christian play' has troubled many critics. Some see Cordelia as a Christ-like figure, who redeems Lear (thus his sufferings have not been in vain). Cordelia and Edgar's Christian virtues are commented upon and Lear too is recognised as displaying the virtue of patience. There are obvious problems with the Christian view, which fellow critics have been keen to point out. Why do the good characters' calls for justice from the gods go unheeded? Why does the ending feel so bleak? The agnostic view has tended to dominate. W.R. Elton (1966) refutes the Christian critics' positive readings of *King Lear*. He sees Cordelia's hanging and Gloucester's blinding as proof of 'the wilful operations of an upside down providence in an apparently deranged universe'. In his *Penguin Critical Studies: King Lear* (1986), Kenneth Muir, a humanist critic, agrees with Elton. 'In *King Lear*', Muir says, 'he [Shakespeare] starts from the hypothesis, whatever his personal beliefs, that the gods are indifferent, or hostile, or inexplicable, or even a man-made fiction, and that there is no after-life in which the injustices of life on earth may be set right. It follows that human beings are entirely responsible for their actions, and that if these lead to disaster, the tragedy is absolute'. After these pessimistic comments, however, Muir finds a reason to be more optimistic. He notes that many characters act with Christian morals, seeking to do good, regardless of the chaos that surrounds them. Thus, Shakespeare does not present man as completely evil.

CONTEMPORARY CRITICISM

Now, scholars are interested in the political and social implications of *King Lear*. Debate is focused on class, gender, race, the family, authority, the structures of power, and the meanings and functions of literary criticism itself. Some of the most interesting work on *King Lear* has come from **feminist** and **new historicist** critics.

NEW HISTORICISM

In *Radical Tragedy* (1984), Jonathan Dollimore completely reassesses *King Lear*. For him the play is not about the heroism of human endurance, or the moral growth of a hero who comes to know himself more thoroughly. Dollimore moves away from the analysis of character and individual suffering favoured by Bradley. He suggests that Lear's identity is a social construction; 'What makes Lear the person he is – or rather was – is not kingly essence (divine right), but, among other things, his authority and his family'. Lear loses his mind when he loses his social status. As the play progresses Lear is stripped of his 'conceptions of self'; he is forced to question his identity, 'Does any here know me?' … 'who is it that can tell me who I am?'

Dollimore believes *King Lear* is really about 'power, property and inheritance'. In this play Shakespeare focuses on what happens when there is 'a catastrophic redistribution of power'. Society is 'torn apart by conflict' because of its 'faulty ideological structure'. Looking at the end of Act V Scene 3 Dollimore sees a total collapse. Edgar and Albany try vainly to 'recuperate their society in just those terms the play is subjected to sceptical interrogation'. Thus, for Dollimore, *King Lear* is a subversive, radical tragedy which questions the Jacobean status quo.

Leonard Tennenhouse refutes Dollimore's subversive reading. For him *King Lear* shows us the opposite: the dangers of not following the 'old ways' of the patriarchal hierarchy. He sees the play as reconfirming oppressive structures, as being conservative in impulse. Tennenhouse would also deny that Shakespeare's portrayal of the sufferings of the poor and his concern with justice in *King Lear* are proof that the playwright viewed his society with a critical eye. However, other new historicist critics point to Lear's abuses of power as being direct comment on the vagaries of James I and his monarchy. In these readings, Shakespeare emerges as a social commentator.

FEMINIST CRITICISM

Feminist criticism of Lear incorporates a similar range of contrasting views. For Coppelia Kahn *King Lear* is a play about 'male anxiety'. Kahn suggests that Lear breaks down when he refuses to accept that he is dependent on his daughters, that he needs the feminine. Lear goes mad because he cannot face his feminine side; he refuses to cry. When Lear learns to weep, and rediscovers a loving non-patriarchal relationship with Cordelia, he is redeemed. In Kahn's view the play affirms femininity as a positive force.

Kathleen McLuskie's reading of *King Lear* asserts the opposite view. For her, Lear is an 'anti-feminine' play. She suggests 'the misogyny of King Lear, both the play and its hero, is constructed out of an ascetic tradition which presents women as the source of the primal sin of lust, combining with concerns about the threat to the family posed by female insubordination'. Her arguments are based on her recognition that the 'action of the play, the organisation of its points of view and the theatrical dynamic of its central scenes all depend upon an audience accepting an equation between "human nature" and "male power"'. McLuskie points out that the play forces us to sympathise with the patriarchs, Lear and Gloucester, and the masculine power structure they represent. She does not feel that Shakespeare presents a movement towards the feminine in *King Lear*, rather the reverse. 'Family relations in this play are seen as fixed and determined, and any movement within them is portrayed as a destructive reversal of the rightful order'. For McLuskie 'Cordelia's saving love, so much admired by critics, works … less as a redemption of womankind than as an example of patriarchy restored'. The audience is forced to agree that evil women (Gonerill and Regan) create a chaotic world, and must be resisted. The feminine must either be made to submit (Cordelia) or destroyed (Gonerill and Regan).

To explore these diverse ideas further it is best to consider your own response to the play and then return to the critics themselves in full. You will find some of the critics mentioned here in the books listed in Further Reading.

PART SEVEN

BROADER PERSPECTIVES

FURTHER READING

THE TEXT AND ITS SOURCES

G.K. Hunter, ed., *King Lear*, The New Penguin Shakespeare, Penguin Books, 1972

This is the edition of the text used in the preparation of these Notes. It includes full comments on the text itself, helpful notes on the Quarto and Folio texts of *King Lear* and an interesting discussion of the play in the introduction

Kenneth Muir, ed., *King Lear*, The Arden Shakespeare, Methuen, 1959

The Arden edition of King Lear includes extensive annotations, extracts from sources used by Shakespeare in the appendices and a fine and comprehensive introduction to the play

Gary Taylor and Stanley Wells, eds, *The Complete Works*, Clarendon Press, 1986

The Quarto and Folio texts of King Lear are printed separately and the editors provide a detailed discussion of their histories. There is also a compact edition of *The Complete Works*, published in 1988

✳ Kenneth Muir, *King Lear: Penguin Critical Studies*, Penguin Books, 1986

For a full discussion of Shakespeare's sources for *King Lear*, the section called 'The Making of the Play' is excellent

CRITICISM

This list represents only a very small tip of an enormous critical iceberg. Collections of criticism are very useful since they provide a range of views of the play. Some of the best recent collections include:

Frank Kermode, ed., *King Lear: A Casebook*, Macmillan, 1969

This collection covers a range of criticism of *King Lear* up to the 1960s, including the views of some of the play's early critics

Kiernan Ryan, ed., *King Lear: A Casebook*, New Casebooks, Macmillan, 1993

Concentrates on contemporary criticism of the 1980s. Some essays are less immediately accessible than others, but for a survey of current views this is an excellent selection. Four critics referred to in the section on Critical History – Dollimore, Tennenhouse, Kahn, McCluskie – can be found here. Ryan provides a helpful explanation of the current trends in literary criticism

John Drakakis, ed., *Shakespearean Tragedy*, Longman, 1992

Again, a selection of contemporary views. There are four essays specifically about *King Lear* and other references to the play in other essays. In the introduction Drakakais provides a detailed summary of views about tragedy, which is particularly helpful for undergraduates. The Dollimore essay is reprinted here

Other well known critics who are worth reading on *King Lear*:
A.C. Bradley, *Shakespearean Tragedy*, 3rd edition, ed. by J.R. Brown, Macmillan, 1992

An influential critic from the beginning of the twentieth century, Bradley focuses on character and motivation

Harley Granville-Barker, *Prefaces to Shakespeare II*, London, 1927, reissued in 1982

As a playwright and director, Granville-Barker provides useful insight into staging Shakespeare's plays

G. Wilson Knight, *The Wheel of Fire*, 4th edition, Routledge, 1989

Includes two fine essays, '*King Lear* and the Comedy of the Grotesque' and 'The *Lear* universe'

W.R. Elton, *King Lear and the Gods*, San Marino, California, 1966

For a full discussion of religion and religious attitudes in the play

SHAKESPEARE'S THEATRE

For anyone interested in the history of the Elizabethan playhouses, staging practices and acting companies the following book is invaluable: Andrew Gurr, *The Shakespearean Stage*, Cambridge University Press, 1980

CHRONOLOGY

World events	Shakespeare's life	Literature and the arts
1492 Columbus sails to America		
		1513 Niccolò Machiavelli, *The Prince*
1534 Henry VIII breaks with Rome and declares himself head of the Church of England		
1556 Archbishop Cranmer burnt at the stake		
1558 Elizabeth I accedes to throne		
	1564 Born in Stratford-upon-Avon	
1568 Mary Queen of Scots taken prisoner by Elizabeth I		
1570 Elizabeth I excommunicated by Pope Pius V		
1571 The Battle of Lepanto		
		1574-87 John Higgins, *A Mirror for Magistrates*
1577 Francis Drake sets out on round the world voyage		**1577** Holinshead, *Chronicles of England, Scotland and Ireland*
		1581 Sir Philip Sidney, *Arcadia*
1582 Outbreak of the Plague in London	**1582** Marries Anne Hathaway	
	1583 His daughter, Susanna, is born	
1584 Raleigh's sailors land in Virginia		
	1585 His twins, Hamnet and Judith, are born	
1587 Execution of Mary Queen of Scots after implication in plot to murder Elizabeth I		**1587** Christopher Marlowe, *Tamburlaine the Great*
	late 1580s-early 90s Probably writes *Henry VI (Parts I, II, III)* and *Richard III*	
	c1585-92 Moves to London	
1588 The Spanish Armada defeated		
1589 Accession of Henri IV to French throne		
		1590 Edmund Spenser, *The Faerie Queene (Books I-III)*
1592 Plague in London closes theatres		
	1593 Writes *Titus Andronicus*	
	1594 onwards Writes exclusively for the Lord Chamberlain's Men; writes *Richard II*	**1594** First performance of *The True Chronicle History of King Leir*

World events	Shakespeare's life	Literature and the arts
	1595 Writes *Romeo and Juliet*	
1596 Drake perishes on expedition to West Indies	**1596** Hamnet dies; William granted coat of arms	
	1599 Buys shares in the Globe Theatre; writes *Julius Caesar*	
	1600 *The Merchant of Venice* printed	
	1600-1 Writes *Hamlet*	
1603 Death of Queen Elizabeth I	**1603** onwards His acting company enjoys the patronage of James I as The King's Men	
	1604 *Othello* performed	
1605 Discovery of Guy Fawkes's plot to blow up the Houses of Parliament	**1605** First version of *King Lear*	**1605** Cervantes, *Don Quijote de la Mancha*
	1606 Writes *Macbeth*	
	1606-7 Probably writes *Antony and Cleopatra*	
	1607 Writes *Corialanus, Timon of Athens*	
	1608 The King's Men acquire Blackfriars Theatre for winter performances	
1609 Galileo constructs first astronomical telescope	**1609** Becomes part-owner of the new Blackfriars Theatre	
1610 Henri IV of France assassinated; William Harvey discovers circulation of blood; Galileo observes Saturn for the first time		
	1611 *Cymbeline, The Winter's Tale* and *The Tempest* performed	
1612 Last burning of heretics in England		
	1613 Globe Theatre burns down	
	1616 Dies	
1618 Raleigh executed for treason; Thirty Years War begins in England		
		1622 Birth of French dramatist Molière

alliteration a sequence of repeated consonantal sounds in a stretch of language. The matching consonants are usually at the beginning of words or stressed syllables. Alliteration is common in poetry and prose, and is one of the most easily identifiable figures of speech e.g. the repeated 'd' in Kent's lines in Act V, 'All's cheerless, dark, and deadly. / Your eldest daughters have fordone themselves, / And desperately are dead.' (V.3.288–90)

Aristotle a Greek philosopher (384–322BC), whose Poetics (observations about Tragedy collected by his followers) is an early and influential example of empirical criticism. By the examination of examples Aristotle attempts to analyse those features that make some tragedies more successful than others. He focuses on the nature of the plot and its connections with a moral pattern, the typifying features of the tragic hero, and the play's intensity of focus in time and place (later called the Unities)

aside an aside is a common dramatic convention in which a character speaks in such a way that some of the characters on stage do not hear what is said, while others do. It may also be a direct address to the audience, revealing the character's views, thoughts, motives and intentions

blank verse unrhymed iambic pentameter: a line of five iambs. One of the commonest English metres. It was introduced into England by Henry Howard, Earl of Surrey, who used it in his translation of Virgil's *Aeneid* (1557). Thereafter it became the normal medium for Elizabethan and Jacobean drama. The popularity of blank verse is due to its flexibility and relative closeness to spoken English. It allows a pleasant variation of full strong stresses per line, generally four or five, while conforming to the basic metrical pattern of five iambs

characterisation the way in which a writer creates characters so as to attract or repel our sympathy. Different kinds of literature have certain conventions of characterisation. In Jacobean drama there were many stock dramatic 'types' (see Machiavellian, malcontent) whose characteristics were familiar to the audience

chorus (Gk. 'band of dancers') in the tragedies of the ancient Greek playwrights the 'chorus' is a group of characters who represent the ordinary people in their attitudes to the action which they witness as bystanders, and on which they comment. The Fool is in some ways a choral character, who comments as an observer on the action of the play. The choral character is not a major participant in the events witnessed, but his comments are full of ironic insight

closure the impression of completeness and finality achieved by the ending of some literary works: 'and they all lived happily ever after'. *King Lear* is now seen as a play which defies closure; it refuses to leave the reader or audience with a feeling of comfortable satisfaction. It is hard to reach conclusive judgements about many issues in *King Lear*

denouement (Fr. 'unknotting') the final unfolding of a plot: the point at which the reader's expectations, be they hopes or fears, about what will happen to the characters are finally satisfied or denied

dramatic irony a feature of many plays: it occurs when the development of the plot allows the audience to possess more information about what is happening than some of the characters themselves have. Characters may also speak in a dramatically ironic way, saying something that points to events to come without understanding the significance of their words

feminist feminism is, broadly speaking, a political movement claiming political and economic equality of women with men. Feminist criticism and scholarship seek to explore or expose the masculine 'bias' in texts and challenge traditional ideas about them, constructing and then offering a feminine perspective on works of art. Since the late 1960s feminist theories about literature and language, and feminist interpretations of texts have multiplied enormously. Feminism has its roots in previous centuries; early texts championing women's rights include Mary Wollstonecraft's *A Vindication of the Rights of Women* (1792) and J.S. Mill's *The Subjection of Women* (1869)

humanism the word 'humanist' originally referred to a scholar of the humanities, especially Classical literature. At the time of the Renaissance European intellectuals devoted themselves to the rediscovery and intense study of first Roman and then Greek literature and culture, in particular the works of Cicero, Aristotle and Plato. Out of this period of intellectual ferment there emerged a view of man and a philosophy quite different from medieval scholasticism: in the ninetieth century this trend in Renaissance thought was labelled 'humanism'. Reason, balance and a proper dignity for man were the central ideals of humanist thought. The humanists' attitude to the world is anthropocentric: instead of regarding man as a fallen, corrupt and sinful creature, their idea of truth and excellence is based on human values and human experience. They strive for moderate, achievable, even worldly aims, rather than revering asceticism.

'Humanism' in a general sense has been revived at various times since the Renaissance. The domination of society by science and industry during the nineteenth century led many writers to stress humanist values in an attempt to define a properly rounded education as a counter to the cultural aridity they saw spreading around them.

Nowadays 'humanism' refers vaguely to moral philosophies which reject the supernatural beliefs of religion: many twentieth-century 'humanists', in this loose sense, are actively opposed to Christianity

imagery (Lat. 'copy', 'representation') a critical word with several different applications. In its narrowest sense an 'image' is a word-picture, a description of some visible scene or object. More commonly, however, 'imagery' refers to the figurative language in a piece of literature (metaphors and similes); or all the words which refer to objects and qualities which appeal to the senses and feelings. Thematic imagery is imagery (in the general sense) which recurs throughout a work of art: for example, In Shakespeare's *Macbeth* (*c.*1606), images of animals, birds, darkness and disease are common, and they are used in such a way as to underpin the play's them of the battle between unnatural evil and goodness. Similar patterns of images are used in *King Lear* to explore the same theme (see Images and Themes)

Machiavellian the Machiavel was a villainous stock character in Elizabethan and Jacobean drama, so called after the Florentine writer Niccolo Machiavelli (1469–1527), author of *The Prince* (written 1513), a book of political advice to rulers that recommended the need under certain circumstances to lie to the populace for their own good and to preserve power. Embellishment of this suggestion (which was only one small part of his analysis of political power and justice) made Machiavelli almost synonymous with the Devil in English literature.

Machiavels are practised liars and cruel political opportunists, who delight in their own manipulative evil. The topic of dissembling and disguising one's true identity amount almost to an obsession in plays in the early seventeenth century

malcontent the malcontent was a familiar figure in Jacobean drama; sometimes a tragic hero e.g. *Hamlet*, but not necessarily so. Malcontents also appeared in comedies (Jaques in *As You Like It*) and as villains (Flamineo in Webster's *The White Devil*). Being 'malcontented' was fashionable in the Jacobean period. It meant being disaffected, melancholy, dissatisfied with or disgusted by society and life. Gripped by a feeling of malaise, many malcontents scorned or railed against the world of the court in particular. The state of being malcontented was thought to be brought about by the dominance of black bile in a man's system. Edmund is not a true malcontent, although he shares some of the characteristics described here. He is unhappy with his position in life and on the fringes of society, which he mocks and seeks to undermine

metaphor (Gk. 'a carrying over') a metaphor goes further than a comparison between two different things or ideas by fusing them together: one thing is described as being another thing, thus 'carrying over' all its associations. When Shakespeare remarks in sonnet 116 (1609) that love 'is the star to every wandering bark' he defines exactly that aspect of the star which he wants to associate with love: its constancy and secure fixedness in a world of change and danger

new historicist the new historicism refers to the work of a loose affiliation of critics who discuss literary works in terms of their historical contexts. In particular, they seek to study literature as part of a wider cultural history, exploring the relationship of literature to society

pathos (Gk. 'suffering', 'grief') moments in works of art which evoke strong feelings of pity are said to have this quality. Tragic drama is full of moments of pathos: for example, Gertrude's description of the death of Ophelia at the end of Act IV in *Hamlet*

poetic justice Thomas Rymer devised this term in *The Tragedies of the Last Age Considered* (1678) to describe the idea that literature should always depict a world in which virtue and vice are eventually rewarded and punished appropriately. The deaths of the evil characters in *King Lear* can be viewed as examples of poetic justice

soliloquy (Lat. 'to speak alone') a curious but fascinating dramatic convention, which allows a character in a play to speak directly to the audience, as if thinking aloud about motives, feelings and decisions. The psychological depth which the soliloquy gives to Shakespeare's tragedies is inestimable. Part of the convention is that a soliloquy provides accurate access to the character's innermost thoughts: we learn more about the character than could ever be gathered from the action of the play alone

tragedy (Gk. 'goat song') possibly the most homogenous and easily recognised genre in literature, and certainly one of the most discussed. Basically a tragedy traces the career and downfall of an individual, and shows in the downfall both the capacities and the limitations of human life. The protagonist may be superhuman, a monarch or, in the modern age, an ordinary person.

Aristotle analysed tragedy in his *Poetics*. He observed that it represented a single action of a certain magnitude, that it provoked in the audience the emotions of pity and terror which were then resolved or dissolved by the catharsis of the play's climax, and that certain features of the plot were common, notably the existence of some connection between the protagonist's downfall and preceding behaviour and the process of 'the reversal of fortune' and the moments of discovery by which the protagonist learned the truth of his or her situation. Many of Aristotle's ideas are still accepted as valuable insights into the nature of tragic drama.

Seneca was the most influential Roman tragedian: his plays were probably not meant to be performed on stage, though he borrowed his subjects from the Greek playwrights.

In the Middle Ages tragedy was regarded simply as the story of an eminent person who suffers a downfall. The Classical tragedies and theories of Aristotle were unknown.

In English literature the Elizabethan and Jacobean periods are the great age of tragedy. Seneca provided the model both for the formal Classical tragedy with five acts and elaborate style, and for the popular revenge tragedies of blood, full of horrific violent incidents and sensational elements, in which a quest for vengeance leads to a bloodthirsty climax.

Shakespeare's tragedies are characterised by their variety and freedom from convention, in contrast with those of the slightly later Classical revenge tragedians, Racine and Corneille. Shakespearean tragedy concentrates on the downfall of powerful men and often illuminates the resulting deterioration of a whole community around them. The protagonists are not necessarily good: *Richard III* is a punitive tragedy in which evil is justly punished. Often the extent to which the tragic fall is deserved is left richly ambiguous, as is the case with *King Lear*. The relationship between human evil and the justice of fate is at the core of Shakespeare's tragic interests, as are the morality and psychology of his characters

AUTHOR OF THIS NOTE

Rebecca Warren is a Lecturer in Further Education, where she teaches English Language and Literature. She was educated at the Universities of Stirling, California (Berkeley), Warwick and Leicester. She is also the author of York Notes Advanced on *Othello*.

NOTES

York Notes – the Ultimate Literature Guides

York Notes are recognised as the best literature study guides. If you have enjoyed using this book and have found it useful, you can now order others directly from us – simply follow the ordering instructions below.

HOW TO ORDER

Decide which title(s) you require and then order in one of the following ways:

Booksellers
All titles available from good bookstores.

By post
List the title(s) you require in the space provided overleaf, select your method of payment, complete your name and address details and return your completed order form and payment to:

Addison Wesley Longman Ltd
PO BOX 88
Harlow
Essex CM19 5SR

By phone
Call our Customer Information Centre on 01279 623923 to place your order, quoting mail number: HEYN1.

By fax
Complete the order form overleaf, ensuring you fill in your name and address details and method of payment, and fax it to us on 01279 414130.

By e-mail
E-mail your order to us on awlhe.orders@awl.co.uk listing title(s) and quantity required and providing full name and address details as requested overleaf. Please quote mail number: HEYN1. Please do not send credit card details by e-mail.

York Notes Order Form

Titles required:

Quantity Title/ISBN Price

____
____
____
____
____
____
____

Sub total ________
Please add £2.50 postage & packing ________
(*P & P is free for orders over £50*) ________
Total ________

Mail no: HEYN1

Your Name ________________________
Your Address ________________________
____
Postcode ____________ Telephone ____________

Method of payment

☐ I enclose a cheque or a P/O for £______ made payable to Addison Wesley Longman Ltd

☐ Please charge my Visa/Access/AMEX/Diners Club card
Number ____________ Expiry Date ____________
Signature ____________ Date ____________
(please ensure that the address given above is the same as for your credit card)

Prices and other details are correct at time of going to press but may change without notice. All orders are subject to status.

☐ *Please tick this box if you would like a complete listing of Longman Study Guides (suitable for GCSE and A-level students)*

York Press
Longman

Addison Wesley Longman